Bloomsbury CPD Library: Supporting Children with Special Educational Needs and Disabilities

By Cherryl Drabble

B L O O M S B U R Y

LONDON · OXFORD · NEW YORK · NEW DELHI · SYDNEY

Bloomsbury Education
An imprint of Bloomsbury Publishing Plc

50 Bedford Square	1385 Broadway
London	New York
WC1B 3DP	NY 10018
UK	USA

www.bloomsbury.com

Bloomsbury is a registered trade mark of Bloomsbury Publishing Plc

First published 2016

British Library Cataloguing-in-Publication Data
A catalogue record for this book is available from the British Library.
Boardmaker® is a trademark of Mayer-Johnson LLC. Rights Reserved Worldwide.
Used with permission.
Mayer-Johnson
2100 Wharton Street
Suite 400
Pittsburgh, PA 15203

Cricksoft-for Clicker6 or 7
reproduced with the permission of Crick Software Ltd - www.cricksoft.com

ISBN:
PB: 9781472928092
ePub: 9781472928115
ePDF: 9781472928108

Library of Congress Cataloging-in-Publication Data
A catalog record for this book is available from the Library of Congress.

10 9 8 7 6 5 4 3 2

Typeset by Integra Software Services Pvt. Ltd.
Printed by CPI Group (UK) Ltd, Croydon, CR0 4YY

This book is produced using paper that is made from wood grown in
managed, sustainable forests. It is natural, renewable and recyclable.
The logging and manufacturing processes conform to the
environmental regulations of the country of origin.

To view more of our titles please visit www.bloomsbury.com

Contents

Acknowledgements

This has been the most exciting and challenging task I have ever undertaken in academic terms. I have been on a huge learning curve and I have enjoyed every moment.

I would like to offer my sincerest gratitude to Mary Isherwood (LLE. M.Ed. headteacher at Camberwell Park Special School, Manchester and Lynn McCann (Independent Consultant for ASC) for their continual encouragement and support throughout the writing of this book. Special thanks also to Erica Walwyn for kindly providing assistive technology resources. Heartfelt thanks to Highfurlong Special School, Blackpool and our wonderful pupils who are the inspiration behind my writing.

Thank you to my family who have allowed me the time and space to dedicate to my writing and for their support throughout.

I would also like to give sincere thanks to Holly Gardner, my Bloomsbury editor who has shown amazing patience and support and has guided me through every stage of the book.

Finally, thank you to all the Tweeting teachers for all your wonderful ideas.

@Mishwood1 @MaryMyatt @StuartAllenFCMI @Nichola8o @Sue_Cowley @reachoutASC @DamsonEd @TeacherToolkit @jordyjax @BehaviourTeach @MariaStMarys @SiminKnight100 @matthiasenglish @jwscattergood @bethben92 @rachelrossiter @rpd1972 @naureen @ASTsupportAAli @LeadingLearner @nancygedge @clyn40 @ChrisChivers2 @kylemarshesq @ICTEvangelist @FBanham @BehaviourA @r_brooks1 @DavidBartram @tombennett71 @Malcolm_Reeve @virkjay @warwick_beth @tes @MikeArmiger @StarlightMcKenz @mrs_dyslexia @ajbloor @oldandrewuk @nastyoldmrpike @Gwenelope @rodneyreid68 @RuthieGolding @busby_stuart @mjlongstaffe @michhayw @hannahtyreman @DriverTrust @5N_Afzal @Sian_Rowland @iTeachRE @MsAPPee @FKRitson @bellaale @rondelle10_b @nastyoldmrpike @ycpru @emmaannhardy @A_Weatherall @ellierussell

@MrBenWard @JLP_1969 @NeedhamL56 @bjpren @curlyman66 @KevinBerry03 @ASTsupportAAli @Maz90 @nowMrsBeattie @Trundling17 @SecretPhysicist @StarlightMcKenz @OldPrimaryhead1 @comm_uk @karen_macg @MikeArmiger @bethben92 @isright @MrHeadComputing @MacJude @naughtylilkt @karenGoldup @ballater6 @ian_bec @dawson_serena @Yorks_Bunny @MaeveBeg @specialsciteach @debrakidd @PompeyDog @danpo_ @TryAgainToday @ajbloor @DavidBartram @Malcolm_Reeve @FKRitson @englishcal @Historylecturer @cijane02 @joeybagstock (they are all worthy of a follow!) also Nichola Mott (SEND Teacher) and Alison Widdup (TA) for ideas.

Introduction

Why is there a need for this book?

Why is there a need for a book on teaching those with Special Educational Needs and Disabilities (SEND)? The answer is simple: there is very little training out there. I have consulted with my esteemed colleagues from the education sector via Twitter (if you haven't yet discovered the network of teachers on Twitter you're in for a treat! See p 11 for more details) and found SEND training to be very wanting. There is a huge gap in this field in Initial Teacher Training (ITT) and that gap widens still further after qualification.

Children with special needs may face challenges with behaviour, learning or potentially various medical complications. Sometimes there may be a combination of all three, which makes learning for these children very difficult. During teacher training there is no mandatory time span for special needs training which is a cause for concern. Some universities offer an hour each year with a full one-day special school visit in year two, a full day conference in year three and discrete tasks in all years. This allows the trainee teacher to learn the basics of special needs teaching but will not make them confident when faced with SEND children. More recently, some universities have recognised the need and have incorporated a one-term placement in a special school on their four-year BA Education programme. This allows for some degree of skill to be built up by the teacher and will help the new teacher in the mainstream classroom. I am also aware that universities are beginning to offer specialisms in SEND. I know this because I mentored a superb student last year from University of Cumbria who became a top SEND teacher.

To become a teacher in a mainstream, maintained school in England and Wales, Qualified Teacher Status (QTS) is required, and Scotland requires the Teaching Qualification (TQ). This is fair enough. Teachers have the future of the nation in their hands and should be highly qualified. There are many ways to achieve QTS, including the traditional tried and tested methods such as PGCE, School Centred

Initial Teacher Training (SCITT) and BA Education to name but a few. There are also new and exciting pathways such as Teach First, and Schools Direct run by the Teaching Schools Alliances (TSAs). There is a small SEND element to all of these routes, except Teach First. (I am advised by Sam Freedman, Executive Director at Teach First, that the Government does not currently fund a module for SEND. It is not within their remit at the moment.)

Teaching School Alliances usually offer a full day's placement in a special school and SCITT courses also provide taster days in special schools. Both of these routes take a full year to gain QTS. This is also insufficient to give a newly qualified teacher the confidence to deal with children with special educational needs.

However, there is some tentative good news. TSAs are beginning to look seriously at the issue of SEND. My own TSA, Fylde Coast Teaching School Alliance, in line with many others, currently offers a short placement of a one-day taster at my special school and this adds to the teacher's growing knowledge. Some TSAs are more adventurous and are including whole modules. Simon Knight, Director of Oxfordshire TSA informed me that they are offering a whole SEND specialism – a third of the year in a special school.

I have also recently discovered that SEND Teaching School (@SENDTS) is an alliance of special schools in Surrey who are doing great things with trainee teachers of children with SEND. After tweeting them I was informed that they are offering an option to do a short placement, followed by an extended placement as part of their mainstream SCITT. This is very pleasing news and I am sure that this TSA will be one of the first in the country to offer this.

This is all moving in the right direction, but the gap in teacher knowledge concerning special needs is still there. In the past, many special school teachers learned on the job from their own pupils. They perfected their skills as they needed them. 'Hands-on' is often the best way to learn. The difficulty with this approach is that skills were often kept within the special schools as there was no time for teachers to collaborate with each other and share their skills with mainstream teachers. A further solution is that many teachers, myself included, have studied special needs at Masters level to ensure the children are receiving a good education. This is seen as the best way to fill the gap left by teacher training.

What makes this book different from others written on the subject of SEND?

This book is 'special' in every sense of the word – it has been written by a practising teacher who has 15 years hands-on experience working in a special school. There are places for books based on academic research, but this book has its roots very firmly in classroom experience.

I read most, if not all of the blog posts written by teachers in special schools and Special Educational Needs and Disabilities Coordinators (SENDCos) from mainstream schools that feature on Twitter. The information I have to share is current and relevant and is of benefit to all teachers as it addresses the problems that teachers face on a daily basis. There is of course some research to back up the information, but the main thrust of the book is about addressing problems teachers need help with right now.

Throughout the book, I draw on information shared by experienced teachers in the form of blog posts and tweets and from educational conferences and websites. When addressing each of the different topics covered, I make suggestions of people to follow on Twitter to receive the best SEND tweets and posts. There are also references to teachers and educators who readily share their opinions, knowledge and expertise on Twitter – these are also listed in the Bibliography and further reading at the end of the book.

What will this book cover?

To assist me in assessing the CPD needs of the teachers and would-be readers of this book, and therefore decide which topics to focus on in the book, I canvassed the opinion of my fellow tweeters. I asked Twitter:

> 'Mainstream teachers, if you could choose any SEND CPD what would you choose? Please use #SENDCPD. Thanks.' (@cherrylkd)

I would like to thank everyone who responded to this tweet. I wish I could answer every single issue raised, but to do so would make the book unmanageable. However, there was an over-whelming request for help with the following six key areas, which I have taken as the core areas to cover in this book:

- Autism spectrum condition (ASC)*
- Attention deficit hyperactivity disorder (ADHD)
- Learning difficulties and disabilities (LDD)
- Dyslexia
- Inclusion
- Behaviour for learning.

*Please note: ASC is often known as ASD and the two are used interchangeably. The 'D' is for 'disorder' and has been the cause of much controversy, so it was changed to 'condition' representing the hope that the autism could improve. Simon Baron-Cohen spoke passionately about this on YouTube: www.youtube.com/watch?v=BDEHjLMOhHI. For the purposes of this book ASC will be used.

The six themes above are largely interrelated: if the classroom is inclusive and children feel welcome they will be motivated to learn and this generally leads to improved behaviour. Dyslexia is more of a stand-alone subject and I will give clear and helpful strategies for use with students with dyslexia as I have been asked many times for this support.

This book will be of use to all teachers who need to further develop their knowledge of SEND. There will be top tips for you to use with all your SEND children, and more specific training for the areas outlined above (see How to use this book (p xi) for more details).

The book is primarily aimed at all teachers working in mainstream schools, both primary and secondary. However, I hope that teachers in hospital schools, those from virtual schools and home tutors who are isolated, will also find it useful as well. And likewise, SENDCos, NQTs and teaching assistants (TAs) in all settings and teachers working in special schools who need up-to-date practical information at their fingertips.

This book also recognises that schools often exist on a meagre budget and it is therefore helpful if you can train yourself at a fraction of the cost. This book will help you to do that. With an ever-decreasing budget saving money is paramount. This book will prevent you from feeling isolated. It will be a handy, at your fingertips resource to help you just when you need it most.

Acronyms

AAC	Augmentative and Alternative Communication
ADHD	Attention Deficit Hyperactivity Disorder
ADD	Attention Deficit Disorder
AfL	Assessment for Learning
ASC	Autism Spectrum Condition
ASD	Autistic Spectrum Disorder
CPD	Continuing Professional Development
EHC plan	Education, Health and Care plan
IEP	Individual Education Plan
ITT	Initial Teacher Training
LA	Local Authority
LDD	Learning Difficulties and Disabilities
MLD	Moderate Learning Disability
PECS	Picture Exchange Communication System
PMLD	Profound and Multiple Learning Disability
QTS	Qualified Teacher Status (England and Wales)
SEN	Special Educational Needs (as it was generally referred to pre 2014)
SEND	Special Educational Needs and Disabilities (2014 onwards)
SENDCo	SEND Co-ordinator
SLD	Severe Learning Disability
SpLD	Specific Learning Disability
TA	Teaching Assistant
TACPAC	Tactile Approach to Communication
TEACCH	Treatment and Education of Autistic and Related Communication-handicapped Children
TQ	Teaching Qualification (Scotland)
TSA	Teaching Schools Alliance

How to use this book

The Bloomsbury CPD library provides primary and secondary teachers with affordable, comprehensive and accessible 'do-it-yourself' continuing professional development. This book focuses on the important skill of supporting children with SEND.

The book is split into two halves: Part 1 **Teach yourself** and Part 2 **Train others**.

Part 1: Teach yourself

This part of the book includes everything you need to improve your knowledge and skills for supporting children with SEND in your classroom.

STAGE 1: ASSESS

Stage 1 provides an introduction to Special Educational Needs and Disabilities in schools today and a chance for you to take some time to reflect on what you know and what areas you want to improve your knowledge of, and practice in. Also, we'll look at how to assess the needs of the children in your classroom.

STAGE 2: IMPROVE

In stage 2, we will take a closer look at ADHD, ASC, dyslexia, LDD, behaviour difficulties and inclusion and what this means for the child and the teacher in our schools. There will be practical advice in the form of takeaway activities for immediate use in the classroom. There will be information on key strategies for use in the classroom such as communication and behaviour management.

STAGE 3: EVALUATE

In stage 3, you will be able to evaluate your progress and further embed and develop your skills. You can assess your self-directed training's impact by using a series of reflective questionnaires.

STAGE 4: EMBED

In stage 4, there will be further help and activities to assist you in embedding the practice into your everyday teaching within all of your classes.

Part 2: Train others

The second part of the book is aimed at any teacher who is charged with leading professional development in the area of SEND. There will be top tips for successful Continuing Professional Development (CPD) sessions, information on mentoring and supporting other teachers and feeding back from external courses and training. There will be information on how to manage a CPD budget, and how to manage your training without one. Advice will be given on sharing your skills by coaching and mentoring other teachers and working with schools in your local area. Help will be given on the sensitive subject of training teachers who might be older than yourself. The main thrust of section two gives help with running CPD sessions in various allotted times. Training will cover assessing current staff skills levels, strategies to improve those skills, how to evaluate impact and how to effectively share best practice. There will be links to online materials, printable resources and worksheets included to help with planning CPD sessions. There will also be some advice for rectifying specific common training problems.

Part 1

Teach yourself

1

What's it all about?

What do we mean by SEND?

Current figures from the Department for Education show that in England alone 15.4% of pupils in January 2015 had a Special Educational Need or Disability (SEND).

SEND refers to any child who requires 'extra or different' help other than that provided by the school for all pupils. This may include the provision of outside specialists such as teachers of visually impaired children or teachers of hearing impaired children. It may also mean speech and language therapists or it could refer to differentiated work to allow a child to access the curriculum alongside their peers.

A brief history of SEND in the UK

To understand the current situation with children with SEND, let's take a quick look back in time. Way back in the dim and distant past, 1978 to be precise, *The Warnock Report* produced by Mary Warnock, a former headteacher, laid the foundations for the introduction of statements and coined the phrase 'SEN' for children with 'special educational needs'. This was a huge leap for children who were often previously categorised as 'educationally subnormal'. Back then, the child had to adapt to their surroundings and not the other way around.

The report led to the Education Act 1981, which introduced the idea of inclusion into a mainstream school for all children and also the idea of statements of special educational needs. A statement was a formal document which gave details of the child's difficulties and the help that they would require to reach their educational objectives.

By 1988 the National Curriculum had become an entitlement for all children including those with special needs. The advent of league tables saw some schools avoiding admitting children with disabilities for fear of damaging their league standing while other schools took more children with special needs in order to attract more money.

In 1997, the green paper *'Excellence for all children: meeting SEN'* openly supported the idea of mainstream education for children with special needs. There were to be high expectations for all children who should be in mainstream schools, where possible, with trained staff. Prevention and early intervention was also brought in for these children.

The *Special Educational Needs and Disability Act* (2001) saw further commitment to the Government's inclusion in mainstream schools which in turn saw the closure of many special schools. It became normal for those children with SEN, as it was then known, to be educated in mainstream schools unless it was incompatible with efficient education or against the wishes of the parents. Mainstream teachers found themselves faced with children they were untrained to teach. The Code of Practice also said the views of the children should be sought and parents should share their knowledge. Children with special needs were also entitled to the same broad and balanced curriculum alongside their mainstream peers.

In 2003, Warnock made a famous U-turn and declared that statements were a barrier to good education and called for their removal and also the removal of the commitment to mainstream schools. She wished to see a return to small specialist schools. This did not happen.

In 2004 'Removing the Barriers to Achievement' was a new initiative from the Labour Government. The aim was to personalise learning for all children and thereby improve the achievement of those with special educational needs. The strategy was based on early intervention; removing all barriers to learning; high expectations; and encouraging partnerships between education, health and social care to meet the needs of the child and the family. This document stated that all schools should play a part in educating children locally, whatever their background and whatever their ability. Mainstream continued to be the order of the day. This was to include all pupils with disabilities, those with behaviour challenges, minority ethnics, faith groups, travellers, those with English as an additional language and many more children considered to be at risk of underachievement. This situation has gone backwards and forwards for years, as those with special needs have been used as a political football by successive governments.

The notion of inclusion continues to be a hotly debated topic in 2016 with many proficient and established bloggers and writers putting forward their views.

In 2009 the Department for Children, Schools and Families (DCSF) worked with the national strategies to develop the progression guidance for children with SEN including those working below level 1 of the National Curriculum. Mainstream teachers received little training on this even though the use of P Scales or P levels as they are also known became statutory.

Finally in 2014 there came a change in the form of The Children and Families Act. And when change came – it really came! There were sweeping changes. Gone are all the old categories of Special Educational Needs (SEN) and in have come just four areas of Special Educational Needs and Disabilities. The term 'SEND' had been in use previously but was not widespread. The use of the new terminology became common after June 2014 when the Revised Code of Practice was published and was full of references to SEND.

The old categories of School Action and School Action Plus were removed under the new reforms and were replaced by a graduated approach of SEN support. The idea behind SEN support is to remove any barriers to learning to enable the child to make progress and participate fully in school life. Teachers should remember that all children can make progress and all children can achieve. Progress and achievement is personal to each child and this person-centred planning is at the heart of the 2014 reforms. Teachers also need to remember that we are all teachers of those with special educational needs and disabilities. This is where you as the teacher need to have special knowledge.

The sweeping changes brought about by the new act have major implications in the classroom. The old areas of difficulty have been condensed into four new areas of SEND and these are:

1) Communication and interaction
2) Cognition and learning
3) Social, mental and emotional health
4) Sensory and/or physical needs.

Behaviour and English as an Additional Language (EAL) which formed part of the old 'categories of need' from pre-2014 have disappeared as neither necessarily equals a special educational need and neither is a disability. Other categories have been condensed in to the four areas detailed above.

What is required of mainstream teachers today?

Mainstream teachers today are responsible for children with SEND in their classes and all are responsible for ensuring they make good progress. Many children with SEND are not destined to be high-flyers, but with the correct support they should achieve their personal best. Many mainstream teachers find themselves faced with children with a wide range of needs that they have not been trained to deal with, including: behavioural, medical, physical, moderate and severe learning difficulties, ASC or ADHD. They often find that their lessons are disrupted by children who are displaying behaviours that again they have not been trained to deal with. They may have no understanding of why the child is disrupting their class. Under the banner of 'inclusion', it is tempting for teachers to resort to generic teaching where all with SEND are treated to the same lesson with no personalisation aimed at catering for their individual needs. TAs have been drafted in in large quantities to assist teachers in the mainstream classroom, and the teacher–TA team do their utmost to be all things to all children.

However, many teachers are unhappy with this approach, and simply feel they need more help. I know this, because I am increasingly contacted on Twitter, as are my special school colleagues, by teachers, student teachers and NQTs all asking for help with specific children. As we have already discovered (see the introduction, p vii), today's teachers have little training in this area and, with the best will in the world, they are ill-equipped to help these children achieve their full potential. My colleagues and I do our best to offer helpful advice. We have become very aware of how difficult it is for teachers who may have little experience and no training.

Twitter tip

Follow @SpcialNdsJungle for up to the minute advice and information

Follow @DiLeed for information regarding EAL

Parents are often in the dark about any changes and quite often the first person they will turn to will be you in your trusted position as the teacher. Here is a whistle-stop tour of the basic facts. Let's start by having a quick look at the main changes and what this means for you as a classroom teacher. The following information is in accordance with the DFE's Special educational needs and disabilities: a guide for parents and carers.

Local Authority duty

Local Authorities (LAs) must identify all education, health and social care services in their area for children with SEND. They must provide a directory of services known as the 'local offer'. A good local offer will include information that parents may need for their child that is not provided within their area. The LA is responsible for a child with SEND as soon as they are aware of their need and must ensure they receive the support required to help them achieve their best educational outcomes. The LA, not the parents, is responsible for carrying out an Education, Health and Care plan (EHC plan) if a child needs more support than their school can provide, but parents should always be consulted.

Personal budgets

Local Authorities may be required to identify a personal budget for children and young people who have an EHC plan. This is an amount of money required to provide parts of the provision set out in the EHC plan. The personal budget may include money from education, health or social care depending on the needs of the child or young person.

What are EHC plans?

An EHC plan:

- is only intended for individuals with more complex needs which cannot be met from the resources normally available through the LA's local offer.
- brings the child's education, health and social care needs into one single document from age 0–25 years, if needed
- replaces the previous 'statements'
- is child-centred, and must involve parents, carers and the child
- focuses on outcomes for the child
- can be requested by a parent, teacher, doctor or health visitor
- is drawn up as a multi-agency task, involving every professional who works with the child or young person (see below)
- must be reviewed at least annually.

Top tip

For further information about EHC plans, IPSEA (Independent Parental Special Education Advice) have a fantastic website: www.ipsea.org.uk.

As a teacher of a child with SEND it will be useful to know who will be involved in drawing up an EHC plan. It is a multi-agency task. Every professional who works with the child or young person will be involved. This can include:

- The child
- The child's parents
- SENDCo
- Class teacher
- TA
- Occupational therapist
- Physiotherapist
- Health visitor
- Social worker
- Nursery nurse
- Speech and language therapist
- Any other specialist who works with the child.

The most important people are of course the child and the child's parents. They must always have a say in the EHC plan.

SEN support for children who will not be assessed for an EHC plan

Children who have special needs but who will not be assessed for an EHC plan will still be able to access SEN support. According to the *SEND Code of Practice: 0 to 25 years* (2015), 'All settings should adopt a graduated approach with four stages of action: assess, plan, do and review.' This is summarised below:

Assess	Assess the child's difficulties through discussions with all professionals involved, looking at records and reports and observing. Use any available data.
Plan	Educational setting agrees the intended outcomes and the impact on the child. A time to review is agreed. All involved should be made aware of the child's needs.
Do	Put in place the required support. Teacher remains responsible for progress although pupils may access support from TAs or specialist staff.
Review	Review the support received. Amend if necessary.

Fig. 1 SEN support and the graduated approach

The graduated approach detailed above should be revisited regularly, reviewed and amended until the best support is provided for the child. There is no set number of Assess, Plan, Do, Review cycles before the decision is taken to ask for a statutory assessment for an EHC Plan. This is personal to each child.

Effective SEN support should be provided where the school cannot meet the needs of the child from within their own resources. Furthermore, to be effective it should also:

- be a whole school buy-in
- have the class teacher as the key driver
- provide CPD for the teacher to enable them to effectively teach the child
- involve the SENDCo giving support to the teacher and providing CPD
- involve the parents
- involve the child where possible.

The Code of Practice at a glance

Pupils and families	The pupil should be at the heart of the assessment. Pupil to have more input. Parents/carers to share their knowledge.
Teachers	High expectations for all and quality-first teaching for all children with special needs.
New language	SEND in widespread use as distinct from SEN support as part of the Graduated Approach.
School Action and School Action plus	To be replaced by SEN support.
EHC plan	Replaces statements and learning difficulty assessments up to the age of 25. Existing statements will stay in force until transitions are completed. All to be transferred by 2017.
Personal budgets	Parents/carers can choose to hold their own budgets and buy in the support they require.
Local Authority	Consider how to provide the best education for the child with special needs and arrange that support. Responsible for carrying out EHC plan.
Class teachers	Class teachers will be more accountable for SEND through performance-related pay.

Fig. 2 Code of Practice at a glance

So this is what the requirements are. Take some time to have a look at the policy, which can be found here: www.gov.uk/government/uploads/system/uploads/attachment_data/file/398815/SEND_Code_of_Practice_January_2015.pdf

What are the main areas of special educational needs?

Below is a breakdown of the four main areas now specified as SEND:

1) Communication and Interaction which includes:
    • Autistic Spectrum Condition (ASC)
    • Asperger's Syndrome (intellectually higher with different language development from most with ASC)
    • Speech, Language and Communication Needs
    • Use of verbal and non-verbal communication
2) Cognition and Learning which includes:
    • Attention Deficit Hyperactivity Disorder (ADHD)
    • Moderate Learning Difficulty (MLD) – only if additional help is required

- Profound and Multiple Learning Difficulty (PMLD). This is severe learning difficulties which are accompanied by physical disabilities, sensory impairments such as visual impairment or severe medical difficulties.
- Severe Learning Difficulty (SLD). These children have severe cognitive impairments.
- Dyscalculia. Difficulty with mathematical skills.
- Specific Learning Difficulty (SpLD). This may include dyspraxia, dyscalculia, dyslexia.
- Dysgraphia. Lack of fine motor skills which leads to difficulty with numbers and writing, language processing and visual spatial difficulties.
- Dyslexia. Difficulty learning to read, write, punctuate and spell. Comprehension skills may be impaired along with sequencing and organising.
- Dyspraxia. Gross and fine motor difficulties leading to difficulty with movement.

3) Social, Emotional and Mental Emotional Health includes:
- Obsessive Compulsive Disorders
- Anxiety disorders
- Adjustment disorders

4) Sensory and/or Physical includes:
- Visual impairment (VI)
- Hearing impairment (HI)
- Multi-sensory impairment which might be a combination of VI and HI plus other complex disabilities.
- Physical Disability (only including those with associated difficulties with learning) such as cerebral palsy, muscular dystrophy, muscular difficulties, neurological impairments, hydrocephalus, spina bifida, meningitis, fine motor difficulties, gross motor challenges, juvenile arthritis.
- Medical needs if there are associated learning difficulties. This may include cystic fibrosis, asthma, colostomy, ileostomy, diabetes, eczema, epilepsy, incontinence.

In the 2001 SEN Code of Practice for behaviour, emotional and social difficulties (BESD) was listed as a separate category of need. The reforms of 2014 removed behaviour from the list as it is not deemed to be a disability. While I whole-heartedly agree that behaviour challenges are not a disability, I do feel that children with challenging behaviours are on the increase in our schools. I cannot speculate as to the reasons for this but I do know that I am frequently asked for help in this area. Teachers ask me to suggest strategies and provide resources to deal with children with some extremely challenging behaviour. It is for this reason that I have decided to include behaviour advice in this book. Other areas of ADHD, ASC, LDD, inclusion and dyslexia all rated highly on my questionnaire directed at teachers on Twitter and are therefore included by popular demand.

Chapter 1 takeaway

Teaching tip

Make the most of social media

My first top tip is to join Twitter. This is quite possibly the best piece of CPD advice a teacher will ever hear. I highly recommend it. I have been a tweeting teacher now for four years and have learned so much – and all for no financial outlay.

As a teacher, I once posed a question about how to plan to teach the topic of the Victorians for my sensory learners. I was overwhelmed with the responses from people planning to teach the same theme. Between us we drew up a medium term plan in a very short space of time.

As a leader, I am able to ask for advice on leadership issues and the headteachers and leadership teams are supportive in the extreme. As a specialist leader of education and a teacher myself I can give a little back. I also happily mentor NQTs and willingly share my teaching strategies with anyone who asks.

Using Twitter also directs you to blog posts. Written by leaders in their own fields of expertise, they all educate me in their different ways. High-ranking and important officials such as Sean Harford, Ofsted's National Director of Schools, regularly blogs and tweets about Ofsted. He keeps the profession up-to-date and canvasses opinions from those in the classroom. There are many more reasons for using Twitter to further your own knowledge and these are just a few.

Facebook is also growing in popularity as a tool for educators. There are several groups using Facebook for educators who wish to further their knowledge of children with SEND. I can recommend the 'Special Needs Jungle' Facebook page for information, blogs and resources. I also recommend 'Special Education Resources for Kids' as a good starting point. They post book recommendations and resources and other posts for children with SEND.

Useful information can also be found on Linkedin, Google plus and MSN. For the purposes of this book I will be referring to the views and opinions of the teachers on Twitter.

Pass it on

Share and tweet

@SENexchange is a place to share news, ideas, resources and chat about issues related to SEND. It is established and run by @Mishwood1 and @Cherrylkd. Weekly discussions are on Wednesdays 8–8.30 p.m. Follow #SENexchange.

CPD book club recommendation

The SEND Code of Practice 0-25 Years by Rona Tutt and Paul Williams.

This book aims to ensure you are meeting all the requirements and also improving the education of children with SEND.

Bloggers' corner

SENBlogger has some high-quality posts on the subject of SEND that are well worth a read. Visit their blog at: www.senblogger.wordpress.com.

TO DO LIST:

- ☐ Read The SEND Code of Practice 0-25 Years.
- ☐ Check if any children in your class have an EHCP.
- ☐ Join Twitter and tweet your questions using #BloomsCPD.
- ☐ Read *The SEND Code of Practice 0-25 Years* by Rona Tutt and Paul Williams.
- ☐ Follow #SENexchange each Wednesday evening at 8pm to learn more about specific special educational needs.

2 Self-assessment

In this chapter we will really begin to get to grips with your knowledge of your children with SEND. What do you know? What do you need to know? Take a moment to look at the children in the class and think about their needs. Are you addressing them all? Are you doing the best job that you possibly can? Think about your continuing professional development and what would be the most valuable training you could have at this moment in time. What is your greatest area of need?

How to complete the self-assessment questionnaire

On pages 17–31 there is a self-assessment questionnaire to encourage you to start the 'teach yourself' process by thinking very carefully about the current support you provide for your SEND children before you jump into trying to improve it.

When you are looking at your own SEND practices and trying to form a clear view of where you are now and what the next steps will be, there are many ways of approaching it – it will depend on you as a person. For some people, it is useful to go with your gut and listen to the first thing that comes into your mind – your instinctual answer. For others, it is a better approach to spend a good amount of time really mulling over the self-evaluation questions slowly and in detail.

Quick response approach

If your preference for the self-evaluation is to go with your gut only, then simply fill in the quick response section after each question with the first thing that comes into your mind when you ask yourself the question. Do not mull over the question too long, simply read carefully and answer quickly. This approach will give you an overview of your current SEND understanding and practice and will take relatively little time. Just make sure you are uninterrupted, in a quiet place and able to complete the questionnaire in one sitting with no distractions so that you get focused and honest answers.

Considered response approach

If you choose to take a more reflective and detailed approach, then you can leave the quick response section blank and go straight onto reading the further guidance section under each question. This guidance provides prompt questions and ideas to get you thinking in detail about the question being answered and is designed to open up a wider scope in your answer. It will also enable you to look at your experience and pull examples into your answer to back up your statements. You may want to complete it a few questions at a time and take breaks, or you may be prepared to simply sit and work through the questions all in one sitting to ensure you remain focused. This approach does take longer, but it can lead to a more in-depth understanding of your current SEND practice, and you will gain much more from the process than the quick response alone.

Combined approach

A thorough approach, and one I recommend, would be to use both approaches together regardless of personal preference. There is clear value in both approaches being used together. This would involve you firstly answering the self-evaluation quick response questions by briefly noting down your instinctual answers for all questions. The next step would be to return to the start of the self-evaluation, read the further guidance and then answer the questions once more, slowly and in detail forming more of a narrative around each question and pulling in examples from your own experience. Following this you would need to read over both responses and form a comprehensive and honest summary in your mind of your answers and a final view of where you feel you stand right now in your marking and feedback practice.

This is the longest of the three approaches to this questionnaire but will give you a comprehensive and full understanding of your current SEND practice. You will be surprised at the difference you see between the quick response and the considered response answers to the same questions. It can be very illuminating.

• I have done this self-assessment before. • I only want a surface level overview of my current understanding and practice. • I work better when I work at speed. • I don't have much time.	Quick
• I have never done this self-assessment before. • I want a deeper understanding of my current understanding and practice. • I work better when I take my time and really think things over. • I have some time to do this self-assessment.	Considered
• I have never done this self-assessment before. • I have done this self-assessment before. • I want a comprehensive and full understanding of my current understanding and practice and want to compare that to what I thought before taking the self-assessment. • I have a decent amount of time to dedicate to completing this self-assessment.	Combined

Fig. 3 How should I approach the self-evaluation questionnaire?

Rate yourself

The final part of the self-evaluation is to rate yourself. This section will ask you to rate your confidence and happiness in each area that has been covered in the questionnaire, with a view to working on these areas for improvement throughout the course of the book. The table below shows how the scale works: the higher the number you allocate yourself, the better you feel you are performing in that area.

Rating	Definition
1	Not at all. I don't. None at all. Not happy. Not confident at all.
2	Rarely. Barely. Very little. Very unconfident.
3	Not often at all. Not much. Quite unconfident.
4	Not particularly. Not really. Not a lot. Mildly unconfident.
5	Neutral. Unsure. Don't know. Indifferent.
6	Sometimes. At times. Moderately. A little bit. Mildly confident.
7	Quite often. A fair bit. Some. A little confident.
8	Most of the time. More often than not. Quite a lot. Quite confident.
9	The majority of the time. A lot. Very confident.
10	Completely. Very much so. A huge amount. Extremely happy. Extremely confident.

Fig. 4 Rate yourself definitions

SEND self-evaluation questionnaire

QUESTION 1: How many children in your class have an identified special educational need or disability?

Quick response:

_____
_____
_____
_____

Questions for consideration

- Do they all have an EHC plan?
- Are you aware of the support they require?
- Do they have a one page profile?
- Do they have a designated teaching assistant?

Considered response:

_____
_____
_____
_____
_____
_____
_____
_____
_____
_____
_____

Rate yourself

QUESTION 1: How knowledgeable are you about the needs of the children in your class?

1   2   3   4   5   6   7   8   9   10

QUESTION 2: Can you identify each child's barrier to learning?

Quick response:

_____

_____

_____

_____

Questions for consideration

- Does the child interact with their peers?
- Does the child prefer the company of adults which in turn limits group work?
- Does the child display any behavioural difficulties?
- Is the child able to participate in a full lesson?

Considered response:

_____

_____

_____

_____

_____

_____

_____

_____

_____

_____

_____

_____

Rate yourself

QUESTION 2: What is your current knowledge about the barriers to learning in your class?

1   2   3   4   5   6   7   8   9   10

QUESTION 3: Can you identify any of your class who may have ADHD, LDD, ASC or dyslexia?

Quick response:

_____

_____

_____

_____

Questions for consideration

- Are you aware of how ADHD manifests in the classroom and the difficulties it brings?
- Are you aware of how LDD manifests in the classroom and the difficulties it brings?
- Are you aware of how ASC affects a child in your class?
- Are you aware of how dyslexia affects a child in your class and the difficulties it brings?

Considered response:

_____

_____

_____

_____

_____

_____

_____

_____

_____

_____

Rate yourself

QUESTION 3: How much knowledge do you have of the way children are affected by ADHD, ASC, LDD and dyslexia?

1   2   3   4   5   6   7   8   9   10

QUESTION 4: Do you have children displaying challenging behaviours as a result of the above conditions?

Quick response:

_____

_____

_____

_____

Questions for consideration

- Is the behaviour more challenging than is usual?
- Do you need support to manage the behaviour?
- Do you have routines in place to help with challenging behaviours?
- Are your strategies having an impact?

Considered response:

_____

_____

_____

_____

_____

_____

_____

_____

_____

_____

_____

_____

_____

Rate yourself

QUESTION 4: How comfortable are you with your knowledge of challenging behaviour?

1	2	3	4	5	6	7	8	9	10

QUESTION 5: What do you need to improve within the classroom to help all children to stay on task?

Quick response:

_____

_____

_____

_____

Questions for consideration

- Have you checked the environment for distractions?
- Have you consulted with the TAs in your class and considered their opinion on how to keep the children on task?
- Have you discussed with the children what distracts them?
- Are your displays too busy for the children?

Considered response:

_____

_____

_____

_____

_____

_____

_____

_____

_____

_____

_____

Rate yourself

QUESTION 5: How aware are you of how to keep all children on task?

1   2   3   4   5   6   7   8   9   10

QUESTION 6: Do you know where to get help and support within school for any aspect of SEND if required?

Quick response:

_____
_____
_____
_____

Questions for consideration

- Have you asked the SENDCo for help?
- Can the SENDCo provide you with strategies for behaviour?
- Can the SENDCo sign post any outside help that may be required?
- Is there another member of staff you can ask for advice and support?

Considered response:

_____
_____
_____
_____
_____
_____
_____
_____
_____
_____
_____

Rate yourself

QUESTION 6: How comfortable are you with requesting help when needed?

1   2   3   4   5   6   7   8   9   10

QUESTION 7: Are you confident that you are operating a full inclusion policy for all children?

Quick response:

_____

_____

_____

_____

Questions for consideration

- Have you asked the child if they feel included?
- Have you spoken to the teaching assistant; are they happy with the support they give?
- During all lessons are all children equally involved?
- Are the parents sending in positive messages about the way their child is included?

Considered response:

_____

_____

_____

_____

_____

_____

_____

_____

_____

_____

_____

_____

Rate yourself:

QUESTION 7: How confident are you that all children can access your lesson?

1   2   3   4   5   6   7   8   9   10

QUESTION 8: Think about the term 'inclusion'; what does it mean to you?

Quick response:

_____

_____

_____

_____

Questions for consideration

- Should children with SEND be included in mainstream schools or special schools? Your thoughts on this will affect your teaching.
- How does inclusion relate to your lessons?
- How could you ensure all children are included and not just present in the lessons?
- What is the biggest barrier to inclusion you encounter?

Considered response:

_____

_____

_____

_____

_____

_____

_____

_____

_____

_____

_____

Rate yourself

QUESTION 8: How happy are you that every member of your class can access your lessons equally?

1   2   3   4   5   6   7   8   9   10

QUESTION 9: How will ASC affect a child in your class?

Quick response:

_____

_____

_____

_____

Questions for consideration

- Are you confident you can teach a child with ASC?
- Who would you ask for support if not your SENDCo?
- Would you ask the parents in to discuss their strategies?
- Would your teaching assistant need extra training?

Considered response:

_____

_____

_____

_____

_____

_____

_____

_____

_____

_____

_____

_____

_____

_____

Rate yourself

QUESTION 9: What is your current knowledge of ASC and how it affects the child?

1   2   3   4   5   6   7   8   9   10

QUESTION 10: How does ADHD affect the child in your class?

Quick response:

_____

_____

_____

_____

Questions for consideration

- Are you confident you can teach a child with ADHD?
- Have you looked at the classroom through the eyes of a child with ADHD, what do they see?
- Would you or could you visit another school to see how they teach children with ADHD?
- Can you think of practical strategies to help this child?

Considered response:

_____

_____

_____

_____

_____

_____

_____

_____

_____

_____

_____

_____

Rate yourself

QUESTION 10: What is your current knowledge of ADHD?

1   2   3   4   5   6   7   8   9   10

QUESTION 11: What do you know about the umbrella term 'Learning Difficulties and Disabilities'?

Quick response:

_____

_____

_____

_____

Questions for consideration

- Are you aware of the vast number of areas this term covers?
- Where will you go for advice if the child has no diagnosis but is displaying difficulties with learning or behaviour?
- How will you teach a child with LDD?
- How could you personalise the learning for the child if there is no diagnosis?

Considered response:

_____

_____

_____

_____

_____

_____

_____

_____

_____

_____

_____

_____

Rate yourself

QUESTION 11: What is your current knowledge of LDD?

1   2   3   4   5   6   7   8   9   10

QUESTION 12: Are you aware of the difficulties caused by dyslexia?

Quick response:

_____

_____

_____

_____

Questions for consideration

- Have you identified the child's main area of difficulty?
- How is the child's learning affected?
- What strategies can you use to help?
- Where will you go for advice?

Considered response:

_____

_____

_____

_____

_____

_____

_____

_____

_____

_____

_____

_____

_____

Rate yourself

QUESTION 12: What do you know about dyslexia and how it affects a child's learning?

1	2	3	4	5	6	7	8	9	10

QUESTION 13: What are the underlying causes of many behaviour challenges?

Quick response:

_____

_____

_____

_____

Questions for consideration

- Do you need to change the environment to help with behaviour challenges?
- Do you need to put strategies in place to help individual children?
- Do you need to discuss with your teaching assistant and check you are working as a team?
- Can you isolate the difficulties for individual children?

Considered response:

_____

_____

_____

_____

_____

_____

_____

_____

_____

_____

_____

_____

Rate yourself

QUESTION 13: How comfortable are you with behaviour management?

| 1 | 2 | 3 | 4 | 5 | 6 | 7 | 8 | 9 | 10 |

QUESTION 14: Have you considered all the different aspects of SEND you may encounter in your classroom and all the challenges this will bring you in terms of resources?

Quick response:

_____

_____

_____

_____

Questions for consideration

- How will you ensure each child has a voice? Will you need symbols, Makaton, visual resources or iPad apps to help them to communicate?
- How will you ensure each child has specialist reading, writing and PE equipment?
- Are you aware of where to source these things?
- Are you aware that you may have to change the physical layout of the classroom to accommodate all the child's physical equipment?

Considered response:

_____

_____

_____

_____

_____

_____

_____

_____

_____

Rate yourself:

QUESTION 14: Are you happy that you can provide all the resources needed to make the classroom a successful experience for the child with SEND?

1   2   3   4   5   6   7   8   9   10

QUESTION 15: How will you evaluate your progress in terms of providing full inclusion for all children in your class?

Quick response:

_____
_____
_____
_____

Questions for consideration

- Will you ask the children if they feel included?
- Could you observe the class and see if everyone is participating in all of your lessons?
- Will you ask the parents if the child is happy when they return home from school?
- Will you create an action plan to improve things further?

Considered response:

_____
_____
_____
_____
_____
_____
_____
_____
_____
_____
_____
_____

Rate yourself:

QUESTION 15: How happy are you that your strategies are having an impact?

1   2   3   4   5   6   7   8   9   10

The results

Well done; you have self-evaluated your SEND practices and have taken a step forward in the right direction to becoming an inclusion expert! You have considered your current knowledge and how you can further improve your knowledge of the various SENDs. You have begun to think about where you can turn for extra help and advice if needed. You have also considered some of the strategies you may need for full inclusion. It is a lot to take in so take the time to let your self-evaluation sink in and sit with you for a while.

Take a look at how you rated your answers for each question in the questionnaire and compare your ratings with the chart below which will guide you to taking the next steps in your SEND provision.

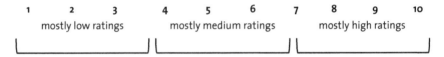

1	2	3	4	5	6	7	8	9	10
	mostly low ratings			mostly medium ratings			mostly high ratings		

Fig. 5 How did you rate yourself?

Mostly low ratings
You have assessed your knowledge and worked out that you have a fair amount to learn. Don't be disheartened; you have been very honest with yourself and this will help you on your journey to becoming an inclusive teacher. Remember to take it slowly. There is a lot to learn and a lot to take in.

Mostly medium ratings
You have discovered that you have a reasonably good idea about the various SENDs that you may face in your classroom. You now need to determine your own next steps for learning. Prioritise your personal needs and work on a plan of action according to the needs of your class.

Mostly high ratings
You are quite an expert in SEND. You have assessed yourself highly and are in the wonderful position of being able to help other people to learn how to fully include and teach all children. Do remember everyone can improve. Continue to discuss with others, continue to learn from others and continue to collaborate with experts and further your knowledge. No one is perfect and we all have the capacity to improve.

Now what?

You have now completed your self-reflection on SEND and you are aware of exactly where you are up to in terms of learning about the different conditions. Use this knowledge wisely. Plan when you will begin your training and make yourself a plan. Consider how you can fit your training in alongside planning for and teaching your class. Take your time with this step and be clear about your own priorities.

Chapter 2 takeaway

Teaching tip
No man is an island
Ask for help! There is no shame in asking for help from more experienced colleagues or from those who are experts in their own area. We all need help from time to time. Our job is to be the best teacher we can for the children who are experiencing difficulties in our classrooms. We also need to be sure that every child has access to the curriculum and we can't do that by ourselves. Asking for help is a good thing.

Pass it on
Be generous! Two heads are always better than one; we all know that. Share your knowledge; pass it on to those who have less experience. The most powerful model is the collaborative model. Collaboration is a good thing and should be encouraged in schools where doors are often firmly closed to visitors.

CPD book club recommendation
Teaching Children and Young People with Special Educational Needs and Disabilities by Sarah Martin-Denham

This book is designed to help teachers teach and work with young people in an inclusive way.

Bloggers' corner
Jules Daulby authors some excellent posts on SEND. Her posts are often thought provoking and are always informative. I have referred to some of her posts in quick training sessions with my newly qualified teachers on some occasions. Jules can be found on staffrm.com/@jules

TO DO LIST:

- ❑ Reflect on your questionnaire; what is it telling you?
- ❑ Prioritise your areas for learning; what is most important to you?
- ❑ Make yourself a training schedule.
- ❑ Tweet out your discoveries or any questions you may have using: #BloomsCPD.
- ❑ Read *Teaching Young People with Special Educational Needs and Disabilities*.
- ❑ Have a read of some of Jules Daulby's posts.

3 Class assessment

Now that you have assessed your own knowledge and practice, it's time to assess the needs of the children in your class. In order to know how to support every child in your class, you need to be able to answer the question: what specific needs do they have?

The child in the classroom

So, the child has arrived in your classroom. They may or may not have an EHC plan (see p 7). If the child has an EHC plan, the job could be deemed to be slightly easier at this stage as their area of special educational need has already been identified. This of course does not make teaching any easier, but it does remove the issue of what is the main barrier to learning. Sometimes a teacher can find himself or herself faced with a child who won't or can't learn. The task for the teacher is to find out why and put measures in place to ensure progress. I suggest a good place to begin is with a one page profile.

One page profile

A one page profile is an excellent way to learn about a child. They are not statutory but they are good practice and most schools are using them. It is a summary of what is important to them, how they want to be supported and how they like to live their lives. It is personalised, child-centred and is a key part of working with children with SEND, especially those with more complex needs. It is an 'at a glance' view of everything that is important to the child as specified by the child themselves rather than an adult working with them. It helps anyone who is unfamiliar with the child to quickly learn what is important to them.

The best way to make a one page profile is to involve the parents if possible. Many schools have developed their own templates to send home for parents to fill in to help teachers to learn key information about the child. This is particularly helpful if the child in question has communication difficulties. Once you have your information it is often best to work on an individual basis with the child. Take your time. It is more important to get the basic facts about what is 'important to' them and what is 'important for' them correct rather than producing a document at speed. It may take several attempts to get the profile just right but your attention to detail will be worth it when it perfectly describes the child and what they need and what they want for themselves.

As well as the one page profile there are other documents you create to help you audit the needs of the children in your classroom.

Here is an example of a one page profile. This one is made for a child that you may encounter in your own class and is an example of good practice.

My one page profile

Things I like

- Going swimming
- My trampoline
- Going to the park
- Going on the computer at school
- People talking and interacting with me
- Going to McDonald's

Things people like about me

- Sense of humour
- Always happy
- Make friends easily
- Caring
- Love being with people

Poppy

Important to me

- Going out for tea
- Going shopping
- Being busy
- Being around my friends
- People giving me time to answer

Things I don't like

- Sudden loud noises
- Not being told what is happening
- People talking about me like I'm not there
- Total darkness

Important for me

- Eating plenty
- Doing activities that keep my hands and fingers flexible
- To do my stretches and to go in my standing frame
- Having plenty to drink
- To be given the opportunity to make choices
- To make sure I always have my communication aid charged and on me all the time so I can contribute
- To be told what is going to happen next

Fig. 6 One page profile

Pupil passport

A pupil passport is similar to a one page profile. Again, they are not statutory but are considered good practice. It is a summary of important information about the child such as name, age, photograph, family members and pets. It contains information the child wants to share with others and should be written with the child and also, as with one page profiles, written in the first person.

Individual Educational Plan (IEP)

IEPs are not compulsory but are considered good practice. Many schools have changed the name of these documents and are making their own versions of them since the new Code of Practice, but the basic information remains the same. They give details of specific targets which arise from the EHCP and the strategies which will be used to meet those targets. The targets should be SMART targets: specific, measurable, attainable, relevant and time bound. More information on SMART targets later.

An example of a school that is using IEPs but has changed their approach to it is from Camberwell Park Specialist Support School in Manchester. Headteacher Mary Isherwood and her team have produced a new format for supporting their children. They are using 'My Learning Targets' (MLTs) which are produced following the Annual Review and directly link to EHCP outcomes. Staff monitor and consult with parents or carers at parents' evenings in the two terms in between Annual Reviews to evaluate the progress the child is making. They record on their MLT pro-forma and add in any multi agency collaborative working which informs the next review. This is thorough and effective practice for children who need it.

If you choose to use IEPs you need to be aware of some introductory information on the subject:

- The IEP is designed to help teachers and all school staff to work on specific targets arising from the child's statement (if they still have one) or EHC plan.
- The targets and strategies for achieving them are different from or additional to those required by all children.
- There should be no more than four targets; they should be SMART targets, and they should be short term and reviewed regularly.

Provision maps

Once again provision maps are not compulsory. Paragraph 6.76 of The Code of Practice says they are an efficient way of showing all the provision the school makes which is additional to and different from that which is offered through the school's curriculum.

To make a provision map:

- Gather all information about your children with SEND, including data, past interventions, previous successes
- Identify any new areas of need for your children
- Determine which staff will work with the children
- Remember – Paragraph 6.76 of The Code of Practice states that provision maps are an efficient way of showing all the provision that the school makes which is additional to and different from that which is offered through the school's curriculum.

It is worth remembering that schools have different names for all this paperwork and they will choose which paperwork they wish to use.

Conducting an audit

Now you know what is important to the child, it is vital that you identify the SEND or find out what is the barrier to learning. It is worth remembering that you the teacher are responsible for the progress of all the children in the class and performance-related pay has ensured that this is built in.

I suggest looking at the whole cohort of children in your class and conducting an audit. It is important to establish how a child with SEND interacts with the rest of the class and how the class responds to the child with special needs. You can then discover what needs you have in your class, combine this with the results from your self-assessment in the previous chapter and define the areas you need to improve.

As mentioned in the introduction, this book will focus on ADHD, ASC, LDD, dyslexia, inclusion and behaviour for learning. The next few pages provide you with auditing skills for these conditions and key areas of SEND practice. Chapter 4 (p 50) includes an overview and advice on the most common special educational needs you are likely to find in the classroom and details on where you can find more expert information on them.

A good audit is based on certain key principles: there must be whole school buy-in to any agreed action and information must be disseminated to everyone who works with the child.

First of all have a good look around your classroom and check:

- Is the lighting correct? (i.e. not too bright, no broken lights, no flashing lights.)
- Can the child hear you as you move around the classroom?

- Can the child see you as you move around the classroom?
- Is anybody prodding/teasing them?
- Are they showing off for others?

If there is nothing immediately obvious, it is time to look at the particular behaviours the child is displaying.

Behaviour audit

Use the questionnaires below to assess what examples of low-level and high-level disruption are going on in your classroom.

Observe ➡ What behaviours is the child displaying?

Low-level disruptive behaviours	Yes	No
Chatting/muttering		
Lip twanging		
Velcro		
Pen clicking		
Letting taps drip in the science lab (S)		
Pencil tapping		
Rudeness (S)		
Calling out		
General silliness/showing off		
Turning gas taps off and on in science labs (S)		
Being off-task		
Muttering under breath		
Using mobile phone (S)		
Fidgeting		
Arriving late (S)		
Constantly dropping pens/pencils		
Sitting doing nothing (S)		
Constantly asking to borrow equipment (S)		

* Those marked (S) were highlighted as being more prevalent in secondary schools.

Fig. 7 Low-level disruption questionnaire

Observe ➡ What behaviours is the child displaying?

High-level disruptive behaviours	Yes	No
Throwing chairs		
Throwing iPad		
Fighting		
Continual use of mobile phone		
Use of imitation guns to intimidate staff (S)		
Listening to music and ignoring lesson (P)		
Screaming		
Setting off fireworks (S)		
Vandalism		
Destruction of resources and fittings		
Foul and abusive language to teacher and peers		
Fighting so badly that whole class has to be evacuated		
Running around classroom		
Setting off fire alarms (S)		
Complete refusal to engage		
Streaking (S)		
Physical violence towards the teacher, e.g. headbutting		
Jumping out of the window		
Hitting other child with badminton/tennis racket (S)		
Smoking/preparing cigarette before leaving lesson to smoke (S)		
Stabbing with compass		
Throwing stool through window (Sp)		
Squirting with acid (Sp)		
Knife brandishing (S)		
Totally trashing classroom (Sp)		
Open confrontation		
Leaving the room (Sp)		
Running out of school		

Key
S =Secondary specific
P= Pru
Sp=Special

Fig. 8 High-level disruption questionnaire

Glance down the columns you completed in the questionnaires above and see where your ticks lie. Are they predominantly in the yes or no column? This will give you an idea of what you are dealing with.

If your ticks lie mostly in the 'yes' column, your child could have Attention Deficit Hyperactivity Disorder (ADHD) or Attention Deficit Disorder (ADD) as it used to be known in the 1980s. It is now thought that the two terms are similar, but where there is no hyperactivity, the difficulty is termed ADD. We will learn more about this in the next chapter (P 51). Of course it is important to be sensible. Not all disruptive behaviour has a medical diagnosis. ADHD is more than normal, child-like disruptive behaviour. ADHD often disrupts the classroom so much that normal teaching cannot take place. It is a problem for the teacher, the rest of the class, the child themselves and the parents.

Let's assume your child has a problem with behaviour, quite possibly ADHD. You need to plan the next steps. How are you going to deal with this? How are you going to make this work for the rest of the children in the class, you, the teacher, and the child?

Taking action

1. The first step would be to consult your colleagues. Pertinent questions need to be asked. Does the child behave like this for every teacher or is it confined to your own lessons? It is hard for any teacher to accept that a child may only play up for them, but it does happen. The behaviour may not be present for every teacher and in every lesson. Again, this is a clue to ADHD. If no one else reports a problem, it is time to look more closely.
2. Have a colleague observe your teaching. Look for specific triggers. Does the behaviour happen at key times such as just after break, or is it random? Is anyone else involved in causing the behaviour, another child perhaps?
3. Ask the SENDCo to visit your lesson and observe the child.
4. Have a frank and open conversation with the parents or carers. How is the child's behaviour at home?
5. After all this research and questioning a decision needs to be made. Do you need to access SEND support for this child? Discuss with SENDCo. Discuss with parents.

Autism audit

It is important to remember that autism is a spectrum and children will be affected in different ways. We will learn more about this in the next chapter (P 55) but here are some signs that a child may be on the autistic spectrum.

Observe ➡ What behaviours is the child displaying?

Behaviours observed	Yes	No
Speech and language difficulties		
Lack of social skills		
Lack of eye contact		
Prefers the company of adults		
Dislikes social situations, such as parties		
Hand flapping/rocking		
Inappropriate facial expressions		
Inappropriate gestures		
Lack of interest in others		
Difficulty understanding other people's emotions		
Dislikes being touched		
Dislikes playing with children their own age		
Speaking in an unusual tone		
Taking spoken word too literally e.g. 'pull your socks up' will result in an attempt to pull their socks up.		
Difficulty communicating their needs/desires		
Repeating words and phrases		
A need for strict routine		
Clumsiness/prone to falling		
Over-emotional/unable to control emotions		
Unable to follow instructions		
Lack of concentration		
Does not understand more than three choices; will be overwhelmed		
Lack of understanding of sarcasm		

Fig. 9 ASC questionnaire

Once again, it is important to remember that each child is different. As with ADHD there is a need to be sensible. Are your ticks mainly in the 'yes' column? If so, there is a greater chance that the child may be somewhere on the spectrum. Presenting with one or two of these signs is not conclusive evidence that there is a real difficulty.

Taking action

1. Let's assume there is a strong reason for suspecting ASC, as there are many ticks in the 'yes' column. Chat to the parents to see if this type of behaviour is also occurring at home.
2. Talk to your TA and gather their opinion. Could the two of you together come up with an immediate plan of action to help the child?
3. Ask the SENDCo for their opinion. Should SEN support be accessed?
4. Remember at this point the diagnosis of ASC is important for securing funding but it is not important to you in terms of teaching strategies. Your role is to teach the child in the best way you can. If ASC-like behaviours are occurring there are some very simple measures you can put in place immediately to support any child that you suspect of being somewhere on the autism spectrum (see Chapter 5, p 81).

Dyslexia audit

In this book I will look at both dyslexia and Irlen Syndrome, as there is much confusion between the two. We will learn more about both conditions in the next chapter (p 65) as it is quite a complex area. To begin we need to look at the signs from the child that all is not well. We need to know what we are looking for. We need to audit the signs and symptoms observed.

Observe ➡️ What signs is the child displaying?

Signs observed	Yes	No
Delayed speech development		
Jumbled phrases		
Lack of understanding of rhyming words		
Problem learning letter names		
Inconsistent spelling		
Letters/figures reversed		
Confused order of letters		
Slow reading		
Errors when reading aloud		
Words jumping on the page		
Difficulty writing answers but able to answer orally		
Difficulty following instructions		
Problems copying		
Not identifying words within words to aid reading		

Signs observed	Yes	No
Poor spelling		
Difficulty with note-taking		
Difficulty remembering sequences of numbers		
Rereading the same line		
Missing out whole lines		
Moving closer to or further from the page when reading		

Fig. 10 Dyslexia questionnaire

It is important to remember that each child is unique. Not all children who are eventually diagnosed with dyslexia will display all these signs. Where are your ticks? Are they mainly in the 'yes' column? If so, your child may have dyslexia.

Taking action

1. Again, a chat with the SENDCo and the parents is in order to decide if extra help should be accessed.
2. Remember again, the diagnosis of dyslexia is important for securing funding but is not important to you in terms of teaching strategies. Your role is to teach the child in the best way you can. There are some very simple measures that you can put in place immediately to support any child that you suspect of being dyslexic (see Chapter 5, p 83).
3. The British Dyslexia Association (BDA) notes that 'Specific Learning Difficulties' (SpLD) is an umbrella term and generally covers dyslexia, dyspraxia, dyscalculia, AD(H)D and Asperger's syndrome. It is thought that a person who has one SpLD often has traits of others to some extent.
4. You and your TA should observe the child extensively to see if there are signs of any related conditions as suggested by the BDA above. You may be able to add to your teaching strategies if so.

LDD Audit

As with ADHD, ASC and dyslexia we will find out more about this term in the next chapter (p 60). For now, in simple terms, these children are often diagnosed with what used to be termed 'General' or 'Global' developmental delay. This is the term used to describe a delay in the developmental milestones usually acquired by children at certain ages. This might include physical abilities such as sitting up, rolling over and learning to walk. Speech and language and intellectual development is also usually lower. These milestones will generally be met but not until much later. Speech and language and intellectual abilities may never catch up. These are the children who are now usually placed in mainstream schools and experience inclusion first hand. Some may already have a diagnosis and this makes the job a little easier. For others there is a need to decide if the child has LDD or is just taking a little longer to catch up with their peers in terms of maturity and ability to cope with school. First we need to know what we are looking for.

Observe ➡️ What signs is the child displaying?

Signs observed	Yes	No
Difficulty understanding instructions		
Difficulty understanding spoken language		
Poor auditory memory		
Difficulty expressing themselves		
Difficulty staying on task		
Inability to control emotions		
Difficulty forming friendships		
Unable to concentrate/poor attention span/easily distractible		
Low-level disruptive behaviour		
Specific difficulty in reading or writing or other curriculum area		
Unable to organise self for beginning work		
Distracts others		
Unable to participate in group work without support		
Unable to accept change in routine as easily as others		
Working at a level far below age-related expectations		
Needs differentiated work structured to their learning abilities		

Fig. 11 LDD questionnaire

This is not an exhaustive list, as LDD is an umbrella term covering many conditions. It will give the class teacher a head start though, as to the behaviours they can expect to see in children with LDD. Again, we see an overlap with signs of ADHD or ASC.

Once again, look at your ticks. If they lie mostly in the 'yes' column the child may have LDD.

Taking action

1. Talk to your SENDCo and ask for advice.
2. Speak to the parents; they know the child best. What are their thoughts?

3. Decide if the child requires extra SEN support.
4. Chapter 5 (p 84) also offers some quick tips that can be implemented immediately to support any child you suspect of having LDD.

Inclusion

Having audited the behaviours and the needs of the children in your class, we need to look briefly at inclusion.

If the child is in a mainstream school, they must be welcome and be made to feel welcome by everyone involved. There is a heated debate occurring concerning the pros and cons of inclusion in mainstream schools. Some believe that every child has the right to a high-quality education in their local mainstream school no matter what their additional needs may be. Others believe that individual choice is the solution and that not every child would actually be happy in a mainstream school.

> **Twitter tip**
>
> See @NigelUtton for passionate views on complete inclusion for all children.

The Centre for Studies on Inclusive Education (csie.org.uk) summarises inclusion as:

- Reducing barriers to learning
- Reducing exclusion/discrimination
- All children having the right to a high-quality education in their local mainstream school
- Improving schools for staff, carers and parents as well as children
- Supporting everyone to feel that they belong
- Recognising that inclusion in education is one aspect of inclusion in society.

> **Twitter tip**
>
> See @JulesDaulby or @ERA_tweet for a collection of inclusion blog posts from top bloggers.

My personal view on inclusion is that inclusion is not a matter of place; rather it is the quality of the educational experience provided. The child should be educated according to the views and the needs of the child, or if this isn't possible, the views of the parents. It shouldn't be the cheapest option and it shouldn't be about the current DfE diktat. It's about 'Quality First' teaching and graduated support for every single child who needs it.

Chapter 3 takeaway

Teaching tip

Including the difficult to include.

During this chapter we have checked all the signs and symptoms of the main areas of SEND and reached a conclusion as to the barriers to learning faced by the child. Remember, it is your task to fully include them all; the label is the very least of your worries. Think about full inclusion. Don't pay lip service to it. Details such as where the child will sit, friendship group, working with the TA and remaining a part of the class are all important points to consider for your child with SEND irrespective of what that special need is. Give yourself time to work this out; it won't be easy.

Pass it on

Share and tweet

In order to compile the low- and high-level disruption questionnaires at the start of this chapter, I posed this question on Twitter: 'Teachers and TAs: can you give me some examples of low-level and high-level disruption in your classes please? Thanks.'

I thought this would be a good place to begin, by discovering the behaviours that teachers are witnessing. Many tweeters replied, providing a comprehensive list of behaviours to begin to look out for. (See the acknowledgements for details of and thanks to those who answered!)

Try doing the same for a topic you want to know about; ask Twitter and use #asktwitter for collated answers.

CPD book club recommendation

Beating Bureaucracy in Special Educational Needs by Jean Gross

Bloggers' corner

Dare I be so bold as to recommend my own blog? Have a look at cherrylkd.wordpress.com for all manner of posts on SEND.

TO DO LIST:

❏ Think about the children in your class. Ask yourself if you have worked out their individual needs.

❏ Ask your SENDCo for specific advice if you are struggling with any aspect of removing barriers to learning.

❏ Tweet out your questions using the #BloomsCPD.

❏ Have a look at Cherrylkd's blog posts on aspects of SEND.

❏ Read *Beating Bureaucracy in Special Educational Needs* by Jean Gross.

4

Getting to grips with the conditions

In this chapter we will get to grips with the different conditions and special educational needs. Teachers need to know something of the causes and theory behind the difficulties in order to help the children.

Getting to grips with ADHD

What is ADHD?

ADHD is a condition that may seriously affect a child's chances of academic success. As with most conditions the signs and symptoms vary, and not every child will display all of the signs at all times. It is also important to remember that many of these behaviours are normal child-like behaviours. The difference is that a child with ADHD does not outgrow them in time as most children do. ADHD affects around two to five per cent of children and is more commonly diagnosed in boys than girls. An article by Jane Collingwood, 'ADHD and Gender' (psychcentral.com) says that the guidelines used in assessment and diagnosis have traditionally focused on boys but that girls also have problems but present differently. The article says that girls are more likely to have the inattentive form of ADHD and have low self esteem and outwardly show less behaviour difficulties. Boys on the other hand show the outward signs of running around and being impulsive and their behaviour is generally problematic.

The condition ADHD tends to be present in all settings. It is not confined to school or home and will manifest at social functions such as birthday parties and family gatherings, and will therefore harm the child's chances of forming friendship groups.

ADHD has been split in to three subtypes:

1. **Inattentive type** – these children show difficulties with organisational skills, following instructions and paying attention.
2. **Hyperactive-impulsive type** – these children have difficulty sitting still; they may run continually and talk too much. They never stop. They are hyperactive but not inattentive.
3. **Combined type** – these children exhibit signs of the inattentive type and the hyperactive-impulsive type. This is the most common type of ADHD.

('What are the three types of ADHD' www.healthline.com)

Signs and symptoms of ADHD

- Difficulty waiting their turn/turn-taking
- Wants everything their own way

- Difficulty staying on task
- Emotionally incontinent, for example laughing inappropriately
- Prone to serious temper tantrums
- Inability to finish a task
- Fidgeting and inability to sit still when required to do so
- Difficulty focusing on a person who is speaking to them
- Difficulty following instructions
- Often loud in class
- Oblivious of their surroundings
- Inability to make and keep friends
- Inability to control own behaviour
- Little or no sense of danger
- Careless mistakes in work
- Poor organisational skills
- Highly distractible
- Impulsive and restless.

Causes of ADHD and latest research

At the moment very little is known about the causes of ADHD. Studies have shown that a child is more at risk of ADHD if someone in their family already has it. Scientists are in agreement that it is inherited and is the result of chemical imbalances in the brain. It may in fact be a combination of factors including environmental.

For many years there was a suggestion that food colourings and sugar could be the cause of ADHD. In an article entitled 'Food Dye and ADHD: Food Colouring, sugar, and Diet' (www.webmd.com) the evidence was shown to be inconclusive but is more likely to be a combination of environmental factors and heredity. Environmental factors could include smoking or drinking during pregnancy, low birth weight, complications during birth, neglect or abuse, and exposure to lead or other toxic substances.

Twitter tip
Follow #adhd for news about ADHD.

Seven myths about ADHD

1. It isn't a real medical illness.
   False – it is a chemical imbalance within the brain.
2. It will be outgrown.
   False – over 70% still have it as adults.
3. ADHD is restricted to boys.
   False – girls are just as likely to have ADHD but due to this myth boys are more likely to be diagnosed.
4. ADHD is the result of poor parenting.
   False – it is a chemical imbalance in the brain.
5. People with ADHD are lazy.
   False – they are often of above average intelligence.
6. ADHD is over diagnosed.
   False – some believe it is actually under diagnosed.
7. ADHD treatment will make a child lethargic.
   False – if the correct dose is administered, the child will be more focused, more attentive and more in control of their behaviour.

Famous people with ADHD

- Jamie Oliver (celebrity chef)
- Will Smith (actor; self-diagnosed)
- Jim Carrey (actor)
- Richard Branson (entrepreneur and Virgin founder)
- Paris Hilton (hotel heir)
- Michael Phelps (swimmer)
- Wolfgang Amadeus Mozart (composer)
- Salvador Dalí (painter).

Good news for those with ADHD

While ADHD can be a debilitating condition for those who have it, it is not necessarily entirely bad news. There are some positive aspects to it, if it is correctly treated. Those who have ADHD are often able to:

- create order from chaos
- multi-task
- see the bigger picture
- be comfortable talking in front of an audience
- be courageous
- be good in a crisis
- be willing to help others

- be empathetic towards others
- be good at problem-solving
- be good at listening
- be hard-working
- be intuitive
- be optimistic
- be outgoing
- be passionate
- be resourceful
- be able to work well under pressure.

Where to find more information on ADHD

Name: ADHD News
Twitter handle: @ADHD_news
Who are they? ADHD news from around the net
Why to follow them: Regular updates and news on ADHD

Name: ADHD Aware
Twitter handle: @ADHDAWARE
Website: adhdaware.org
Who are they? Empowering the ADHD Community
Why to follow them: Regular updates on research relating to ADHD and related conditions.

Useful websites for information and advice on ADHD:

- www.livingwithadhd.co.uk
- www.add.org
- www.addforums.com

Recommended reading

ADHD: What Every Parent Needs to Know by Michael I. Reiff
A very readable book written for parents to help them cope with ADHD. It encourages teamwork with the whole range of professionals and is a reassuring read.

'ADHD A guide for UK teachers' from the Living with ADHD website:
www.livingwithadhd.co.uk
A clear and comprehensive guide to ADHD which talks the reader through signs of
ADHD, diagnosis, living with ADHD and possible treatments for those with ADHD.

Taking Charge of Adult ADHD by Russell A. Barkley
This talks about all the difficulties faced by an adult with ADHD and will help the
teacher to empathise with children who are living with ADHD.

Getting to grips with ASC

What is ASC?

Leo Kanner first described Autistic Spectrum Condition in 1944. As the name
suggests, ASC is a spectrum; it includes Asperger's syndrome. It is a developmental
disability caused by differences in the brain. According to www.autism.org.uk
around 700,000 people in the UK have ASC. ASC incorporates a whole range of
signs and symptoms. Children with ASC will generally look the same as their
peers but their basic social and communication skills may be severely affected. It
is important to note that every child with ASC is different and even very verbal
pupils can have acute social anxiety. Children with ASC may also have significant
behaviour difficulties. They may be affected in different ways and can be
anywhere on the spectrum from mild to severe. The signs are usually there by the
time the child is three years old, and the condition is there for life. Diagnosis does
not always happen early on and some children are not diagnosed until they are in
their teens.

Quite often the difficulty is in the child's understanding and communication
skills. Although they may be verbal, they often prefer not to join in a
conversation with adults or other children. From an early age there may be
some signs that all is not well. For example, the child may not babble as other
babies do around the age of 12 months. Gestures such as pointing and waving
may not occur, and eye contact will generally be avoided. Speech in general
is delayed and the child may not be using single words by the time they are
18 months old. Children with ASC seem to live in their own private world and
prefer not to interact with others if possible. As with many conditions, not all
children with ASC will display every symptom. Not all will have problems with
communication – this will vary. Some may be completely non-verbal while
others will be able to talk extensively on a subject of their choice. Many children
with ASC will also have difficulty understanding body language and the tone of
other people's voices.

Some children with ASC display extraordinary skills and these are known as 'autistic savants'. Around ten per cent of those with ASC will be termed an autistic savant. The most well-known is Dustin Hoffman's character in *Rain Man* who had exceptional mathematical skills. Music and art are two more areas where autistic savants have been seen. For example, Tim Baley is a concert pianist who has ASC.

Signs and symptoms of ASC

- Delayed speech
- Repetition of words
- Not responding to own name
- Dislike of being cuddled although they may initiate a cuddle
- Prefers to play alone
- Unaware of personal space
- Dislike of crowded parties
- Dislike of social situations
- Often avoiding eye contact
- Repetitive movements known as stimming e.g. rocking, hand flapping
- Enjoying lining things up according to certain attributes e.g. size, colour or shape
- Dislike of strong tastes
- An absolute need for routine and structure
- Taking speech literally
- Sensory issues such as being irritated by the feel of some clothes
- Behaviour may be affected by some patterns on clothing
- May prefer tight clothes.

Causes of ASC and latest research

At the moment scientists are unsure about the exact cause of ASC. They are investigating genetics and heredity as well as other theories. They are agreed that children who have ASC often have abnormalities in the structure and the shape of the brain.

When looking at a possible familial link, there seems to be a pattern of disabilities that are similar in nature to autism. This has led scientists to begin to search for an irregular genetic code that could be inherited. Work is also being carried out in the search for a trigger for autism, as some children are more susceptible to it than others. Research is also being carried out looking at environmental factors such as exposure to chemicals or environmental toxins such as mercury. A further theory surrounds increased chances of autism if the mother ingests harmful substances during pregnancy.

Research is now showing that children with ASC share genetic traits with those with ADHD, schizophrenia, bipolar disorder and clinical depression. This has led the *Cross Disorders Group of the Psychiatric Genomic Consortium* to suggest that these conditions share the same common inherited genetic variation. For some children, ASC is associated with a genetic disorder such as Fragile X Syndrome, a genetic condition causing developmental problems or Rett Syndrome, affecting the development of the brain. It is safe to say that given the extent of the disorder and the wide variation of signs and symptoms, there is probably a combination of causes for ASC.

For many years there has been a large question mark over whether the cause can be attributed to childhood vaccines. Andrew Wakefield started this theory in *The Lancet* in 1998 and this theory although completely discredited continues to make parents wary of having their children vaccinated. The measles, mumps and rubella (MMR) vaccine was thought to be the culprit for a long time. In April 2015, however, the *Journal of the American Medical Association* published a major study that had used over 95,000 children in the research and found no link to ASC from MMR.

> **Twitter tip**
> Follow #asd for news on ASC.

Fifteen myths about ASC

1. All people with ASC have savant qualities and are good at maths.
   False – at most only two in every 200 individuals with ASC will have an extraordinary talent.
2. People with ASC no longer need support after leaving school.
   False – careful planning is required to help them cope with the change.
3. People with ASC can't start friendships.
   False – ASC makes relationships difficult, but some adults with ASC are happily married.
4. People with ASC don't want any friends.
   False – 65 % of those with ASC interviewed in 2012 said they wanted more friends.
5. Those with ASC can't feel emotions.
   False – many feel their emotions intensely.
6. ASC is only diagnosed in children.
   False – it is generally diagnosed under age three years, but it can be diagnosed at any age.

7. Those with ASC require care around the clock for their entire lives.
False – ASC is a spectrum and the level of support varies widely.
8. ASC is a male condition.
False – more males are affected, but girls are affected too.
9. All those with ASC attend special schools.
False – many children with ASC attend mainstream schools. Only those most affected need specialist support.
10. Self stimulatory behaviour or stimming as it is known, repetitive body movements such as hand flapping should be discouraged.
False – it is a coping strategy and should not be discouraged.
11. ASC will be outgrown.
False – the right support will help the child to cope but it will not be outgrown.
12. Only children have ASC.
False – ASC is a lifelong condition.
13. Non-verbal children with ASC are severely cognitively impaired.
False – some may have an associated learning difficulty while others may be above average intelligence.
14. Asperger's syndrome is a fabricated middle class condition to excuse poor behaviour.
False – it is real and disabling.
15. ADHD and ASC are the same condition.
False – some children are diagnosed with both, but the conditions are separate.

Famous people with ASC

1. Wolfgang Amadeus Mozart (composer)
2. Andy Warhol (artist)
3. Lewis Carroll (author; possibly Asperger's syndrome)
4. Courtney Love (singer; mildly autistic)
5. Temple Grandin (professor)
6. Dan Aykroyd (actor; Asperger's syndrome)
7. Susan Boyle (singer)

Good news for those with ASC

It isn't all bad news for those with ASC – there are some positive aspects. For example, many people with ASC:

- are very honest – they may find it difficult to understand others' points of view and how to manipulate others' thinking that is essential to being able to lie. Generally, many don't have the capacity to tell even white lies.
- don't judge others – this is not true of all people with autism as some are incredibly judgemental. But, many are simply not interested in who is richer or who is better looking. Most with ASC tend to see only the real person.

- have fantastic memories – because they like details and therefore remember things intricately.
- don't have hidden agendas – they tell you exactly what they want and when they want it. There is no guesswork involved.

Where to find information on ASC

Name: Lynn McCann

Twitter handle: @reachoutASC

Who are they? Independent consultant for ASC

Website: reachoutasc.com

Why to follow them: Lynn tweets out information and answers questions. She provides support and resources.

Useful websites for information and advice on ASC:
The National Autistic Society
www.autism.org.uk
The leading UK charity for people with autism and their families.

Research Autism
www.researchautism.net
This is the only UK charity exclusively dedicated to research into interventions in autism.

Autism Research Institute
www.autism.com
Keeping everyone up to date with the latest research.

The Centre for Autism
www.autism.org.uk
Established to raise the standard of support and services for people with ASC.

Books

How to Support Pupils with Autistic Spectrum Condition in Primary School by Lynn McCann
How to Support Pupils with Autistic Spectrum Condition in Secondary School by Lynn McCann.

These books give information and strategies for how to support children with ASC in primary or secondary school.

The Autistic Brain by Temple Grandin
As a talented scientist and autistic person Temple Grandin is in the unusual position of being able to offer her own experience and also explain about the autistic brain.

Autism and Asperger Syndrome by Simon Baron-Cohen
This book summarises the current understanding of autism and Asperger's syndrome. It talks the reader through diagnosis and education.

Getting to grips with LDD

What is LDD?

LDD is an umbrella term for any learning or emotional problem that affects a child's ability to learn in the same way and at a similar rate to children of their own age. The term 'learning difficulty' is often used to cover the whole spectrum of learning disabilities. The learning difficulty can include all areas of their life and not just their school life. Quite often it involves an inability to understand instructions and new information. Memory is often impaired and the child may struggle to work or achieve independence. LDD does not affect all children in the same way; the term incorporates many syndromes and conditions. Some common types of LDD are:

- Dyslexia
- Dyscalculia (maths)
- Dyspraxia (fine motor skills, co-ordination)
- Dysgraphia (writing)
- Auditory processing disorder (reading/language)
- Visual processing disorder (maps, charts, symbols)
- Dysphasia (language)
- Down's Syndrome
- Cerebral Palsy
- Language processing Disorder
- Epilepsy
- Pervasive Developmental Disorder
- Delayed Development
- Sensory Processing Disorder
- Chronic Fatigue Syndrome.

It is possible that ADHD, ASC and Down's syndrome may also co-occur under this heading, although all conditions have different traits and characteristics. Some children may be mildly affected and cope well in the mainstream classroom; others will need much support in various forms. Although the specific learning difficulty dyslexia is included under the term LDD, these children show no signs of impaired cognitive ability and so I have chosen to cover dyslexia separately (p 64).

The different terms: Moderate Learning Disability (MLD), Severe Learning Disability (SLD) and Profound and Multiple Learning Disability (PMLD) are also used interchangeably with LDD although these conditions are very different. Those with MLD are mildly affected and require little support; those with PMLD are often dependent on an adult for their care and for every aspect of their welfare. Some learning disabilities are diagnosed at birth or before, and others take much longer to diagnose.

Signs and symptoms of LDD

Many children will show signs of difficulty with certain aspects of their school life but this does not necessarily indicate a learning disability. The signs need to be prevalent for a long time. As we know the indicators are different in each child but there are some common indicators that all may not be well. All the learning disabilities we have mentioned have their own signs and symptoms although there is some overlap as we have seen. Some children:

- are disorganised and have trouble remembering simple instructions to the point where schooling becomes a struggle without support.
- are inattentive
- lack concentration
- are disruptive in class
- have immature speech
- have difficulty understanding their peers
- have problems with reading and writing or maths
- have no concept of time
- may lack a sense of danger which means they need support
- have poor coordination which means they are prone to falling over and can be a danger to themselves and others.

Causes of LDD and latest research

The latest research as reported in www.specialeducationalneeds.co.uk says that for some children, there may be no known reason for their learning disability. For others it is possible to group the possible causes into four broad areas:

- Genetic causes, which includes Fragile X Syndrome and Down's Syndrome – also included in this category are alcohol and drug consumption by the mother during pregnancy.
- Oxygen deprivation during birth – this can sometimes occur and this leads to brain damage and premature birth.
- Environmental conditions such as Meningitis or a child being neglected or abused.
- A combination of all of these factors – being caused by things prior to and post birth.
- As the cause of LLD varies so much between children who are affected it is difficult to accurately find the latest research. Similarly, there is no single recommended treatment. Each child will display different difficulties and these should be addressed according to the needs of the child. For example, one child might have communication as their greatest challenge. In this case a speech and language therapist will be involved as soon as possible. Another child may have Cerebral Palsy and be unable to walk but have no problem articulating their thoughts. In this case a physiotherapist must be involved as soon as possible.

Twitter tip

Follow #learningdifficulties for information on LDD.

Five myths about LDD

1. People with LDD are lazy.
   False – there is a difficulty with the development of the brain.
2. Watching too much TV causes LDD.
   False – there is no evidence to prove this. Children with a poor attention span caused by LDD are often able to concentrate on the TV for long periods.
3. People with LDD can't have successful careers.
   False – many celebrities have a learning disability. Tommy Hilfiger (fashion designer) and Robert Graham (sculptor) both have forms of LDD. Daniel Radcliffe (Harry Potter) lives with dyspraxia.
4. Mostly boys have LDD.
   False – girls are often quieter by nature and are therefore not diagnosed as often.
5. Children can outgrow a learning disability.
   False – as it often has a biological cause it can't be outgrown and will sometimes intensify with adulthood.

Famous people with LDD

- Alexander Graham Bell (inventor of the telephone)
- Napoleon Bonaparte (military leader)
- Cher (singer)
- Agatha Christie (author)
- Walt Disney (cartoonist and film-maker)
- Tom Cruise (actor)
- Thomas Edison (inventor)
- Benjamin Franklin (inventor)
- John F. Kennedy (American president)

Good news for those with LDD

As with most things it isn't all bad news for those children with LDD.

- With support children with LDD can be very successful.
- Society is becoming ever more inclusive; most places are now wheelchair accessible for example. People with visual and hearing impairments are catered for in wider society.
- Famous people like Stephen Hawking have made it more acceptable to be disabled and prove that you shouldn't judge a book by its cover.
- People with LDD learn early on in life that there is no shame in asking for help, a lesson everyone can learn.

We will learn more about the support required for children with various learning disabilities in the next chapter. The key thing to remember is that the actual label given to a child is not important. The support given to the child is the key to their success. The placement or school for the child is also important (see inclusion, p 71).

Where to find more information on LDD

Name: Mencap

Twitter handle: @mencap_charity

Website: mencap.org.uk

Who are they? Mencap is the leading charity that who believes that all children have the right to a good start in life and a good education.

Why to follow them: They will answer questions and they tweet out up-to-the-minute DfE documents and information.

Useful websites for information and advice on LDD:

The British Institute of Learning Disabilities (BILD)
www.bild.org.uk
BILD want people with LDD to be valued equally and be able to participate fully in their communities. They also provide training for school staff on some aspects of LDD such as autism and positive behaviour management.

Learning Disability
http://www.nhs.uk/Livewell/Childrenwithalearningdisability/Pages/Childrenwithalearningdisabilityhome.aspx
Live Well Articles and videos aimed at parents and carers of children with a learning disability. Talks the family through the diagnosis and getting the best education possible.

Learning Disabilities/Reading Rockets
http://www.readingrockets.org/reading-topics/learning-disabilities
This site provides lots of information about different learning disabilities. Resources and articles for different LDD are also provided.

Books

Engaging Learners with Complex Learning Difficulties and Disabilities by Barry Carpenter. Children with complex learning difficulties often have co-existing conditions which can make teaching them extremely complicated. This book gives you strategies to help.

Language for Thinking by Stephen Parsons and Anna Branagan.
This book gives advice for teachers of children who have delayed speech and language due to a learning disability.

The Complete Learning Disabilities Handbook: Ready to use Strategies and Activities to Teaching Students with Learning Disabilities by J M Harwell and R W Jackson. This book gives effective strategies and top tips for motivating students with SEND.

Getting to grips with dyslexia

Before we can begin to work on strategies for helping the child with dyslexia, it is important to make a distinction between Irlen Syndrome and dyslexia. We need to do this as there is some confusion over using certain strategies to help children with dyslexia which are actually for helping those with Irlen Syndrome.

What is Irlen Syndrome?

Irlen Syndrome is often mistaken for dyslexia but it is vastly different, although the two conditions can co-exist. Irlen Syndrome is an impairment of how the brain deals with the visual information it receives. It is not an optical problem. Irlen Syndrome has no bearing on language and no amount of phonics catch-up classes will help with Irlen Syndrome. Those with Irlen Syndrome see different shapes and objects on the page to the ones we see. The words on a page may be blurred or move around. As with many other syndromes, the problems experienced will be different for each person. Areas affected may include: academic output, attention and concentration, fidgeting and behaviour. There will also be sensitivity to light, especially fluorescent lights, bright lights and sunlight.

Signs and symptoms of Irlen Syndrome

- Glare on page
- Headaches/migraines
- Reading difficulties
- Tired eyes
- Lack of concentration
- Lack of motivation
- Problems with spatial awareness
- Sensitivity to light
- Problems tracking
- Slow reading rate
- Inability to speed-read
- Trouble copying work
- Difficulty staying on task
- Feeling sleepy, anxious, irritable
- Low self-esteem.

What is dyslexia?

According to the British Dyslexia Association around one in ten children and adults are affected by dyslexia. An article from www.bdadyslexia.org.uk 'The Science Behind Dyslexia' states that dyslexia is a language-based disorder. It is a continuum and people are affected in different ways and show different symptoms from mild to severe.

There is much research in the area of genetics and it is thought that approximately 40% of children who have a dyslexic parent may have dyslexia themselves and others without full-blown dyslexia will show mild symptoms. This research points to dyslexia possibly being caused by a combination of many different genes.

Dyslexia is a language-based disorder which results in difficulties with processing spoken language. There are also difficulties with memory and organisational skills. Other difficulties are also seen in dyslexic children such as reduced motor skills and a lack of attention. This may result in difficulties with specific language skills and, in particular, reading. There will also be problems with spelling and decoding abilities.

Dyslexia is a family of specific learning difficulties which includes dyspraxia, dyscalculia and ADD. It is unrelated to intelligence and it occurs in children with normal vision; it is not related to eyesight as many people once thought.

There are several signs of dyslexia that are common in many of those who have it. However, as with all the other difficulties we have looked at, it is important to remember that not all people will display the same signs and with the same severity.

Those who have it are often distressed because they fail to make satisfactory academic progress. There is a widely held belief that dyslexia involves letter or word reversals, or words jumping and dancing around on the page. This is simply not true. Most children go through a phase of reading letters wrongly and reversing words such as 'saw' and 'bad'. This is perfectly normal when learning to read and is not an indicator of a problem. There is also another widely-held belief that dyslexia is something made up by 'middle class' mothers who are disappointed that their children are not as bright as they would like them to be. Dyslexia is no respecter of class, and it is not related to a child's intelligence.

Professor Goswami, Director of the Centre for Neuroscience explained in 'Children's Cognitive Development and Learning', Cambridge Primary Review Trust 2015, that dyslexia is a language disorder rather than a visual one as previously thought. Dyslexic children hear language differently from the way other children hear language. Dyslexia is a problem in the way the brain moves sounds into words. Brain rhythms and speech rhythms line themselves up and send a signal, but that process does not work correctly in those with dyslexia. This is the reason why spelling is affected. If a child cannot hear a sound it is hard to spell it.

Children who have dyslexia often struggle with concentration. It is thought that this is because the very act of concentrating so hard causes children to be tired out and they subsequently struggle to pay attention. It is thought that a high number of children with dyslexia also have ADHD. It is important to remember that these difficulties on their own do not indicate dyslexia.

Signs and symptoms of dyslexia

- Poor or delayed speech development
- Jumbling phrases and an inability to pronounce long words
- Difficulty learning the sounds of letters and their names
- Difficulty with spelling
- Confusing the order of letters in words
- Difficulty expressing themselves in writing
- Difficulty with sequences of instructions
- Difficulty with sequencing such as months of the year
- Problems with organisational skills
- Avoiding reading aloud
- Problems remembering facts.

Causes of dyslexia and latest research

Many years ago, early on in the research into dyslexia, it was discovered that dyslexia often runs in families and there was a suspicion that genetics were involved in transmitting it from one generation to another. In fact, recent researchers have suggested that six chromosomes, including numbers 3, 6 and 15, may be related to dyslexia and language difficulties. Four of the genes have been identified as affecting part of the process in the development of the brain that leads to the brain's specialised jobs. Further research using brain scans has also shown problems with the area at the back of the brain. This research into the functioning of the brain has shown that phonological processing is affected and this contributes to dyslexia. Dyslexia is now understood to be a neurological condition and it is accepted that it is passed on through families.

What is phonological processing?

For most of us, our ability to understand spoken language is a reasonable assumption. We hear whole words rather than phonemes. These phonemes, the smallest part of the word, are thought to be a problem for people with dyslexia. In the development of literacy skills – reading and writing in particular – recognition of letters is required, then the identification of phonemes and finally whole word recognition. This is known as phonological processing and those with dyslexia are thought to have phonological processing impairment.

> **Twitter tip**
> Follow #dyslexia for daily news on dyslexia

Eight myths about dyslexia

1. Reversing letters and words means a child is dyslexic.
   False – children often outgrow this.
2. Reading difficulties are caused by visual problems.
   False – reading difficulties are caused by a combination of factors, including incorrect tuition, learning difficulties, hearing difficulties.
3. Children will outgrow dyslexia if given time.
   False – they will learn strategies that will help them cope better.
4. More boys than girls have dyslexia.
   False – boys are more likely to be diagnosed with dyslexia as girls try to hide it.
5. Dyslexia only affects those who speak English.
   False – dyslexia is found all over the world.
6. Those with dyslexia need coloured overlays or lenses.
   False – this is a remedy for those with Irlen Syndrome.
7. Those with dyslexia can never learn to read.
   False – with intensive instruction they can become accurate but slow readers.
8. Dyslexia can be cured.
   False – it is a life-long condition.

Famous people with dyslexia

- Lewis Carroll (author of *Alice in Wonderland*)
- Jim Carrey (actor)
- Jennifer Aniston (actor)
- Richard Branson (entrepreneur and Virgin founder)
- Alexander Graham Bell (inventor of the telephone)
- Albert Einstein (theory of relativity)
- Michael Faraday (inventor and electrical pioneer)
- Leonardo da Vinci (famous painter and scientist)
- Tom Cruise (actor)
- Steve Jobs (founder of Apple)
- John Lennon (Beatles singer)
- Steven Spielberg (film director)

Good news for those with dyslexia

It isn't all bad news for those with dyslexia. There are some advantages that are rarely mentioned. People with dyslexia are:

- Quick problem-solvers as they often think in pictures
- Excellent communicators
- Able to see the whole picture
- Very creative and often have creative careers, such as actor, chef, designer
- Very perceptive
- Articulate in most situations.

There are several generalised strengths that teachers can use to create an environment where children with dyslexia can succeed.

Strengths of children with dyslexia	Areas of weakness
Ability to think logically	Low self esteem
Ability to think outside the box	Co-ordination problems
Good problem-solving skills	May have memory issues
May be good with technology	Poor organisational and sequencing skills
Ability to see the bigger picture	
May be good with DT and other 3D skills	Poor concentration
May be creative	Difficulties with reading

Where to find more information on dyslexia

Name: Sarah Chapman

Twitter handle: @mrs_dyslexia

Website: facebook.com/groups/dyslexia

Who are they? Award-winning campaigner/BDA Ambassador

Why to follow them: Expert in dyslexia and associated difficulties.

Name: DriverYouthTrust

Twitter handle: @DriverTrust

Website: driveryouthtrust.com

Who are they? Charity dedicated to improving the life chances of young people with a focus on those who struggle with literacy and dyslexia.

Why to follow them: Updates information on dyslexia training and research.

Name: Maria Constantinou
Twitter handle: @MariaStMarys
Website: londonleadershipstrategy.com/content/delivery-team
Who are they? Maria is an SLE for SEN and also works as a consultant for London Leadership Strategy
Why to follow them: Maria is my number one person to go to for all things relating to dyslexia.

Name: The British Dyslexia Association (BDA)
Twitter handle: @BDAdyslexia
Website: www.bdadyslexia.org.uk
Who are they? The British voice for dyslexia
Why to follow them: Constant updates on all news relating to dyslexia.

Useful websites for information and advice on dyslexia:

Dyslexia Action
www.dyslexiaaction.org.uk/ (@DyslexiaAction)
A national charity supporting people with dyslexia.

Dyslexia Assist
www.dyslexia-assist.org.uk (@DyslexiaAssist)
A charity run by parents, for parents, formed to share information and experience about dyslexia.

Drive for Literacy
www.driveforliteracy.co.uk
Specifically for free downloadable resources: http://driveforliteracy.co.uk/resources-how-do-i-adapt-my-teaching/

The Dyslexia-SpLD Trust
http://www.thedyslexia-spldtrust.org.uk/

Interventions for literacy
www.interventionsforliteracy.org.uk

Books

Reading Difficulties and Dyslexia: An Interpretation for Teachers by J. P. Das.
This gives teachers and parents a complete source of current knowledge and answers frequently asked questions.

Specific Learning Difficulties (Dyslexia) by M. Crombie.
A complete up-to-date guide for dealing with dyslexia in the classroom. The book is aimed at primary but has a section for secondary school teachers as well.

How to Detect and Manage Dyslexia by P. Ott.
An essential reference book for SENDCos, specialist, non-specialist teachers and parents and anyone involved in helping those with dyslexia.

Getting to grips with inclusion

What is inclusion?

Put simply, inclusion is about equal opportunities for all pupils. There should be no discrimination on the grounds of age, gender, ethnicity, background or disability. A school that can call itself 'inclusive' values the teaching and learning and achievements of every child.

In education at the moment, inclusion is possibly one of the most hotly debated topics. Everyone has an opinion on inclusion and what that means for the child. Twitter has a lengthy thread devoted to #inclusiondebate and many bloggers have written passionately on the subject, including myself.

There is however, no single certain answer. Personalisation is the key. Whatever is best for the child is the way forward. There should be no hard and fast rules in an ideal world. The British Government is currently committed to the principle of inclusive education in mainstream schools. The latest Code of Practice (2015) states:

> 'Where a child has SEND but does not have an EHC plan they must be educated in a mainstream setting except in specific circumstances.'

The Code of Practice also states there should be a focus on inclusive practice and removing barriers to learning. The new code reminds us that all teachers are teachers of children with SEND. Children and their parents will be included in the decision-making process and if a request for a special school is made it will be considered carefully despite the general rule for mainstream education.

I asked my teaching colleagues on Twitter for their thoughts on inclusion and I received this answer from Amjad Ali @ASTsupportAli who is the biggest champion of inclusion in a mainstream school that I am aware of. In his school his official title is 'Director of Inclusion.'

'Inclusion to me is the ability of teachers/schools to ensure their students make progress and socialise equitably.'

Twitter tip

Follow @ASTsupportAli for top tips on inclusion

As Amjad has pointed out, it is not just about the expectation of progress; it is also about the socialisation. Friendship groups are a key component in a child's happiness and this is often an area that is neglected both in special and mainstream schools.

John Scattergood's (@jwscattergood) response to my tweet highlighted removing the barriers to learning:

'Ensuring that barriers to learning are removed and every child can progress to the best of their ability.'

As teachers in mainstream schools, it is imperative that we do this in order to become inclusive. More information on the practicalities of making the classroom inclusive will follow in the next chapter (p 91).

Advantages of inclusion

There are many advantages of a mainstream inclusive education for a child with SEND and for their mainstream peers. Here are a few that teachers can aim for:

- Increased friendship groups
- Provides role models for those displaying behaviour difficulties
- Prepares children for an inclusive society
- Acceptance of diversity
- Improves teachers' ability to adapt to the different ways children learn
- Attends the local school with children from same area.

Disadvantages of inclusion

- For children with PMLD, or children with complex medical needs, mainstream school can be very intrusive. For a child who is fed via a tube, or who has other medical interventions in the classroom it could be unfair to expose them to prying eyes.
- Teacher knowledge of teaching children with LDD and other conditions may be scant – training would be required.
- Less chance of meaningful friendship groups as classes are very small.
- Attends a school often outside their own area.

Where to find more information on inclusion

Name: Chris Chivers

Twitter handle: @ChrisChivers2

Website: chrischiversthink.weebly.com

Who are they? Ex-headteacher, School VC of governors.

Why to follow them: Quite simply the best quote I have seen to describe inclusion is this from the very knowledgeable @Chrischivers2: 'The mantra for each school and each individual within a school should be, 'Inclusion is what we do.'

Useful websites for information and advice on inclusion:

The Centre for Studies on Inclusive Education
www.csie.org.uk
A national charity that works to promote equality and eliminate discrimination in education.

Alliance for Inclusive Education
www.allfie.org.uk
A national campaigning and information-sharing network led by disabled people. They campaign for all disabled learners, both inside and outside the classroom.

The Inclusion Quality Mark
www.inclusionmark.co.uk
A site providing a complete audit of what is happening in a school and helps schools to further improve their inclusion practice.

Books

Working Towards Inclusive Education: Social Contexts by Peter Mittler.

This book provides an overview of current issues arising from today's inclusive policies in education.

Teaching and Learning in Diverse and Inclusive Classrooms: Key Issues for New Teachers edited by Gill Richards and Felicity Armstrong.
This book focuses on diversity in education and the inclusion of all children in all aspects of school.

The Language of Inclusive Education: Exploring Speaking, Listening, Reading and Writing by Elizabeth Walton.
This book considers the writing, speaking, reading and hearing aspects of full inclusive education.

Chapter 4 takeaway

Teaching tip

Happiness levels

Have a think about all your pupils. Are they all happy in the classroom? If they are all happy and they are participating in your lessons this is a good start. Happy children = progress. Also, keep an eye on your staff; are they happy? This is an obvious yet often overlooked point. Happy staff = happy children!

Pass it on

Keep sharing

Remember to share your ideas. All too often in teaching we close our doors and do the job never thinking for a moment that what we are doing might be of great benefit to others. Blogging is a good way to share your ideas. Have a look at some of the education blogs on Twitter and think about starting your own blog.

CPD book club recommendation

Inclusion for Primary School Teachers by Nancy Gedge.

Nancy is a teacher and a mum to 3 children. She won @TES blogger of the year and now writes regularly for TES.

Bloggers' corner

Nancy also blogs passionately about SEND, Down's Syndrome, education and motherhood. Follow her blog at https://notsoordinarydiary.wordpress.com/ and on Twitter: @nancygedge

TO DO LIST:

- [ ] Work your way through the audits and see what they are telling you.
- [ ] Think about the environment of your classroom and decide if it is conducive to inclusion.
- [ ] Check out the recommended websites and become acquainted with the various special educational needs and disabilities you are likely to encounter in your classroom.
- [ ] Read *Inclusion for Primary School Teachers* by Nancy Gedge.
- [ ] Follow Nancy Gedge's blog.
- [ ] Tweet your ideas and thoughts from this chapter using the #BloomsCPD.

5 The strategies

In the last two chapters we have looked at the cohort of children in our classes and completed an audit. We have identified the possible causes, conditions and difficulties for individual pupils we have concerns about. We have raised this with our SENDCo and put together any measures we can implement immediately. We have done our research into ADHD, ASC, LDD, dyslexia and behaviour difficulties and thought about how we could aim for full inclusion for the children in the class. Now we need to work on a plan to help us to create that inclusive classroom where all children feel safe and happy and make progress.

ADHD and ASC

Information from The National Autistic Society shows that a number of children are now being diagnosed with both ADHD and ASC. For this reason, children with ADHD and children with ASC share some similarities in terms of the way they behave in the classroom. Many of the strategies described for helping children with ASC to cope in the classroom will be beneficial for the child with ADHD. You should keep this in mind when deciding on the strategies to use with the individual child.

There are many books written on the subject of autism. As we know, ASC is a spectrum and children can be anywhere on that spectrum. The child with ASC in the mainstream classroom will usually be at the more able end of the spectrum. They will have a learning disability associated with their ASC and will often have problems controlling their behaviour due to their lack of understanding of the world. There are, however, some very bright and well-behaved children with ASC who experience social anxiety and still have difficulty with change. These children, although not poorly behaved will require support. There remains a lack of understanding concerning autism amongst teachers in mainstream schools. Even where they have the resources they often still lack the training. School provision has improved enormously over the years as a greater understanding of ASC has been reached, but there is still much room for improvement.

The first thing we need to do is to look at the difficulties experienced by the child.

ASC: difficulties experienced by the child

Children with ASC are sometimes described as being 'locked in their own world' and they struggle with everyday activities. Children with ASC often have a problem with sensory perception. For most of us our brain adequately processes all the sensory information it receives and helps us to deal with the world around us. Those on the autistic spectrum have a neurological disorder that prevents them from processing information from their senses. They receive the information but cannot process it correctly. This makes life very difficult for them. In children with ASC, the frontal lobe of the brain does not receive the information needed to deal with the sensory information.

In order to help the child with ASC in the classroom we need to see how it affects them. There are some common aspects that are widely known to affect the child with ASC.

Area of difficulty	How the child is affected
Lack of communication	• May be able to verbalise but cannot use speech to communicate • Lack of eye contact • Inappropriate facial expressions
Lack of flexible thinking and rigid patterns of behaviour	• Clings to strict routine • Development of repetitive behaviours • Difficulty coping with change
Lack of understanding of the spoken word/lack of auditory processing	• Lack of interest in other children and adults • Hears the word but fails to understand, potentially resulting in 'shutdown' or behaviour problems
Sensory processing difficulties	• Gives rise to difficulty with movement and balance • Child may be terrified of space or crowded places • May be clumsy and fall over continuously • May be frightened of climbing • May actively seek sensory stimulation and climb on tables and twirl around the classroom

Fig. 12 ASC difficulties experienced by the child

Practical strategies

As we can see, our child with ASC is quite complex. Here are some simple strategies to help you to focus your thinking when beginning to work with a child with ASC:

- **Start at home** – I would always recommend starting with the family. Make contact and establish a good relationship. Find out what works at home and see if you can implement the strategy at school. The family know the child best and their views are important. It is good practice to continue with routines established at home when in school. Routine is key for a child with ASC; it makes them feel safe and secure.
- **Make routines whole school** – any routines established in school should be implemented by all teachers. Spread the word around your colleagues that there is an expected routine to follow and consistency is vital for success. Also, remember that each child is an individual and should be treated as such. There is no correct way with children with autism; there is only a correct way for each individual child.

- **Make it visual –** many children with ASC are known to be visual learners, often due to their lack of verbal communication. This is also true of those who are good verbally. Use this information and provide visuals for instructions. Give the child plenty of time to understand what is required. What may seem like a simple request to you could be a mammoth task for a child on the spectrum. See chapter 6 for more information on the use of visuals.
- **Think about communication methods –** teach the child how to inform you if they don't understand. This is often overlooked and results in a 'shutdown' or a tantrum. If the child is using a communication book, prepare a page that requests help. This could be something simple such as a speech bubble. When they don't understand or need help they can show you the speech bubble and prevent a shutdown or a behaviour tantrum.

Fig. 13 Icon shown by the child with ASC to request help

- **Make lists –** encourage children with ASC who are cognitively able to make lists. Lists help them to sequence steps towards solving a problem or working through a lesson.
- **Have a plan –** if the worst comes to the worst and there is a shutdown from the child with ASC, have a plan in place. Many schools have a 'chill-out room' or 'calming room' these days. Some schools call them 'safe spaces'. Chapter 6 describes how to create a suitable chill-out room (p 105).

Quick tips for working with a child with ASC

1. Use visual aids to help children understand the structure of their day.
2. Create an ASC-friendly classroom, e.g. plain walls, fewer bright colours.
3. Have less clutter, easy access, calm spaces and a place to go to if stressed.
4. Use Picture Exchange Communication System (PECS) as a means of helping the child to communicate their needs or wants. PECS is a form of augmentative and alternative communication system. It uses icons and teaches the child to initiate conversation rather than being passive. (This can only be implemented by a speech and language therapist until staff are properly trained.)
5. Use clear, short sentences and give thinking time.
6. Say the child's name first to ensure the child knows you are talking to them personally rather than the whole class.
7. Use pictures or symbols as many children with ASC don't understand gestures, or be consistent and use Makaton.

8. Use fewer words and allow them time to digest the information.
9. Stick to routines and have a structure to your day.
10. Aim to keep the volume in the classroom low.
11. Structure sensory or 'time out' breaks into their day so they know when it's coming and don't have to resort to poor behaviour to get it.
12. Be wary of the child becoming too reliant on a particular TA or other adult.

Top tip

See autism.org.uk for 'A quick guide to an ASC-friendly classroom'.

Once you have implemented as many of these strategies as you are able to, your child with ASC will be much happier. Your classroom will be far more autism-friendly and all students will benefit from the calm and quiet atmosphere.

ADHD: difficulties experienced by the child

With the correct support, children with ADHD can be successfully included in mainstream classrooms. As teachers it is our role to work closely with the child, discover their barriers to learning and remove them wherever possible. In order to do this teachers should have a thorough knowledge of how a child is affected by their ADHD and how it impacts on their learning.

The first thing we need to do is to examine the difficulties faced by the child with ADHD.

Area of difficulty	How child is affected
Inability to effectively handle ordinary environmental situations	• Displays defiant behaviour
Anxiety disorders	• Feeling of isolation • Constant feeling of panic • Needs constant reassurance
Inappropriate interaction with peers	• Lack of friendship group • Peers may become fed up with requests for reassurance
Inability to sit still in classroom	• Constantly moving around the classroom
Inability to follow a list of instructions	• May inadvertently get into trouble for being in the wrong place at the wrong time due to a lack of understanding of instructions
Inability to work in a group	• Acts out during group work and may be ostracised by those in the group

Fig. 14 ADHD difficulties experienced by the child

Practical strategies

Here are some simple strategies to help you focus your thinking when working with children with ADHD. As explained above, many of the strategies used for children on the autistic spectrum are also beneficial for children with ADHD.

- **Identify their main difficulty** – the key to helping children with ADHD to conform to school life is to identify their main difficulty. This will be different for each child. Is it communication? If so the visuals mentioned for children with ASC will be useful for this child. A communication book or a communication chart will help them to understand your instructions (see Chapter 6, p 99).
- **Develop a good structure to your day** – all children are happier in a routine but those with ADHD need it as a matter of high importance. Think about the lessons. Do you like to know what lesson is coming next? Children with ADHD need to know as a coping strategy. Set achievable goals for them. For example, if the first lesson lasts for an hour set a target of 30 minutes to work and then a short break. Structure your day in this manner. Remember to structure playtime if possible. Non-lesson times are potential flash points for children with ADHD. Again set an achievable target such as playing outside for ten minutes and then a ten minute break to do something fun of their own choosing.
- **Consider the use of a visual timetable** – a visual timetable is useful to help the child see the structure of their day. Symbols or words which have previously been taught to the child are used to represent the lessons or activities. They are known to reduce the anxiety and frustration experienced by many children with ADHD.
- **Remember, all behaviour is communication** – attend to the communication and you will usually get to the heart of the problem.
- **Think outside the classroom** – non-class time should be considered when working on strategies for children with ADHD as these are the times when routine and structure are changed. This includes break and lunch time and even time spent in the corridor waiting for entry to the next lesson. These are the times when problems occur and can escalate quickly.
- **Create a behaviour plan** – behaviour plans are an important part of the strategy for success for any child who shows difficulty managing their behaviour. This is an important area so we will look at Behaviour for Learning in a separate section (see p 87).

Quick tips for working with a child with ADHD

1. Set achievable goals – break down large amounts of time into manageable sizes.
2. Build in times to 'chill out' to release frustration.
3. Use visuals if appropriate with either words or symbols.
4. Have a behaviour plan and share it with all staff.
5. Find the child's motivator and use it as a reward for staying on task.
6. Ensure the room is ADHD friendly. This means not too busy, not too cluttered and not too noisy.
7. Use short clear sentences with one or two directives, no more.
8. Allow time for the child to think through your instructions.
9. Be aware of the 'Velcro effect' with your TA. Avoid the child becoming too reliant on them.
10. Build in some errands for the child with ADHD. Sometimes a 2 minute trip down the corridor to deliver a message is enough to change the mood of the child for the entire day.

Learning difficulties and disabilities

We know that teachers receive very little training for those with LDD in their classes. According to my tweeting colleagues, this is the area of teaching SEND that causes our teachers the most anxiety. Training often consists of learning on the job. The plain fact of the matter is that the teacher has to identify the barrier to learning and remove it. That sounds easy but is actually far from the truth.

Teaching children with LDD is far and away the most prevalent area that teachers struggle to find strategies for. The reason is that children with LDD often have no single diagnosis. Without a diagnosis – with no 'label' to identify the area of need – it is hard to identify a strategy that works. My advice is always to deal with the child in front of you. A label may help the parents and the school to secure extra funding to help, but in general it will not help you to find the best way to educate the child. As we have seen, even when a child is in possession of a label they will not display all the signs and symptoms and certainly not all of the time. That is the reason why it is crucial to educate the child in front of you rather than seeing the label as a cure all.

LDD: difficulties experienced by the child

Area of difficulty	How the child is affected
An activity-led classroom	• The child is often on the fringes, not joining in
Teacher tries to ensure the child is included in everything for full inclusion as is their right	• Being treated the same as all other children when actually they aren't the same and allowances must be made where necessary
Child will learn more slowly than peers	• May end up being left behind and having to work permanently with TA
Speech and language difficulties	• Child may be withdrawn from class to attend therapy and miss key lessons
Child may have mobility difficulties	• Inability to move around the classroom in a wheelchair or without support from adult
May have seizures	• May not be room for the child to have a fall due to a seizure without hurting themselves
May be incontinent	• May need to leave the classroom frequently resulting in missing further lesson content
May need assistive technology for writing and speaking.	• TA needs to find time to set this up while attending to the needs of all the children

Fig. 15 LDD difficulties experienced by the child

Practical strategies

The first thing we need to do with children with LDD is to observe them closely. Watch and learn from them. What are their experiences while in the classroom? Here are some simple strategies to help you focus your thinking when working with children with LDD.

- **Make sure the child is involved** – what is the child doing during whole class discussions? Ensure the child is contributing by asking them direct questions and giving them time to contribute. Build in time for them to use assistive technology to answer your questions and make sure the whole class waits for them to answer.
- **Review how the child is behaving** – ensure the child is not disrupting the rest of the table by checking they understand the lesson. Talk to them and gauge their understanding. Give them a choice of 3 answers to allow them to demonstrate their developing knowledge. Ensure the child is working with a group and not being distracted by a group working close by. Place your TA with their group but not directly with the child. Keep activities occurring close to the child to a minimum to avoid distracting them from their lesson.
- **Evaluate their working environment** – how can you change your classroom or your teaching to improve the experience for the child? Consider whether the child needs any obvious modifications. Would they benefit from writing

pencils, a slanted desk for writing or different coloured paper? Make these obvious changes.

- **Personalise the learning** – focus on the individual child and what they can achieve. Personalise the learning for them and tailor your resources to suit their individual need.
- **Expert advice** – call in the experts for advice if appropriate. You may need an assessment from a child psychologist, an occupational therapist or similar professional. Be prepared to ask for their help.
- **Consider technology** – decide whether any of your students would benefit from the use of technology in the form of a communication aid, a PC or an iPad.
- **Develop trust** – most of all, establish a purposeful and trusting relationship with the child.

Quick tips for working with a child with LDD

1. Stick to a routine; children feel safer in a routine.
2. Plan the work with your TA so they are aware of the child's overall targets.
3. Use assistive technology (software apps) for reinforcing learning and introducing new topics.
4. Do not react to silly behaviour; you are playing into their hands – poor behaviour is often a cry for help through lack of understanding.
5. Help the child with organisational skills through use of visual overlays.
6. Keep the noise level down in the classroom.
7. Use a PC Program such as Clicker6 for a child who struggles to write.
8. Have audiobooks for struggling readers to enable them to keep up with class text.
9. Establish a good relationship with parents so that strategies may be continued at home.
10. Reward positive behaviour – this is a hotly debated topic, but if you are a believer in extrinsic rewards then now is the time to use it. I firmly believe in extrinsic rewards, especially for children with SEND.

Dyslexia

As we know, dyslexia may occur in any child and it is not associated with a lack of cognitive ability. There may be some co-occurring difficulties experienced by the child with dyslexia, but these are not as a result of dyslexia. There are many strategies for helping children with dyslexia and it is important that as teachers we work out the ones best suited to the needs of our child.

Dyslexia: difficulties experienced by the child

Area of difficulty	How the child is affected
Difficulty with auditory short-term memory	• Problems remembering sounds in spoken words
Inability to follow instructions	• Looks like poor behaviour
Underachievement due to problems with reading, writing and spelling;	• Looks like lack of effort
Problem with spoken language	• Difficulty expressing themselves clearly which may result in misunderstanding
Difficulty with organisational skills	• Will struggle to handle information given to them in a logical and useful manner – this will affect all areas of the curriculum
Lack of confidence and self esteem	• May result in behaviour difficulties as child begins to feel worthless
Poor sequencing skills	• Difficulty sequencing numbers and letters
Very little written output	• Looks like lack of effort
Lack of motivation	• Looks like indifference to lessons and to school
Poor concentration and attention span	• Looks like poor behaviour

Fig. 16 Dyslexia difficulties experienced by the child

Practical strategies

Here are some simple strategies to help you focus your thinking when working with children with dyslexia.

- **Take the time to get to know the child** – find out what makes them tick and what they are successful at and build a trusting relationship. Discover how they learn and use this to your advantage.
- **Use your TA creatively to help a dyslexic child** – TAs can reduce the strain by writing down homework and other non-essential writing for the child. They can break the work into smaller chunks and can spend time organising their activities for them.
- **Make help with reading a priority** – a child who struggles to read yet has no cognitive impairment will feel a mixture of embarrassment and frustration. It is for these reasons that we as teachers must do our utmost to alleviate the pressure for them. Use a structured reading scheme involving much repetition. Avoid asking them to read aloud. Encourage the child to read books on their level to boost confidence. Make sure reading is always fun and not a difficult task.
- **Use visual clues** – dyslexic children prefer pictures to text.

- **Evaluate your teaching** – regularly review your lesson to check understanding. Speak to the child and check they are on track. The last thing you want is to reach the end of the lesson and discover your child hasn't achieved the objectives. Conduct a quick mini plenary for the whole class so that your child is not singled out.
- **Prepare handouts** – for older children, prepare notes to avoid them having to write. Also, avoid children having to write objectives and the date in books. Use pre-prepared labels as a substitute.
- **Chunk it up** – break up instructions into small chunks whenever possible and ask for them to be repeated back to check for understanding.
- **Don't rephrase things** – avoid rephrasing questions and instructions too quickly. Allow processing time rather than adding another layer of information for working memory to work through.

If difficulties are not identified early, children with dyslexia may suffer a lack of self-esteem and a lack of confidence. This may in turn result in behaviour difficulties developing. As teachers we should do our utmost to prevent this.

Quick tips for working with children with dyslexia

1. Change PC font to green
2. Ask the child which style of font they prefer
3. Use pictures to make writing easier to read
4. Keep paperwork uncluttered and use short sentences
5. Use a text reader which converts writing to speech
6. Help the child to organise their subjects with colour co-ordination
7. Teach touch typing to help with spelling
8. Avoid white paper as this can be too dazzling. Use cream or pastel colours to alleviate the glare. Remember that coloured paper won't actually help with dyslexia but light pastel colours will prevent glare.
9. Use a spell checker
10. Encourage reading aloud with CD books

Useful Apps for dyslexia

ClaroRead for PC

Claro Apps for ios devices
http://www.callscotland.org.uk/common-assets/cm-files/posters/ipad-apps-for-learners-with-dyslexia.pdf – this links to several more apps.

Behaviour for learning

Behaviour difficulties have been given several different names over the years. These have included SEBD, EBD and BESD. The reality is that no matter what term we use, these children have some severe behaviour difficulties that need attention. I make no secret of the fact that I am not a fan of labels. They are only useful for securing extra funding and resources. We have to deal with the child in front of us and the behaviour they are displaying, irrespective of whatever fancy term it is given.

Children who display severe behaviour problems in mainstream classrooms will generally have an underlying cause for this. All children have a tendency to push the boundaries on occasions but that is very different from a child who permanently disrupts lessons by running around, climbing on furniture, provoking others, causing fights or even throwing chairs and other objects.

Behaviour is a form of communication and should be treated as such. A child displaying challenging behaviour is attempting to give you a message. Something is wrong in their world. Research from the Speech and Language therapist Sasha Bemrose (2013) informs us that as many as 75% of young people who have BESD also have communication problems. Their area of difficulty may be a lack of understanding of the spoken word or they may not be able to articulate their thoughts and feelings effectively. Behaviour is often their only way of showing you there is something wrong.

There are several prominent tweeters who post on the subject of behaviour. Possibly the most well known one is Tom Bennett. Tom writes for the *Times Education Supplement* (TES) as their behaviour advisor and has written four books. He was recently appointed as school Behaviour Tsar and his remit is to work out how to train teachers to tackle low-level disruption which costs pupils an average of 38 days of learning a year. I highly recommend you follow Tom on Twitter. He is a thoroughly decent man and always answers my questions as promptly as he is able. Just don't call him a Tsar; he doesn't like it!

Name: Tom Bennett
Twitter handle: @tombennett71
Website: about.me/tom_bennett
Who are they? Behaviour advisor for TES and director of Research Ed
Why to follow them: He offers excellent advice on behaviour for learning.

Behaviour for learning: difficulties experienced by the child

Area of difficulty	How the child is affected
Disruptive behaviour such as hitting, calling out, throwing things, running around, name calling.	• Aggression • Impulsivity • Defiance
Anti-social behaviour which is not outgrown, provoking others by prodding, spoiling work, teasing.	• Lack of friends, feelings of isolation
Challenging the teacher or TA on every occasion, refusing to keep quiet.	• Becomes ever more unpopular with the class as children want to work
Refusing to complete their work.	• Does not do their own work and falls behind the class
Refusal to work and leaving the classroom	• Child is unpopular for disrupting lesson, leads to lack of friends, leads to lack of self esteem leads to more attention-seeking behaviour. Becomes cyclic.

Fig. 17 Behaviour for learning difficulties experienced by the child

Practical strategies

Here are some simple strategies to help you focus your thinking when working with children to improve behaviour for learning.

- **Improve communication –** having attributed much behaviour to poor communication skills, we need to look towards improving communication. There are several resources which will help the child better understand their world, such as communication charts, visual time tables and social stories and these are explored in detail in the next chapter (p 99). If the child is non-verbal or really struggles to get their message across, I would consider the use of 'Augmentative and Alternative Communication' (AAC). This title is the umbrella title covering all communication aids for those with speech and language impairments. They range from low tech to high tech devices and must be suited to the needs of the user. This is definitely an area where one size does not fit all. This is all about giving the child a voice when otherwise they would be silent. Again, this is discussed in detail in the next chapter.
- **Create a whole school behaviour for learning policy –** this is important if your school is to succeed. I have had extensive conversations with my colleagues on Twitter about this and we have reached the conclusion that children need to learn 'behaviour for learning' just like they learn anything else. For these reasons it is vital that there is whole-school buy-in. Every single adult in a school must be trained in and stick to an agreed set of rules. Consistency is everything: a child must know that a certain behaviour will always bring the same result, be it good or bad.

- **Implement behaviour management strategies** – personally I am a fan of positive behaviour management strategies and I believe that prevention is better than cure. I would rather arrange my classroom, staff and resources in such a manner that good behaviour is the norm. My own opinion of behaviour management is that the class staff should deal with behaviour themselves. I personally wouldn't call in senior leaders as, in my opinion, the teacher loses credibility. I would consider calling for backup from a fellow teacher if a pupil was aggressive, but would be reluctant to call in SLT. However, when I raised this question in a Tweet to teachers, it appears that opinion on this is very much divided. The best solution came from @ oldandrewuk who suggested the system of dedicated support staff. This is a system I have seen first hand and it works well. I recommend this to all schools. With this system there is a whole team trained specifically for behaviour management. The team know the children and the best way to deal with any behaviours that may occur. This is no substitute for classroom management but it will help if there is an incident and is a better solution than calling in SLT in my opinion.

There are two accepted types of unacceptable behaviour, low- and high-level disruption. Low-level disruption is a well known problem in our classrooms. It is particularly problematic because teachers have different definitions of what constitutes low-level behaviour. What irritates one teacher may not even register for another teacher. Low-level tends to include minor offences such as talking, tapping and fidgeting. High-level disruption tends to be a point blank refusal to work, refusal to comply with class rules, swearing or violence. See the questionnaires in chapter 4 for more detail.

Quick fixes for low-level disruptive behaviour

1. Be a physical presence – stand next to the ringleader to quell the behaviour.
2. Begin each lesson with a quick reminder of class rules – quietly remind them who is in charge.
3. Be fair and be consistent.
4. Tempting as it may be, don't enter into a discussion about the behaviour.
5. State your expectations, then follow up with agreed sanctions.
6. Keep a positive outlook and a smile on your face – by doing this you are modelling expected behaviour.
7. Stick to your routine – all children are happier in a routine, especially those with SEND.
8. Remember to give a child a chance to redeem himself/herself without losing face. For example, give them time out to reflect on their behaviour and don't insist on a public apology immediately as this may inflame the situation further – most children will offer an apology of their own free will eventually.

9. Set the child a task as a distraction/mood changer.
10. Repeat instructions to an individual child and have them repeat them back to check understanding and therefore reduce their distracting behaviour.

Twitter tip
Follow #BehaviourChat Mondays 8-8 30 pm.

Suggestions to help with high-level disruptive behaviour

There are no quick fixes for high-level disruptive behaviour. This type of behaviour should be tackled as part of a long-term strategy but these ideas will help you to prevent some of the actions mentioned in the questionnaire from happening in the first place.

1. Have a routine and stick to it – remember children like routines.
2. Be consistent in everything you say and do.
3. Meet them at the door and greet them with a smile.
4. Show them respect – we all like to be respected, even children.
5. Be firm but fair.
6. Reiterate your rules at the start of each lesson.
7. Have a seating plan.
8. Be a role model.
9. Differentiate your lesson so that you are sure children can actually achieve their objective.
10. Position your TA carefully for maximum impact.
11. Display your rules and adhere to them.
12. Acknowledge correct behaviour.

You will notice that several of these quick fixes are the same as the quick fixes for low-level disruptive behaviour. The reason is that non-compliant behaviour or disengagement is often due to poor communication skills. The child cannot articulate their thoughts and feelings and their behaviour may be a cry for help. It may be their way of revealing that they cannot do the work or that they find the work too easy. Whatever the cause, we have to deal with the behaviour.

Inclusion

As we have seen, it is commonplace for children with SEND to be included in mainstream schools. In 1994 92 governments formed the World Conference on Special Needs Education in Spain and the report is known as The Salamanca Statement. They agreed between them to promote the idea of inclusive education for all, especially those with SEND. The theory is sound but it is not always simple to achieve. From a child's perspective there can be some difficulties.

Area of difficulty	How the child is affected
Friendship groups	Lack of real friendship, may be isolated from peers Mothered by other children
Work not personalised or differentiated for each child	Inability to understand the work
Often working with a TA	Dependent on adult support Sometimes the child receives too much support
Lack of specialised resources due to lack of funding	Child unable to do the work due to lack of equipment
Teacher may be untrained to work with children with SEND	Child left to work with TA and receives little teacher time
Difficult to meaningfully include all physically challenged children in all lessons	May be withdrawn from some lessons such as PE
Difficult for a mainstream teacher to fully include a child with visual or hearing impairment	Child will be with TA who should be appropriately trained but all children are entitled to a teacher
Some children require invasive procedures during school time.	Child may be withdrawn for physiotherapy or tube feeding, both of which would continue during lessons in a special school

Fig. 18 Inclusion difficulties experienced by the child

Practical strategies

Many mainstream teachers welcome children with SEND into their classes but often report that they feel inadequately prepared to teach them. Here are some simple strategies to help you.

- **Break teaching into small steps –** one of the key strategies in achieving inclusion is to remember to teach in tiny steps for your children with SEND.
- **Be adaptable –** involve much repetition and be prepared to re plan your objective mid lesson.

- **Use sensory-based learning** – as teachers we talk about teaching the way our children learn and for some this means sensory-based learning. The rest of your class might be completing traditional work on the learning of shape, space and measure while your sensory learner may be completing a cooking task and learning to weigh in a fun manner.
- **Be practical** – always follow up your learning with practical activities where possible and use visuals to aid their learning.
- **Get outdoors** – a good strategy for children with ADHD who have high energy levels, for example, might be to take them outside to exhaust some of their energy. Maths and science activities can be completed in a fun and practical manner by using the great outdoors for counting, measuring, multiplying and learning times through races. Science is best when completed outside using trees, rocks, plants and shadows. Keep it practical and use the resources in your environment

Quick fixes for successful inclusion

Here are some quick tips to help you to ensure your classroom is inclusive. Some are provided by colleague Mary Isherwood, headteacher of Camberwell Park Specialist Support School in Manchester.

1. Ensure every child is welcomed physically, socially and emotionally.
2. Consider how you can involve and include all children in every aspect of school life including after school activities – what adjustments might you need to make?
3. Understand that all behaviours are a communication – what is the child trying to tell you through their behaviour?
4. Use Individual Education Plans (IEPs are still in use but schools have their own names for them) to meet each child's specific needs – what are their barriers to learning? E.g. such as concentration, behaviour, personal independence skills. Linking to outcomes from the EHC plan is very important.
5. Ensure all staff are trained to work with children with SEND – whole school philosophy and commitment.
6. Ensure displays are meaningful and relevant and include symbol communication where appropriate.
7. Consider the physical environment e.g. furniture that is height adjustable and appropriate seating.
8. Have separate workspaces for children who need to work quietly and on their own.
9. Avoid clutter in the classroom – look at the room from a child's perspective and see how distracting clutter can be.
10. Provide visual timetables to support the understanding of the day. Check the lighting and have blinds to support children with VI.

11. Flexible use of staffing and pupil groups to ensure the child has experience of whole class, small groups and individual time and so that the child does not become over-reliant on one adult.
12. Have a range of resources to support access to reading and writing, e.g. book holder and easy grip pencils and pens and writing slope.

Remember – good practice for an inclusive classroom for learners with SEND is good practice for all learners.

Chris Chivers on his blog states 'Inclusion is just doing your job'. In a post of the same title (http://chrischiversthinks.weebly.com/blog-thinking-aloud/inclusion-and-sen) states that inclusion should not be an 'add-on' but rather an integral part of practice. As we have seen, teachers in mainstream schools strive to achieve this despite lack of funding and lack of staff.

From my perspective, inclusion means personalising the lesson for each child and aiming for individualised tasks. This is a mammoth task for teachers but there is much good practice going on around us. It also means having a whole school policy on inclusion to ensure everyone is pulling in the same direction. The essence of it is to know your children well, know how they learn and adapt your resources, staff and teaching to meet their individual needs.

The final word on this section goes to Unesco 2001:

A UNESCO definition of inclusive education

"Inclusive education starts from the belief that the right to education is a basic human right and the foundation for a more just society.

Inclusive education takes the Education for All (EFA) agenda forward by finding ways of enabling schools to serve all children in their communities....

Inclusive education is concerned with all learners, with a focus on those who have traditionally been excluded from educational opportunities - such as learners with special needs and disabilities, children from ethnic and linguistic minorities".

UNESCO, 2001

Chapter 5 takeaway

Teaching tip

Remember, failing to plan is planning to fail.

Having a master plan in place is crucial to the successful running of your class. As a teacher you are aware that you are responsible for the education of every child in your class including those with special educational needs. Gone are the days when you could hand them over to a skilled TA. Consider your class, consider their difficulties and plan your lessons accordingly. Your plan should include personalised targets for children with SEND, behaviour for learning plans where needed and some strategies to ensure all children are included in practical lessons. Discuss with your TA. They are often full of fantastic, innovative ideas and may be champing at the bit to be included in lesson planning.

Pass it on

Online chats

Get involved in some of the education chats on Twitter. By doing this you can pass on your own knowledge and learn from others. There are several most nights and these chats in; particular include topics; on SEND.

Monday 8-9pm: #primaryrocks; Wednesday: 8-8 30pm #SENexchange; Thursday 8-9pm: # UKedchat; Sunday 8-8 30pm: #SLTchat #SpEdSC The SEND slow chat runs from Saturday to Saturday.

CPD book club recommendation

Key Issues in Special Educational Needs and Inclusion by Alan Hodkinson and Philip Vickerman.

This book will help you to understand special educational needs and disability. It gives historical context and supports the reader to understand inclusion for all children.

Bloggers' corner

Amjad Ali @ASTsupportAAli runs a free teaching and learning toolkit which people are invited to contribute to. Some of these are on the subject of SEND. Amjad himself blogs on inclusion, SEND and leadership. His blog is well worth a read: cheneyAgilityToolkit.blogspot.co.uk

TO DO LIST:

❏ Discuss inclusion with your TA. Bounce your ideas off each other.
❏ Create a spidergram containing all your ideas for inclusion; think how you can incorporate them into your classroom.
❏ Read the book *Key Issues in Special Educational Needs and Inclusion* by Alan Hodkinson and Philip Vickerman.
❏ Have a read of Amjad's blog; there's plenty to keep you going.

6 Putting it into practice

So far we have looked at all the children in the class and identified some of the major difficulties that the children may be facing. We have looked at the nature of their special educational needs and disabilities and learned about how this affects the child in the classroom, and we have looked at some quick tips for immediate success. The next step is to create that master plan for success. In order to be successful and create an inclusive classroom we need to look at practical strategies that can be used for any child who needs them, with or without a label.

Practical ideas for teaching children with ASC

Communication and ASC

Children with ASC (and ADHD and LDD) experience real barriers to learning in terms of their communication. As discussed in the previous chapters, communication is at the heart of most behaviour issues. There may be a lack of understanding on the part of the child or there may be a breakdown when the child attempts to express their feelings. When having a conversation, there is so much more going on than just talking: there is gesture, facial expression, tone, and body language. A child on the ASC spectrum (or a child with ADHD) may have difficulties with all of these aspects of communication. One way to combat this is to introduce a method of AAC.

As explained briefly in the previous chapter, AAC is the term used to describe the various methods used to help those with communication difficulties to communicate. AAC includes any alternative form of communication including signs, symbols, gestures, pictures or the use of electronic devices. They range from low tech to high tech devices and must be suited to the needs of the user. Supplementing speech with some form of AAC is thought to improve speech development. Things have progressed a long way for the non-verbal child and any of these high or low tech devices will help the child with behaviour difficulties.

- **Visual resources** – these low-tech devices are powerful in mainstream schools and include: communication books, communication charts, communication passports (see below, p 98) and Picture Exchange Communication Systems (PECS). www.pecs-unitedkingdom.com They are easy to make, relatively easy to use and cost very little to use after the initial outlay for the software. They do not require a power source.
- **A BIGMack Communicator** – from Inclusive Technology is also a very useful low-tech device www.inclusive.co.uk/ablenet-bigmack-p2039 It requires a

power source but is easy to use and requires little training. The teacher or TA can record a message on this and the child is only required to press it to activate it. There is also a LITTLEmack Communicator which has different levels and can be used for multiple messages. The child cannot initiate their own conversation using these devices but it does allow them to join in a conversation with some support and also enable them to make simple choices.

- **iPads** – the most popular of the high tech devices is the iPad. There are several apps that can be downloaded for iPad that facilitate conversation. My favourite is Proloquo2Go (http://www.assistiveware.com/product/proloquo2go). Training is required for staff and for the user and the child needs to have a relatively high cognitive ability to be able to use it. Another useful app is iCommunicate (http://www.grembe.com/icommunicate). Initiating conversation is easier with this one but the user remains restricted in the conversations they may join in with.

- **Eyegaze** – another high tech device to give a child a voice is the Eyegaze. As the name suggests the Eyegaze works through eye tracking technology. Through the use of this wonderful piece of equipment the child is able to track words, send emails or browse the internet.

- **Symbols** – there are two big contenders for producing the symbols to make the visual resources with: Boardmaker (www.mayer-johnson.com/category/symbols-and-photos) and Widgit software (www.widgit.com). Boardmaker has a full library of picture communication symbols to suit all scenarios for all learners of different ages and abilities. Widgit software is similar as it provides picture support for reading and helps those with communication difficulties to make sense of their world. Both systems are expensive but both are valuable as they are capable of transforming the lives of our children with SEND. Whichever symbols you choose, it's important that you always use the same system. The child needs to know that the symbols will never change: the same one will be used to announce each lesson or each part of the day. There should be whole school buy-in for consistency and the whole staff should have training in the use of visuals, as they are generally referred to. (More about training in part two of the book.)

Communication books

A communication book is a book comprising symbols made for and personalised to suit the individual child. The books are portable and may also be clipped to the child's clothing or wheelchair. Each page is dedicated to a different topic depending on the child's interests, or it could be dedicated to the different curriculum areas. The layout of the book will depend on the child's cognitive ability and their age. It is possible to make the different curriculum areas colour-coded so it is simple for the child to find the relevant page.

This one is made to show choices for a PE lesson:

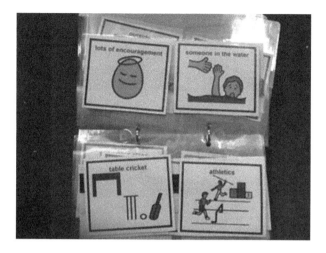

Fig. 19 Communication book example

Communication chart

Staying on the theme of communication for our child with ASC, communication charts are very effective. They are similar in design to the communication book but the symbols are arranged on one sheet. You could have different charts relating to different areas of their school day or relating to the child's interests.

This communication chart has been made to allow the child to express an opinion on the television programme they wish to watch. It is easy to use to use and the child can simply point to the picture they want to use to help them to express their wish.

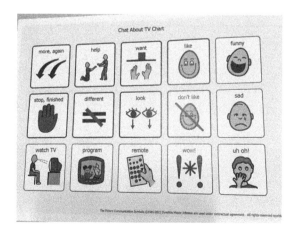

Fig. 20. Communication chart example

Communication passport

For children with more complex difficulties, a communication passport gives basic information about them. It is child-centred and tells anyone who looks at it how the child likes to communicate, how old they are, the things that interest them and their own views on life. These are ideal for anyone to get to know a new child, and they are portable and simple to make. The example in Figure 21 below has a chain that allows it to easily be clipped onto clothing or a wheelchair.

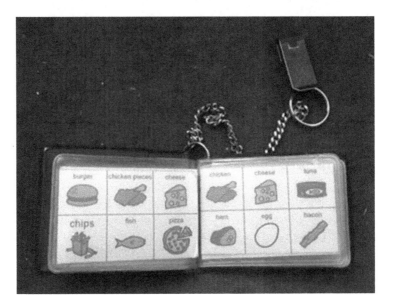

Fig. 21 Communication passport example

Top tip
Enlist the help of a speech and language therapist for a child with ASC.

PECS

The Picture Exchange Communication System, or PECS, allows children with autism or other social educational needs who have little or no communication abilities a means of communicating non-verbally. Children using PECS are taught to approach another person and give them a picture of a desired item in exchange for that item. Training should be given before any one attempts to use PECS as the system goes through various stages and becomes very advanced. Each stage builds upon the last stage and it is important that the stages are embedded before moving on. For this reason I will not give too much detail about PECS.

TEACCH *(www.autism.org.uk/teacch)*

Treatment and Education of Autistic and Related Communication-handicapped Children (TEACCH) was developed for working with children with ASC. (It is also beneficial for children with ADHD). TEACCH works on the principle of providing a structured environment, an individualised plan and using visuals to enforce communication. TEACCH also advises working collaboratively with parents for consistency at home and at school. The system is designed to work best when the child's whole environment is structured in the same way. It helps the child to understand what is happening now and what will happen next. Due to the fact that schools have children with many different challenges and conditions not all schools have chosen to adopt the TEACCH method. If a school chooses to go down this route the whole school needs structuring in this way. Training should be for all members of staff. After the cost of training the only financial cost is for the visuals.

Twitter tip

Follow #teacch for information relating to TEACCH.

Social stories

Social stories are widely used for children with SEND and are particularly useful for those with ASC and ADHD. They can be written or can be visual using the symbols we have discussed above depending on the cognitive ability of the child. (I favour the symbols as the child is already familiar with them.) They were first created by Carol Gray in 1991 as a way of teaching social and life skills for children with autism (see www.carolgraysocialstories.com). They are generally used to introduce new situations to the child to alleviate any anxiety that may occur. For example, a social story might be used to explain to a child about moving to the next class in September. The teacher and TA they have known and trusted for a whole year will be left behind and new ones will be introduced. Another situation where a social story might be of use could be to give advance warning of a new child entering the class. Remember children on the autistic spectrum are all about consistency and routine. A new child in the class is enough to send them in to a shutdown and they should be given the information prior to the arrival of the child.

How to write a social story

- Keep it brief and keep it simple.
- Give accurate information to help the child know what to expect in a given situation.

- Know your end target – what do you wish to achieve?
- Collect relevant information about the child: age, concentration level, whether they need a TA, communication level, etc.
- Think about the information you need to teach the child about the situation, e.g.
  - when do you want it to happen?
  - how long will the situation last?
  - who will be there?
  - what happens during the situation?
- Create your story paying attention to these rules:
  - Use three–five descriptive or perspective sentences for each directive sentence (see below)
  - Avoid 'do not' sentences
  - Write in the first person from the child's perspective
  - Keep your story positive and reassuring.

Sentence type	Example
Descriptive	Describes who, where, why, when or what the statement is about.
Perspective	Describes the child's thoughts, opinions, beliefs, ideas and feelings about the statement.
Directive	Statement from the child of the desired response: 'I will try to', or 'I will do my best to'.

Fig. 22 Types of sentence

Here is an example of a simple social story about not talking in assembly. For a young child or a child with limited reading and/or communication skills you could use symbols rather than words to explain your meaning. Alternatively you can compose your social story using symbols and sentences if your child is working at that level. Lastly, you could make your social story simply using sentences. You will know what will work best for your child.

My name is ....(descriptive sentence).

I like going to assembly every morning. (perspective sentence)

My teacher will be happy if I sit and listen in assembly. (perspective sentence)

I will do my best to be quiet in the assembly. (directive sentence)

Fig. 23 Social story example

Using Boardmaker or Widgit Software (www.widgit.com), a skilled TA can make many of the above resources for a child with ASC or ADHD quickly and easily. If the software is not available you could be very creative and use simple line drawings instead of symbols to get your message across.

Name: Lynn McCann

Twitter handle: @reachoutasc

Website: www.reachoutasc.com

Who are they? Teacher and Independent Consultant for Autism Spectrum Condition

Why to follow them: For a perfect example of a social story on transition to a new class (www.reachoutasc.com/resources/transition-to-new-class)

Twitter tip
Follow #socialstory for examples of social stories.

Objects of reference

Objects of reference are quite simply objects that give a child an idea of what is about to happen. They are generally used for children with severe learning difficulties but may also be useful for children in mainstream classes who may be non-verbal. A good example of an object of reference is a pair of swimming trunks or a part of a towel to symbolise swimming. Another might be a spoon and fork to symbolise lunchtime. As a general rule it is best to add the word as a label even if the child is not at the stage of being able to read. An opportunity to read or associate a word with an object should never be missed. The child carries the object with them to the activity so that they learn to associate the object with the next lesson.

The ultimate goal with objects of reference is that the children learn to select the object associated with the activity they want and take it to the teacher or TA. For this reason they should be easily accessible for the child, e.g. you could have them in a bag next to the child and encourage their use as often as possible. Be consistent in their use.

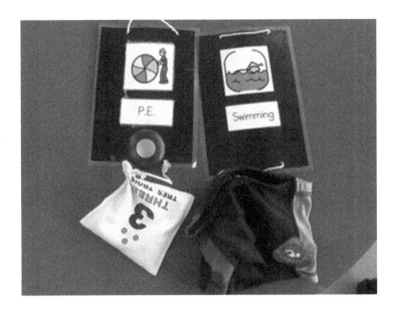

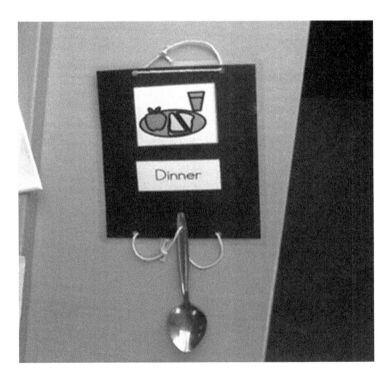

Fig. 24 Object of reference

Chill-out room

A ''shutdown' or 'meltdown' as it may be known from a child with ASC may result in them hitting, kicking, throwing or self-harming. Similarly, a shutdown resulting from sensory overload may result in a child trying to remove themselves from the situation which is distressing them. They may hide under tables or roll themselves into a ball and try to hide. Both scenarios will benefit from a safe space or a chill-out room. As noted in chapter 5 (p 81), it is important to have a plan in place for when the worst comes to the worst and there is a shutdown from the child with ASC. Many schools have a 'chill-out' or 'calming room' these days. Some schools call them 'safe spaces'.

How to create a good chill-out space/room:

- **Think about the physical space** – it needs to be free from clutter to avoid stimulation; the walls should be in a pale colour and be free from furniture associated with classrooms.
- **Make it relaxing** – this should not be seen as a punishment area, more a chance for the child to be away from the situation and calm down. Beanbags are very useful as they allow the child to be in comfort while they are relaxing.
- **Think about how it should be used** – a chill-out room provides the opportunity for a child to reflect on what has happened and regain their composure without an audience. It should provide a place of safety for the child who needs to feel secure. A child who is cognitively able could also request to visit the chill-out room when they feel they are not coping in the classroom. Many mainstream classrooms now have areas set aside where a child can take themselves away from the group and be alone. This is a good second best if there are no available rooms.

Takeaway activities to use immediately for a child with ASC

Some activities can be implemented immediately and will have a huge impact on your classroom and the child with ASC. These are levelled depending on resources available and the level of your own experience as the classroom practitioner (beginner level being for teachers with relatively little experience working with children with ASC, and/or fewer resources).

Beginner level	Intermediate level	Advanced level
Check your environment: noise level, seating, lighting, view for child.	Create a visual timetable for the child. (It is good practice to create one for the whole class too!)	Assemble barriers on the child's desk to restrict their view and avoid distractions. This helps the child to concentrate on their own work and removes any view of other children or activities.
Use as much repetition as necessary to reinforce the instructions and aid learning.	Build time into the day for the child to carry out any personal rituals they might have – they are a comfort to the child.	Organise their desk with baskets for work to do and work completed.
Avoid the temptation to speak for the child – allow them time to formulate an answer.	Do not offer too many choices – children with ASC often struggle to make choices.	Use PECS – this is an AAC system for anyone with communication difficulties (p 100) – training is required but PECS is very beneficial in breaking down communication barriers.
Encourage independence – this may sound obvious but there is a temptation to not allow them to fail.	Give plenty of warnings and time for transition to different activities to avoid a shutdown.	Sign language or Makaton to aid communication.
Children often need motivators to help them learn new skills. Present the child with a few edible or sensory items and see which one they prefer. Repeat until you identify their motivator. Begin to use this as a reward for completing desired activities.	Reinforce your desired behaviours using their identified motivators. When the child displays the behaviour you want to see e.g. staying on task for a certain length of time, present them with their motivator and also use verbal praise. Praise is important as you may not always have their motivator with you.	Set up situations to allow you to reinforce skills you wish to see. For example you could encourage the child to take the register to the office and present with a motivator and verbal praise for the completed task.
Avoid known triggers – again, this seems obvious but there is a temptation to make the child fit in, to 'normalise' them.	Tune in to their language. Are they reversing things? 'I'm too hot' may actually mean 'I'm too cold'.	Teach context clues, e.g. if everyone else is lining up, you should too; if everyone else is quiet, you should be too.
Don't build negative behaviour by rewarding it – a child who is constantly removed from a lesson for poor behaviour will see this as reinforcement of that behaviour.	Scaffold all new learning heavily and reduce over time to encourage independence.	Use specific interventions – do your research and find out exactly how their autism affects their functioning and use issue-based problem solving.
Be aware of sensory issues in the environment, for example the sound of VelcroTM is a known irritant for some.	Make good use of social stories (see p 101) to introduce all new situations and sudden changes of activity.	Seek advice from a speech and language therapist – they have many strategies for helping break down barriers to learning.

Beginner level	Intermediate level	Advanced level
Be aware of the physical contact you have with a child, for example do not ruffle hair or protectively pat their arm as this can actually be painful for some.	Model desired behaviour such as turn taking; pretend to be a part of the group and take a turn to demonstrate.	Enlist the help of a psychologist if necessary.
Be aware that many children with ASC have no understanding of body language – your folded arms in disapproval will have no impact.	Teach social boundaries such as personal space, e.g. remember 'My space, your space'.	Teach social rules to children and young people with ASC. If no one tells them, how will they know? For example, teach them the basics of modesty as they reach puberty. Teach them the rules of unacceptable touching and being touched.
Use direct language rather than requests, e.g. 'Stand up' rather than 'Please will you stand up'. This is because children with ASC best understand concrete use of language as they cannot process emotional expressions or slang.	Try to gain eye contact but be aware that they may not achieve this; avoid this becoming a battle. Also, those on the autistic spectrum have avoidance strategies for this such as looking at your ear to give the appearance of giving eye contact. Settle for this.	Some children with ASC can process only one sensory system at a time. If the child is attempting to focus on your face they may not be able to use their auditory system effectively and will struggle to process your requests. This will cause them some anxiety. It's all about knowing your child as well as you can.

Fig. 25 Takeaway activities to use immediately for a child with ASC

Practical ideas for working with children with ADHD

In this section, I suggest strategies specific to children with ADHD; however, there are also useful strategies in the 'Behaviour for Learning' section that will also help to calm the child with ADHD (p 87). As we know consistency and routine are everything so it is vital to establish your own routines within the classroom and during non-structured times.

Social stories

Social stories (p 101) are particularly beneficial for children with ADHD. Many children with this condition experience difficulty with social skills. They cannot avoid being impulsive and saying what they actually mean. Parents and teachers struggle to explain the concept of inappropriate comments. The child with ADHD may become impatient or frustrated and this in turn leads to poor or aggressive behaviour. Social stories will help with teaching all social situations in a friendly manner.

The most successful ones are the ones that are child-centred. Try to use pictures and draw your information regarding the problem out of the child. Talk through the situation and suggest some possible solutions. Encourage them to choose their own solutions if possible as these will be more meaningful to the child.

Nurture groups

Nurture groups can be invaluable for children with ADHD. They are usually small groups consisting of approximately six children and one teacher and one TA. Each school will have a different way of running a nurture group, but they all work on the principles established by Marjorie Boxall in 1969. (https://nurturegroups.org/introducing-nurture/boxall-profile) She found that many children were entering school with severe behaviour difficulties due to missing out on early nurturing. Put simply, they weren't ready for school. Although children with ADHD have a neurological difficulty, the principles of the nurture group are effective for them. The idea is that specially trained staff work with the children at the developmental stage they have reached and help them to move forward. They help the child's confidence to grow by making them feel accepted and valued. The child remains part of their mainstream class but may spend a small amount of their day in the nurture group.

Since the original nurture groups were established they have now evolved and schools use them in many different ways. The most popular ones tend to have around ten children in them at any one time. The children may share breakfast, share their news and do lessons such as emotional literacy. They re-join their main class for break and lunchtimes and for some lessons. The theory is that the children will form a bond with adults at school who will care for them and see them in a positive light unconditionally. Each school works out what is needed for their own children.

Stop and go cards/traffic lights

These are quick and simple to make, from coloured card and are portable. The child can wear them clipped to their clothes or the TA or teacher can wear them on a lanyard around their neck. They are a visual reminder for the child about their behaviour.

Show the red circle to the child when you need them to stop performing a certain behaviour.

 The yellow or amber one should be flashed up when you need them to calm down or to think about their behaviour.

 The green one gives the go-ahead.

Behaviour plan

Behaviour plans are an important part of the strategy for success for any child who shows difficulty managing their behaviour. These are discussed in detail in the behaviour for learning section (p 87).

Now and next cards/First and then (terms used interchangeably)

Now and next cards are quick and easy to make and are very effective for all children with behaviour or communication difficulties. They consist of a rectangle with the word 'now' on the left side and the word 'next' on the right side. Underneath there may be a symbol or a photograph of the activity the child is doing now and the activity that is coming next. It is used to remind the child that the activity will be changing soon and also to tell the child what is coming next. These are excellent for keeping children on task as you can constantly remind them that there is a change of activity coming soon.

Timer

A whole lesson is a long time for a child with ADHD to sit and concentrate. I suggest using a timer. I have a variety of timers ranging from one minute up to 15 minutes. Some are manual and some are digital. This will depend on the cognitive ability of the child. These can be used in conjunction with the 'now and next' cards. For a very excitable child who is really struggling to attend to your lesson use the one minute timer with the cards. An activity of their choosing should be the 'next' activity. The child will see the time disappearing and will know that the 'next' activity is coming very soon. An important point to remember is that if you promise something you must stick to it. The child will develop a bond with you and learn to trust you if you stick to your word. Eventually they will respond to you without the cards and timers if you are consistent in your management of their behaviour.

Increase the time slowly and the child will respond. Only you and your TA will know how long that child can stay on task for. Increase the time that you expect the child to stay on task for.

Pay attention to the detail. Will the timer be used as a missile? Will the child fiddle with it? If so, be sure it will bounce rather than break and be sure it doesn't break too easily if a child with meddling hands gets hold of it.

Fidget toys

As previously mentioned, children with ADHD struggle to focus and keep still. You are wasting your breath by asking them to stop fiddling with things. They can't. This is beyond their control, so you may as well go with it and provide a fidget toy. A fidget toy is usually something small and often sensory-based. Some children like to have a small ball that they squash with their fingers and run it around in their hands. Others like to hold a balloon filled with sand and others will like a book that they constantly turn the pages of. Anything that prevents the child from running around the classroom or harming themselves or others is to be welcomed.

Takeaway activities to use immediately for a child with ADHD

Some activities can be implemented immediately and will have a huge impact on your classroom and the child with ADHD. These are levelled depending on resources available and the level of your own experience as the classroom practitioner (beginner level being for teachers with relatively little experience working with children with ADHD, and/or fewer resources).

Beginner level	Intermediate level	Advanced level
Use reward systems or motivators for all children and find individual motivators for children with ADHD to encourage desired behaviour.	Provide time out but be sure this is not reinforcing poor behaviour or to avoid work.	Provide ear defenders for the child who is irritated by unpredictable noise.
Remind children of rules at the beginning of each new lesson.	Trust the child – allow them to decide when they need a break and provide a space within the classroom for this.	Provide a weighted blanket or a weighted lap bag to help calm a distressed child with ADHD (or ASC).
Encourage children to use their peers as tutors – children understand each other's language when adults may not.	Send them on errands to break up the lesson – as they are not able to remain seated for long periods, this gives them a purpose to move.	Set clear expectations and do not resort to bribery. For example, first you will do this, then you may have your PC (motivator)
Teach the core subjects (maths, science and English) in the morning when behaviour is better.	Give praise if some work is completed – this is a bone of contention for some teachers, but it helps to increase confidence and provides a willingness to improve.	Keep the child stimulated and willing to participate in the lesson through the use of PC programs rather than worksheets. For example use 'Mr Thorne Does Phonics: Letters and Sounds' or 'Squeebles Spelling Test: Great Spelling' app for kids.
Have the child help you, e.g. let them operate the whiteboard or take photographs. Keep them busy and exhaust their energy.	As with children with ASC, prepare them for transitions by talking, using visuals and picture clues.	Teaching reading using phonics will not usually work for children with ADHD. Teach them to visualise whole words if phonics fails.
Be aware of colours and patterns in the environment – these are well-known triggers for children with ADHD.	Keep your day highly structured and use visual timetables so the child knows exactly what to expect.	Provide a Wiggle Seat (an inflatable sensory cushion) to help the child to exercise their muscles and use up their energy while remaining seated.
Wear plain single coloured clothes yourself and encourage your TAs to do the same. This is calming and avoids sensory overload and hyperactivity.	Play calming music quietly in the background during independent work sessions. This can have a soothing effect and prevent hyperactivity.	Provide Chewelry (safe and chewable jewellery) for a child who takes comfort from chewing their clothes. www.cheapdisabilityaids.co.uk/special-needs-chew-toys-36-c.asp
Avoid brightly coloured and highly patterned resources – these are visually attractive to other children but may be an irritant to the child with ADHD.	Allow a stress ball or fidget toy.	Make sure learning is fun. Ask yourself when planning - is it appropriate to make it play based? For example using dominoes for matching numbers or playing cards for sequencing will encourage a child with ADHD to stay on task much longer. Think about role play during literacy lessons. Think outside the box; what will help to keep the child on task and prevent them from distracting others?

Beginner level	Intermediate level	Advanced level
Provide frequent breaks – build these into the routine and structure of the day.	Use timers to indicate how long is left for a particular activity.	When planning your lesson activities alternate an activity where the child is required to sit with one that allows them to move around. Invent one if necessary as it will pay dividends for the peace and harmony in your classroom.

Fig. 26 Takeaway activities to use immediately for a child with ADHD

Practical ideas for teaching children with LDD

The first thing we need to do with children with LDD is to observe them closely. Watch and learn from them over a few days at the start of the year. What are their experiences while in the classroom? Ask yourself these questions:

- What is the child doing during whole class discussions? Are they contributing or are they disengaged?
- How is the child behaving? Are they disrupting the rest of their table group, indicating a lack of understanding?
- Are they distracted by activities close by such as people in the corridor or children on their table?
- Are they on task and for how long?
- Does the child need any obvious modifications? Would they benefit from writing pencils, a slanted desk for writing or different coloured paper? Tick off the obvious things.
- What is their main area of concern? How can you change your classroom or your teaching to improve the experience for the child?

Seating

Seating and the position of children with LDD within the classroom is important. Pairing the child up with a more able child may be effective. Both may benefit from the experience, although there is a delicate balance to be sought to ensure neither child experiences a lesser educational experience.

Some people advocate that a child with LDD should sit at an individual desk in order to help them to concentrate. I am not an advocate of this, as children are sociable and a child with LDD may already feel isolated for a variety of reasons already without sitting them apart from other children.

Keep in mind that a child with LDD may be a wheelchair user. It is unlikely that they will want to remain in the wheelchair all day long as this would make them very uncomfortable. Generally, specialist seating is provided. Make sure you have enough room for a specialist seat and that your classroom tables will go high enough for the child to be pushed up to them. Be aware that you may be the only person in the room while the child with SEND is in their wheelchair or specialist chair. You may be called upon to make sure they are comfortable and safe.

As with most children, be sure that distractions from windows and corridors are kept to a minimum.

Structure and routine

As with all children, structure and routine is important. In fact, we all like to know what is happening next and we all like to be in our comfort zone. These things are particularly important to a child with LDD. If a routine is embedded into everyday practice it will become second nature, and this will minimise poor behaviour as the child will feel secure and safe. For example, meet your child at the door and direct them to hang up their coat and unpack their bag and sit in their own seat. Once at their desk, their visual timetable, detailing activities for the day should be set out waiting for them. They can see, straight away at a glance what they will be doing all day, or for the period you have provided on their timetable. Do this every day and your child will feel safe and secure. They will know that whatever happens at home or on the journey to school there will be structure and routine once they arrive at school.

Visuals

Some of the visual aids already discussed in the section on ASC and ADHD will be useful for a child in the classroom with LDD, e.g. now and next cards and a timer (p 109), or a communication chart or other communication aid (p 99). You might find that the daily timetable is sufficient for the child or you might find that the child will only respond to what is happening now and what will happen immediately after the current activity. This knowledge will come as you work with and observe your child more.

Use graphics and photographs and symbols where needed. Getting to know your child is important. You might find that one day a photograph of the next activity will be a reasonable tool for the child to introduce the idea of changing activity, whereas the next day, a full blown visual timetable may be required for the same task. Think on your feet and remember that no strategy works all of the time. Think outside of the box! What does the child need in a given situation and invent it yourself if necessary.

> ## Top tip
> Remember, no strategy works for every child all the time. Be prepared to change!

Teacher time

During the lesson try and avoid constantly handing over the child with LDD to your TA. As the teacher you are run off your feet trying to accommodate all children and ensure that all are learning to the best of their ability. However, a child with LDD needs your time and your skills as a teacher more than most. Also they may become too reliant on the TA to provide support for their work. A child who struggles to learn requires your specialist skills.

Build up your relationship with the child. Spend time with them; get to know them and what makes them tick. Use praise at every opportunity and link it to rewards. Be clear and precise with your instructions and make them visual if possible. Make success as easy as possible by making adaptions to your plans.

Age-appropriate reading books

Another important point and one that is difficult to achieve is to remember to keep things age-appropriate. Reading books that allow a struggling reader to practise their skills without feeling patronised are particularly difficult to find. The NUT recommends the following as a starting point:

- Book Trust – an online resource (www.booktrust.org.uk)
- SEN Press – age-appropriate for 14–19 years old
- Download – a series of eight books for teenage boys
- Ransom books – for children aged 11 and older reading at 5–8 years level
- Badger books – from reading age 6 to interest age 14. (www.teachers.org.uk)

Techniques to help with written work

Use PC programs such as Writing With Symbols (www.mayer-johnson.com/downloads/trials) and Clicker 6 or 7 (www.cricksoft.com/uk/products/clicker/home.aspx) to help children who struggle with writing to succeed in their work. Do your utmost to reduce the written output and the reading. Think about pairing them with a more able partner who could do the writing while they collaborate on ideas.

There are also several sensory ideas for writing which children really enjoy. For example write the child's name in sand and encourage them to feel the shape of the letters in the sand. A more able child may begin to copy the letters. Shaving foam is also good for sensory writing practice and children often enjoy the feel of the foam on their fingers. Paint, rice and cornflour and water mixed together are also good for encouraging writing skills.

Where needed provide specialist pens and pencils and a writing slope. An occupational therapist will decide if these are necessary.

If you search Twitter, you will find all sorts of other inspirational ideas. I posed the question on Twitter. I particularly like the variety of methods listed by Kate Thompson – @thepetitioner. She is going for an approach that encompasses any method that helps the child rather than relying on one tried and trusted method.

- Video. A group of children including the one who struggles with writing could make a video to record their learning.
- Recordable whiteboard. Turn an iPad into a recordable whiteboard by downloading an app such as Vittle (www.qrayon.com/home/vittle). This app allows the child to record their ideas about photos taken from their own camera roll or allows them to draw pictures and record their thoughts on their drawings.
- Talking tins. These help children to develop speaking and listening skills. The child can record and play back their own thoughts and ideas which saves them from having to complete too much writing.
- Magnetic letters/words. Encourage the child to use initial sounds chosen from the magnetic letters if possible while also using one of the other methods listed.
- Scribe. Adults write the word the child says. Or pair your child with a good writer and encourage them to share ideas.
- Drawing. A child who is not comfortable with writing may be able to draw their learning.
- Picture sequencing. This is a good activity for younger children who find writing a struggle. Take your activity, break it down into separate pictures and ask the child to sequence the pictures. This can be used for literacy stories, historical events or PSHE activities.
- Signing. A child who struggles with writing and communication may be able to learn some signs to show what they have learned in the lesson.

I also love this answer from @ Ask_Mr_Armitage. Children enjoy QR Codes and it encourages them to use technology in a meaningful manner.

'I discovered this website Vocaroo at a Teach meet last week. Records their voice and produces a QR code for their books.'

Takeaway activities to use immediately for a child with LDD

Some activities can be implemented immediately and will have a huge impact on your classroom and the child with LDD. These are levelled depending on resources available and the level of your own experience as the classroom practitioner (beginner level being for teachers with relatively little experience working with children with LDD, and/or fewer resources).

Beginner level	Intermediate level	Advanced level
Break learning into small chunks.	Use visual timetables and communication passports.	Allow the child with writing difficulties to use specialised PC software such as Writing With Symbols or Clicker 6 or 7.
Give regular feedback and praise as often as possible.	Learn as much as you can about the particular disability in order to aid your understanding. Remember though that all difficulties manifest differently in each child. Know your children well.	Allow the use of iPads or other electronic devices.
Scaffold all new learning.	Teach organisational skills and demonstrate how to organise their work.	Improve communication through the use of Talking Tins, BIGMacks, LITTLEMacks, iPads.
Repeat instructions often using key words only.	Personalise all learning for the child; do not set any generic work.	Plan educational visits/ invite speakers in to school to support learning in the classroom.
Have only one or two activities per page and avoid unnecessary detail.	Use reward systems. Word of warning, do not remove rewards once given, as a child with LDD will not comprehend the concept.	Consult with members of the multi-agency team (e.g. educational psychologist, speech therapist), and ensure their advice is fully incorporated into your planning.
Personalise the work to the child by using their interests.	Find out what is important to the child and use it to gain their trust.	Ensure close liaison with parents/carers to ensure strategies are continued in the home, e.g. by providing relevant homework and advising parents/carers on best strategies to use.

Beginner level	Intermediate level	Advanced level
Create opportunities for success to build confidence.	Have the children work in pairs but beware the more able child does not do all the work.	Ensure pupil voice and pupil self-evaluation are a strong feature of learning – including their views on next steps where possible and where appropriate.
Check whether there is an IEP in existence and follow the advice rather than reinventing the wheel.	Group work is good for the child with LDD and encourages independent work as the TA will move around the whole group rather than sticking closely with the child with LDD.	Ensure outcomes from the child's EHC plan are a part of day-to-day learning. Use of 'child friendly' IEPs. These are written with the child and use language the child understands.
Use sensory resources as mentioned previously to support learning. Sand and shaving foam for writing skills. Keeping the work 'hands on' keeps the child interested.	Use real resources where possible, for example, real coins rather than plastic ones.	Fully embed total communication into the classroom, including relevant and meaningful use of signing, symbols and other relevant AAC systems.

Fig. 27 Takeaway activities to use immediately for a child with LDD

Practical ideas for teaching children with dyslexia

Reading

- **Have a structured reading scheme** – the scheme should involve books with much repetition of words and that introduce words slowly. Ensure you put the child on a level where you know they will succeed. This will help them to develop confidence in their reading.
- **Avoid asking the child to read out loud** – this may be their worst nightmare and could result in damaged confidence. Ask for volunteers. To keep the classroom inclusive other children should not be denied the pleasure of reading out loud if they choose to do so.
- **Individual reading time with the teacher and TA** – create a time for the child to read to both the teacher and to the TA – time with the teacher is important. Remember, every teacher is a teacher of SEND and the child with special educational needs should not simply be left to the TA.
- **Reading rulers** – these are transparent coloured plastic strips overprinted to divide the ruler into 10mm and 30mm transparent strips on the opposite edges. The rulers underline the text and highlight it in coloured tint to relieve the glare from the page. They also help with tracking. They are portable and discrete.

- **E-readers** – some children with dyslexia find it better to read from an e-reader rather than a paper book. The reason is that the size of the font can be altered to suit the child and also the background colour can be dimmed to reduce the glare from the white paper. E-readers include Kindle, Nook, Apple products and Kobo Glo.
- **Use audio books** – audio books allow dyslexic children to enjoy the same stories as their peers and generate enthusiasm for reading without having to read the books for themselves. Audio books were previously CDs or tapes of books and were fairly expensive to buy. Now they are usually narrated by famous actors, are more reasonably priced and can easily be downloaded online. As the teacher you can download the set literacy book to an iPad or tablet and send it home with the child for them to listen to at their leisure.
- **Reading tips** – see Dyslexia Action for more information: http://www.dyslexiaaction.org.uk/page/encouraging-reading-o

Writing

- **Encourage the use of cursive joined up writing** – when children begin to write they often begin by learning to print and then move on to joined up writing. Encourage the child with dyslexia to only learn one style: continuous cursive style. This is where words are written without the pencil ever leaving the paper. By doing this the child begins to memorise the shape of the letter and there is less chance of reversing letters such as p and q and b and d.
- **Key words** – produce a handout containing the keywords to avoid the child having to write them down.
- **Lined paper** – always use lined paper for the dyslexic children to work on.
- **Give them time** – give the children with dyslexia plenty of time to write things down if there is no alternative to writing. Factor this into your lesson.
- **Teach touch typing** – by removing the struggle of the handwriting process and getting dyslexia children to type out their work instead, you are allowing the child to focus on content and they will have a far greater chance of success.
- **Symbols** – explore the use of Writing with Symbols or Clicker7 to help the child to focus on content rather than the actual formation of letters. This may not be appropriate in terms of age or cognitive ability but is worth considering to remove the pressure to write.
- **Record it** – if necessary use a recordable device such as a recording pen to decrease the amount of writing needed.
- **E-dictionaries** – these come in pocket size and desktop size and are perfect for helping with spelling and alternative words. For the A.C.E. Spelling Dictionary (4th Edition) the child only needs to think how the word sounds to find out how to spell it.

- **Reading pen** – (www.readingpen.co.uk/) this allows you to scan over a word and instantly hear the word spoken or receive a spoken definition of the meaning. The pen uses the Oxford English Dictionary, has over 240,000 words and phrases, and turns any text into speech.
- **Voice to text software** – this type of software is very popular and allows the child to convert voice in to text. This gives the opportunity for the child to concentrate on the content of their work rather than being held back by spelling and the actual process of writing. Possibly the best known one is Dragon http://www.nuance.co.uk/dragon/dyslexia-solutions/index.htm include Voice Finger, E-Speaking.com and Windows 7 has a program built in for WordPad.

General strategies to help children with dyslexia

- **Keep instructions simple** – children with dyslexia have difficulties with instructions. For this reason instructions need to be kept simple. Use bullet points as an alternative to a paragraph of instructions. Use highlighter pens to highlight key information.
- **Spellings** – focus spellings on key words used for the topic or lesson.
- **Get organised** – encourage the use of notebooks and checklists to help with organisational skills and independence.
- **Sitting arrangements** – sit dyslexic children at the front of the class close to the teacher. Ensure they have a good view of the Interactive Whiteboard or Apple TV. Also ensure there are no children wandering around which will cause a visual disturbance.
- **Keep it tidy** – as with all classrooms where there are children with SEND ensure the classroom is clutter free.
- **Verbal instructions** – if instructions are verbal, ask the child to repeat them back to you. By doing this you can be sure they have understood your instructions.
- **Homework time** – write the homework in the child's planner or ask your TA to do it. Remember the child with dyslexia often struggles with instructions so may write the work incorrectly. They will also be more tired at the end of the day due to the amount of effort put in to getting through the day. Another reason to ensure the work is written correctly.
- **Give them time** – allow extra time for work to be completed due to the child needing more time to read, write and plan.

Here is a top tip from a child with dyslexia!

"It helps if people tell me in advance instead of just telling me on the day or telling me when something is actually happening. I like advanced warning. With instructions I'm ok if I can remember them, but I usually can't. I prefer people to write them down for me."

Extra practical activities

It may take our dyslexic child longer to master certain skills. Provide more practical activities to enhance learning. This could be in the form of games such as bingo, computer programs and iPad apps.

Structure and routine

As with a child with ASC or ADHD, a child with dyslexia needs structure and routine. Keep this in mind and give them visual reminders of what will happen and when it will happen. Try and keep your classroom structured and organised.

Practical ideas for teaching children with Irlen Syndrome

As we know there is a vast difference between dyslexia and Irlen Syndrome (see Chapter 4, p 65). It is estimated that 50 per cent of children diagnosed with dyslexia actually have the visual perceptual processing disorder known as Irlen Syndrome. Reading difficulties resulting from Irlen Syndrome will not be helped by extra phonics instruction.

Helping those with Irlen Syndrome

- Close classroom blinds to filter out bright sunlight
- Try different coloured papers to avoid the glare of white paper
- Avoid using overhead projector due to intense light
- Use your whiteboard as little as possible
- Avoid asking the chid to concentrate on reading or writing for too long
- Reduce fluorescent lighting by turning some strip lights off
- Remind children to use their coloured overlays in all subjects where reading and writing is required, including maths.

Do remember that if a child has Irlen Syndrome, no amount of extra teaching will remedy this situation. Solutions such as those mentioned above will help. Teaching phonics is important but will not cure Irlen Syndrome.

Takeaway activities to use immediately for a child with dyslexia

Some activities can be implemented immediately and will have a huge impact on your classroom and the child with dyslexia. These are levelled depending on resources available and the level of your own experience as the classroom practitioner (beginner level being for teachers with relatively little experience working with children with dyslexia, and/or fewer resources).

Beginner level	Intermediate level	Advanced level
Use a minimum of 12 point font for handouts.	Use font 'Open Dyslexic' if possible.	Use electronic dictionaries.
Change background theme colour to green when working on a PC.	Allow extra time for work and factor this into the day.	Use a Reading pen to scan the text, enlarge it and make it easier to read.
Ariel, Verdana and Comic Sans may be beneficial for some but do experiment with font and find the best one for the child.	Stick to one or two verbal instructions and have the child repeat them back.	Use e-readers for the set literacy text or for reading passages for homework. This means the teacher can use a book that is slightly above the child's reading level.
Use whole line spacing to make chunks of text easier to read.	Teach different memory skills such as mnemonics. To remember lists encourage the child to make up a story which links the words together. By doing so their brain will associate the words together and remember the list.	Encourage use of different voice recorders to reduce writing.
Use bullet points to break up texts containing lots of instructions. This makes it easier to read.	Use pictures to back up or replace text.	Use voice to text software such as 'Dragon'.
Use a reading ruler to help the child to read independently.	Stick spellings all over the classroom to allow the child to process them.	Encourage the use of audio books to allow books of a higher level to be accessed.
Avoid damaging a child's confidence by correcting every error in spelling.	Play Kim's game to develop the child's ability to observe and extend memory. Place about 20 items on a table and give children around one minute to look at them. Cover with a cloth and ask the child to write down as many as they can remember.	Use PC programs for additional practice for new activities. Apps are available in most subjects and many are free. For example visit Nessy and see what's on offer: www.nessy.com/uk.
Flow charts may be easier to follow than text – use them when you can.	Use coloured overlays if helpful (especially for children with Irlen Syndrome).	Remember to consider all your strategies for a child with dyslexia. There is no single strategy that works for all children. The likelihood is that you will need a combination of all strategies mentioned.

Beginner level	Intermediate level	Advanced level
Start each lesson with a brief outline of what the lesson will contain. This is good for all children with SEND as they are happier when they know what to expect.	Have a dyslexic child working in a pair with a non-dyslexic child when doing writing exercises.	Plan daily routines and share them in advance with the child.
Use a blank sheet of paper to blank out upcoming work to avoid distractions.	Use a highlighter to pick out salient information before the lesson begins.	Teach the child to use chunking technique to help with reading. This is when you break long words in to groups of 3 or 4 letters.

Fig. 28 Takeaway activities to use immediately for a child with dyslexia

Practical ideas for teaching children with behaviour difficulties

Pass it on!

Jason Bangbala, Behaviour Consultant (www.jasonbangbala.co.uk) is a must-see for Behaviour for Learning.

Behaviour does not just occur because children wish to misbehave. It is always as a result of something occurring. It could be:

- a lack of understanding of instructions on the child's part
- that the standard of the work set is too high for the child
- the result of loud noises or other distractions around the learning environment.

It is our job as teachers to find the reason for the behaviour and address it at source. A quick and helpful tip is to teach self-regulation or calming techniques. For example, teach the child to count to ten before they respond to anyone or anything they find annoying. Consider teaching a child with behaviour difficulties that they may have a few minutes' time out of the classroom when they feel themselves losing control of their behaviour. This might be just to stand outside the classroom and calm down and should not involve any kind of reward.

As professional teachers, you will have your own theories on behaviour management.

Chris Chivers is one of my favourite tweeters. He was a headteacher for 16 years and his school career spanned 32 years. He is knowledgeable on many topics and has extensive knowledge of behaviour management. Chris is a master of one line mantras and my favourite one regarding behaviour is this:

> *'Simple advice: know your children well, read the signs, spot and deal, keep calm, be firm, be positive.'*

In his blog, 'Behaviour management and ITE', Chris advises the following points:

- Catching them being good and acknowledging that is important, so that positive messages support good behaviours.
- Have a clear rewards scheme in place, so that there is benefit in being good.
- Decide whether rewards are to be intrinsic or extrinsic. Organise properly.
- Know the school rules and approaches to behaviour issues.
- Articulate school expectations clearly and regularly.
- Spot and deal with issues as they arise.
- Involve parents as appropriate.
- Report and record as needed.

Name: Chris Chivers

Twitter handle: @ChrisChivers2

Website: chrischiversthinks.weebly.com

Who is he? Ex Headteacher and Learner/teacher

Why to follow him: Informative tweets and blogs on all educational topics.

Seating plans

I advocate the use of seating plans for classes where there are children with behaviour for learning plans. With a seating plan, you can pair children in your class with those they work best with rather than those they chat best with. By using a seating plan you are sending a powerful message that you are in control of their learning. You can create working partners for your child with SEND and pair them with those who will help them achieve while not becoming distracted themselves.

Planned ignoring

This is difficult to do but is very effective. Simply ignore poor behaviour. Do not rise to it. You and your TA should only pick the arguments you actually need to win. Some behaviours are not worth the fight and may result in you losing your cool. This strategy involves you denying the attention that the behaviour is aiming to illicit. This includes verbal discussion, eye contact and body language. Simply guide the child back to the required activity and continue as though nothing has happened.

Circle time

Circle time is invaluable for helping to change children's behaviour. The class will literally sit in a circle, talk about undesired behaviour that is occurring in their class and will suggest solutions to the problem. It is in their best interests to help with behaviour management as they don't want their learning disturbed. It is used mostly with children in primary schools but may also be used in the early years of secondary school.

From a TA's perspective

Recently I have been working with a group of TAs from a cluster of local primary and secondary schools. I asked them for their best positive management strategies. Out of a group of 20, every one of them said that they looked for good behaviour throughout the lesson and acted upon it immediately rather than rewarding good behaviour at the end.

Here is a selection of other methods they use.

- Individual prize for best contribution in a lesson.
- Class Dojo for staying on task. This is an online app used as a positive behaviour management tool. It is used by schools in many different ways but is always successful. It has the capacity to let the teacher send home photos of how well the child is working throughout the day. Schools run schemes in individual classes or as part of a whole school behaviour tool. See www.classdojo.com/en-gb/ for more information.
- Behaviour points leading to free time at the end of the lesson.
- Plain and simple praise.
- Marbles in a jar leading to free time at the end of the lesson.
- Behaviour ladder with promise of free time at the end of the lesson if all work is completed.
- Add information to Facebook page for parents to see best worker.
- Token economy. This is where tokens are provided to reinforce desired behaviour from children. They can be used to increase the frequency with which the behaviour occurs. The idea is that children collect the tokens as a payment and trade them for something they want as a reward. Rewards might include choosing time, time on PC or anything else that motivates the child.

Long-term behaviour strategies

Where there are several competing behaviour challenges it is important to make a priority list. Not all behaviour challenges can be solved with immediate reward systems. Some require the behaviour to be broken down into small steps and tackled individually. For example a child who cannot be taken on a school trip because they lash out at other pupils if they annoy them, have shutdowns if they are not allowed to have their own way and verbally or physically attack staff will need these behaviours broken down in to small steps. First, identify a long-term goal that the child really wants to achieve such as joining the class trip. Next, prioritise what is most important for your child and the class as a whole and work on that one difficulty. Rewards and motivators should be used at this stage to work on the highlighted behaviour. Remind the child that they are also working towards a long-term goal. Continue with this method until the child is able to join the trip.

Examples of long-term goals might include:

- receiving a Children's University award
- winning a Year 11 special reward for outstanding contribution to school life
- winning a sporting achievement over the year

Strategy/technique	Name of Tweeter
Tokens given for behaviour (may also be removed). 10 tokens = reward	@JulesDaulby Teacher: literature, language, SEN, English and drama
Lego pot and lego as reward/marbles in jar	@nancygedge Mother, writer, teacher
Class Dojo	@gill_ower Year 3 teacher
Ignore poor behaviour and praise good	@JulesDaulby
Bingo card with key targets, winner gets phone call home	@Andyphilipday Life-long Geographer. Some-time teacher.
Marbles in tube – other children can say child deserves this too	@Daydream512 Educator: lifelong learning
Spiders/bugs on wall, personalised to child	@Daydream512 Educator
Get children to agree acceptable behaviour and then have monitors for who sticks to the rules	@Daydream512 Educator
Smileys on board for instant praise, no reward	@nancygedge Mother, writer, teacher
'Caught you being good' raffle tickets leading to prize	@lilybeth80 Mum, wife, Y3 teacher.
Fabulous Friday, Wonderful Wednesday, teacher tries to focus on positive behaviour all day	@lilybeth80 Mum, wife, Y3 teacher

Fig. 29 Behaviour management strategies

- winning attendance awards ranging from weekly or termly to yearly across the whole school, e.g. £5 draw for those with perfect attendance to buy a book
- winning the Stamp system (pride) leading to cinema tickets termly
- receiving a free breakfast for attending early revision sessions.

I consulted my colleagues on Twitter about their behaviour management strategies and these are some of the best answers I received.

Each Monday at 8pm there is a grand Twitter chat #behaviourchat. I strongly recommend you have a look at this and join in if the topic is of interest to you. The chat is hosted by a Key Stage 1 co-ordinator who is a member of SLT and a Specialised Leader in Education (SLE).

One week I logged on to participate in the chat and found it was being hosted by @Parkinson_best whose name is Chris. The topic was the creative use of sand timers in the classroom. The chat dealt with reward strategies. Here are a few of the tweets I was most interested in:

Strategy/technique	Tweeter
Time out	@BehaviourTeach AHT, SLE in behaviour Y2 teacher, Bloomsbury Author
Transition period to avoid rushing pupil	@reachoutASC Teacher and independent Consultant for Autism Spectrum Condition.
Use a game to teach waiting, long and short waiting	@reachoutASC Teacher and independent Consultant for Autism Spectrum Condition.
Give a child 'take up' time if behaviour is oppositional	@Parkinson_best AHT for inclusion. Med. NPQML, NASENCO.
Independently take time out without need for adult input if lesson becomes too much	@Parkinson_best AHT for inclusion. Med. NPQML, NASENCO.
Timer reduces need for auditory input or perceived demands	@jw_teach AHT in a special school specialising in ASD.
Timer helps adult keep their responses appropriate	@beyondbehaviour Leadership, wellbeing and behaviour consultant.
Raffle tickets used to reward attendance	@garycorbett7 Teacher
Give out raffle tickets for good work/behaviour, then put them in a hat and draw out the winner at the end of the day, lesson or week	@ cherrylkd AHT. MA in inclusion. SLE for SEND.
Raffle tickets for children to give to each other for things they see as kind	@reachoutASC Teacher and independent Consultant for Autism Spectrum Condition

Fig. 30 Reward strategies

Takeaway activities to use immediately for a child with behaviour difficulties

Some activities can be implemented immediately and will have a huge impact on your classroom and the child with behaviour difficulties. These are levelled depending on resources available and the level of your own experience as the classroom practitioner (beginner level being for teachers with relatively little experience working with children with behaviour difficulties, and/or fewer resources).

Beginner level	Intermediate level	Advanced level
Greet the child at the door and welcome them to the room.	Use circle time to discuss desired behaviour and reinforce behaviour.	If you are able to, remove the child from the room, when they display challenging behaviour to avoid the added attraction of an audience.
Listen to any concerns that are troubling the child at the start of the day so they are in the right frame of mind for learning.	Have equipment out ready and accessible for the child for the start of the lesson.	If the child cannot be removed due to them physically lashing out or assaulting staff and the situation is extreme, consider evacuating the whole class.
Run a quiet and calm classroom – if you shout, you are teaching that it is fine to shout. Also they will shout louder to be heard.	Ensure good pupil grouping which sees the child mixing with those with desired behaviour.	Make use of a 'chill-out' room or 'calming room' (see 105). Everyone needs time and space to calm down from time to time. As adults we should provide the child with behaviour challenges with that space if possible.
Include children in making the rules so they have ownership.	Every child who needs it should have a clearly written behaviour plan. This is known as a behaviour for learning plan. This should be collaboratively written with staff who know the child well. Ensure whole school buy-in for consistency.	Some schools have staff trained in the use of 'Team-Teach'. This is a holistic approach to behaviour management and trains staff to use the least intrusive positive handling strategy possible. If Team-Teach is in use in your school and the behaviour is escalating consider the use of this. Also, don't back the child in to a corner. Give them a way out of their behaviour. Sometimes their behaviour becomes so poor they forget the original trigger. Offer them chances to redeem themselves and be the bigger person.
Give a reminder of the class rules at the start of each lesson.	Re-visit the behaviour rules as many times as necessary during the lesson. Have the children remind each other of the rules.	Involve parents – home/school partnership is desirable.

Beginner level	Intermediate level	Advanced level
Have rules displayed in text and in symbols or pictures.	Use positive language and give directives rather than a request which could be denied.	Use Tactile Approach to Communication (TACPAC) www.tacpac.co.uk. This is an activity for sensory and neurologically impaired children to learn to make contact with their own bodies in a safe manner. You begin with a simple touch followed by a sensory experience from something lovely to feel while listening to music. My class staff and I found this to be extremely effective for calming children with behaviour difficulties.
Send a postcard home to a child's parents outlining good behaviour, or phone home. Share the behaviour for learning plan with parents.	Keep calm at all times – this is difficult when faced with challenging behaviour; walk away if needed.	Peer massage. This is effective for calming children and also for using up children's excess energy. It is a 15 minute clothed daily massage routine on the head, back, arms and hands, led by an adult. There is a range of activities, which use visualisation and touch and encourages positive touch throughout the curriculum. See more at: www.touchlinetraining.co.uk/Massage-in-Schools.aspx
Keep sentences short and use only key words. Check for understanding.	Remember a child with SEND may not be able to understand your body language and therefore explain things verbally.	Promote self-motivation techniques as described by Stewart Biddle. www.fitnessfirst.co.uk/globalassets/press-content/51220_0114-report_cracking-the-code-lr.pdf. Give choices and expect the right choice to be made to build lasting confidence and self-esteem.
Paint your room a soothing colour such as calming green.	Only pick the important battles – a teacher can't win every single one so choose your battle carefully.	If you promise something it must happen no matter if it is good or bad. For example if you tell the child that their behaviour will result in the loss of their break time you must stick to that even if it means the loss of your own break time to supervise the child. Therefore, don't make promises you can't keep. For example, telling a child you will make them leave the room could be an empty threat if you are alone and have no means of making this happen.
Reduce anxiety by telling children the routine for the day in the morning.	Take ownership of the end of any behaviour conversation and make a clear signal that you have done so: 'I will not discuss this further'.	Start every new lesson with a clean slate. Don't hold grudges. The child must know that every new lesson is a new experience and they won't be judged on what's happened before.

Fig. 31 Takeaway activities to use immediately for a child with behaviour difficulties

Pass it on!
Model the behaviour you want to see. Teach the behaviour you want to see!

Practical ideas for inclusion

As professional teachers we have all developed strategies to aid full inclusion. When working with children with SEND, remember to personalise everything and tailor your strategies to the individual child. There is no right or wrong way; there is only the best way for each child.

Here are a few general ideas to help you to ensure all children are included:

- Make sure the child is seated correctly, close to the teacher and away from distractions.
- Ensure your TA understands the learning objective and where it fits in to the child's IEP. You may need to spend time on this one depending on the level of knowledge your TA has.
- Take account of non-academic targets such as being able to find their own PE equipment. Take every opportunity to encourage independence skills.
- Think about any off-site trips. Think about how you can include your child who may have physical difficulties and be in a wheelchair. They must also be able to access educational trips. Consider the toileting and feeding needs of your child with SEND.

Strategy/technique	Tweeter
Pupil passports, like a 'user guide'–strengths, successes, challenges and strategies to support	@rachelrossiter SENDCo SLT 9-13 school
Good relationships with every student in the class, knowing your students well, question-level analysis in test to set differentiated work, differentiated questioning, showing it is ok to make a mistake	@r_brooks1 Biochemist, Registered scientist, KS3 Teacher and science co-ordinator, Deputy HOY.
Build a team ethos-supporting each other in learning, looking out for each other all the time	@goodman_ang Global Learning Programme Leader. Deputy head
Have regular staff meetings so everyone knows the needs of the child	@rodneyreid68 Ex DH – Exp in behaviour/attendance/mentoring.
Get students to explain what they have learnt to rest of class, they know their language better than us and others may understand	@GMacademic Teacher of science.

Fig. 32 Strategies to achieve a fully inclusive classroom

Many mainstream teachers welcome children with SEND into their classes but often report that they feel inadequately prepared to teach them. I have gathered some expert advice from my teaching colleagues on specific strategies for how to achieve a fully inclusive classroom.

Specialist tech

When working with children with special educational needs its important to have all the correct equipment ready for them at the start of the lesson. It takes them longer to achieve their targets and they need to make a prompt start so that they may be included in the plenary section at the end of the lesson. Here are some examples of the equipment used in the lessons below.

- A switch accessible camera is simple to set up. First, connect the switch for the child to press into the socket on the interface box and plug the lead in to the USB on the camera. Turn on the camera, press the switch and the camera works like any other camera. Outlay is expensive to begin with but once you have it you will find it good value.
- The mixer mentioned in the maths lesson on fractions should be set up in exactly the same way as the camera.
- The iPad is also switch accessible by following the same instructions. Again, your lesson will be inclusive in an easy to achieve way.
- To make any lesson involving writing accessible for children with SEND you need Clicker 6 or 7 (www.cricksoft.com/uk/products/clicker/home.aspx) or Writing with Symbols www.widgit.com/wws2000prog/) These are PC programs which you need to purchase. If you are a skilled PC user you can train yourself to use either of these programs.
- Boardmaker is one of my favourite software tools and is very versatile. (http://www.mayer-johnson.com/boardmaker-software). It is excellent for communication using symbols, animation, speech and much more. Explore it and see!
- A roller ball is an alternative mouse and uses fingers rather than the whole hand. Change the mouse options and make the curser coloured or change it to a different icon so the child can see it. Similarly, joysticks are easier to grip and easier to manoeuvre for a child with hands that do not work efficiently.
- Keyboards have a number of different options. You could purchase a smaller one which is easier to position, or one with larger keys which is better for a child with various conditions that make using a conventional keyboard difficult. A keyguard is very useful. This is a metal plate with holes over each of the characters which makes it easier to isolate one letter. Most keyboards can be made switch accessible for the child who uses their head or another part of their body to access and operate the PC.

- Explore the accessibility options on your iPad. A few of the things that can be done include altering the size of text and button shapes, increase contrast, add subtitles, access assistive touch and make the iPad switch controlled.

Here are some examples of best practice working within lessons.

Main activity	Differentiated for SEND
History. Most students are matching Victorian inventors to descriptions of what they invented.	Use a switch accessible camera and take photographs of things invented during Victorian era.
Maths. Most students are learning about fractions using IWB and attractive worksheets.	Use switch accessible mixer and bake a cake. Cut in to fractions. Make sandwiches and cut into halves and quarters.
RE. Most students are learning about miracles performed by Jesus and completing independent stories.	Use pre-made Clicker 6 or 7 grids (depending which your school has) or Writing With Symbols to tell the story. Have the children dress up and act out the story using sensory resources.
PE. Most children are playing boccia.	Purchase adapted boccia shutes and adapt the game so that all can play.
ICT. Most children are working on independent projects using the internet to research WW2.	Use Boardmaker to teach the various countries involved. Use switch accessible ipad to listen to audio clips from WW2. Use switch accessible camera to take photographs of ration books and uniforms and make in to a project. Dress the children as soldiers or as refugees.

Fig. 33 Examples of best practice

Takeaway activities to use immediately for a fully inclusive classroom

Some activities can be implemented immediately and will have a huge impact on your classroom and inclusion. These are levelled depending on resources available and the level of your own experience as the classroom practitioner (beginner level being for teachers with relatively little experience working with children with SEND, and/or fewer resources).

Beginner level	Intermediate level	Advanced level
If the child has attended another school previously, invite the TA in to share their knowledge of the child.	Provide someone to listen to the child's perceived problems.	Review your classroom and speak to SLT if you require any specialist resources or equipment for writing or seating etc.
Concentrate on the needs of the child rather than what the 'label' is telling you.	Make use of peer modelling for all aspects of the day including non structured times.	Review the school's policies on inclusion. Does the behaviour policy allow for the child's behaviour to be taken into consideration as a result of the child's disability?
Find as much information as possible about the child: strengths, needs, areas of difficulty.	Provide a space for the child to compete any physical exercises as necessary, also space for their specialised equipment such as standing frames and wheelchairs.	Technology should be readily available, e.g. specialised mouse, rollerball, keyboard, switches, keyguard. Make use of 'Accessibility Options'.
Work collaboratively with other professionals e.g. physiotherapist, occupational therapist, psychologist, speech therapist to determine a full picture of the child.	Create a safe place within the classroom where the child can go to feel calm. This could simply be a pop up tent.	Specialised programs such as Clicker 6 or 7 and Writing With Symbols are useful for those who struggle with writing.
Keep it practical where possible, e.g. include trips to shops to handle real money.	Use a variety of teaching styles – children learn in different ways. Use pictures, symbols, words, social stories and communication visuals.	Make use of audio books and digital recorders for encouraging reading and writing.
Include sensory strategies such as practising numbers in sand, paint, foam etc.	Provide a sensory box relating to the topic or lesson you are working on. For example, a lesson on Victorians might include sensory items such as lace, chalk, child's chalkboard, dolly hat, dolly pegs and any other items from that era. This is used for children with LDD and also as a mood changer for those with behaviour difficulties.	Have your positive behaviour management system on show all the time. Encourage others to use it including dinner ladies and anyone else who interacts with the children when you aren't there. In this way you are overseeing their behaviour even when not present.
Plan individual objectives for the child rather than a lower version of class objectives.	If possible plan your objectives with the child. Discuss with them what they would like to learn about the topic and aim to make the targets 'child friendly'.	Make sure you have shared the behaviour for learning plan and the personalised targets and IEP targets with all adults who will have contact with the child. Consistency is key.

Fig. 34 Takeaway activities to use immediately for a fully inclusive classroom

Chapter 6 takeaway

Teaching tip

Consistency is key

All children are happiest in a routine. They may not know it but they have a fundamental need for consistency. They will look for any chink in your armour and they will use it even if it causes them to be frustrated and upset. Communicate your rules to everyone in school and insist that everyone follows them. We have a duty to make sure that all our children are safe and secure and as happy as we can make them and if we do that we will be well on the road to making our schools fully inclusive.

Pass it on

Hold a meeting

Don't keep your ideas to yourself. If you have found a good method for including all children, or a good behaviour strategy remember to pass it on. Ask your SLT if you can run a staff meeting and share your skills. Share it on Twitter using the hashtags #inclusion or #behaviour. Share it on Facebook too; most people appreciate a good behaviour strategy.

CPD book club recommendation

The Principal's Handbook for Inclusive Schools by J. Causton and G. Theoharis.

This book is a guide to building a school-wide vision from theory to practice. It covers the basics of special education to making inclusion work.

Bloggers' corner

Gareth D. Morewood is a SENCo and is also a passionate advocate for inclusive education. He speaks at national conferences and has written papers on provision in mainstream settings for children with complex needs. Follow him on Twitter at: @gdmorewood and check out his blog: gdmorewood.com

TO DO LIST:

- [ ] Check your tech! Make a list of what would be useful.
- [ ] Search #inclusion on Twitter and read the posts it identifies.
- [ ] Pass on your knowledge at a school staff meeting, on Twitter and on Facebook.
- [ ] Read the book *The Principal's Handbook for Leading Inclusive Schools*.
- [ ] Have a look at Gareth's blog and check out his posts on inclusion.

7 Evaluating progress

In the previous chapters we have covered many strategies to help support the children in your classroom with a range of special educational needs, and you should now have had a chance to implement these strategies to make your classroom fully inclusive. Time now needs to be set aside to reflect on your own practice and consider what is working and what needs some more thought. Are the children making the desired progress? Is the classroom more purposeful? Is the learning of the other children less disturbed?

Regular assessment of children's learning is an essential aspect of teaching. It is useful seeing where improvements can be made. The best way to do this is to observe the children, talk to the children and listen to them.

Top tip

Be a reflective teacher! It genuinely helps improve your practice.

Self-evaluation

As a teacher it is your responsibility to reflect on the provision you provide for the children in your care. It is your responsibility to check that:

- every child is included in each lesson
- every child can access each lesson at their personal level
- every child's behaviour is conducive to good learning
- every child's individual needs are catered for
- every room has had the physical adaptations made to it to allow equal access for all children
- every child has the technology they need to communicate.

As the teacher you should maintain the highest expectations of all children at all times and remember that a physical disability or a learning difficulty is not an excuse for lack of effort. As teachers, we are responsible for the progress of all children including those with SEND as is stated in the 2014 Code of Practice.

It is also your responsibility to ensure your own practice improves the practice of the school as a whole. When identifying your own strengths and areas for improvement you should also flag these areas up as areas for whole school continual professional development.

Being a reflective practitioner and carrying out a self-evaluation allows you to seek out and focus on areas where improvement is needed. It will also help you plan further strategies for improving the learning experience of your students.

In this chapter we provide you with a self-evaluation questionnaire to fill in. As well as this, here are some on-going techniques to ensure you are consistently reviewing your teaching and reflecting on your practice:

1. Keep a diary of your own reflective thoughts. There is a good reason why they teach you to do this. Be blunt with yourself. Could you do better?
2. Complete your evaluation on your lesson plan.
3. Possible use of video recording for your own lessons. This is growing in popularity and has huge benefits for reflection.
4. Invite your peers to observe your teaching – not just SLT, as they have a leadership remit.
5. Engage in coaching with peers.
6. Start a blog – many teachers are now blogging and it is helpful to the individual teacher for reflective purposes and also for other teachers. I regularly read the blogs of my fellow tweeters.

How and why to complete the questionnaire

Throughout your reading of this book so far you will have learned a great deal about how to teach and include all children with SEND in your classes. Many practical strategies have been covered and these will be of benefit to you in your every day teaching. Self-reflection is a valuable tool for teachers and that is the next task. Before we can proceed further we need to take stock of what has been learned and what might still be missing.

Completing the self-evaluation questionnaire will give you a quick guide to assessing whether your strategies are working:

- Your planning will be sharper and focused on individual children.
- Children's work will have improved as the whole class is more settled, calm and ready for learning.
- Your colleagues will notice the difference when they are invited to observe your teaching.
- Barriers to learning will be reduced.
- Your classroom will be calmer with a sense of shared purpose.
- All the children will be on task.
- You will be catering for all children in the way they learn best.

You will remember the questionnaire process from Chapter 3 (p 17–31), but here is a reminder.

Quick response approach

If your preference for the self-evaluation is to go with your gut only, then simply fill in the quick response section after each question with the first thing that comes into your mind when you ask yourself the question. Do not mull over the question too long; simply read carefully and answer quickly. This approach will give you an overview of your current SEND understanding and practice and will take relatively little time. Just make sure you are uninterrupted, in a quiet place and able to complete the questionnaire in one sitting with no distractions so that you get focused and honest answers.

Considered response approach

If you choose to take a more reflective and detailed approach, then you can leave the quick response section blank and go straight onto reading the further guidance section under each question. This guidance provides prompt questions and ideas to get you thinking in detail about the question being answered and is designed to open up a wider scope in your answer. It will also enable you to look at your experience and pull examples into your answer to back up your statements. You may want to complete it a few questions at a time and take breaks, or you may be prepared to simply sit and work through the questions all in one sitting to ensure you remain focused. This approach does take longer, but it can lead to a more in-depth understanding of your current SEND practice, and you will gain much more from the process than the quick response alone.

Combined approach

A thorough approach, and one I recommend, would be to use both approaches together regardless of personal preference. There is clear value in both approaches being used together. This would involve you firstly answering the self-evaluation quick response questions by briefly noting down your instinctual answers for all questions. The next step would be to return to the start of the self-evaluation, read the further guidance and then answer the questions once more, slowly and in detail forming more of a narrative around each question and pulling in examples from your own experience. Following this you would need to read over both responses and form a comprehensive and honest summary in your mind of your answers and a final view of where you feel you stand right now in your marking and feedback practice.

This is the longest of the three approaches to this questionnaire but will give you a comprehensive and full understanding of your current SEND practice. You will be surprised at the difference you see between the quick response and the considered response answers to the same questions. It can be very illuminating.

- I have done this self-assessment before.
- I only want a surface level overview of my current understanding and practice.
- I work better when I work at speed.
- I don't have much time.

Quick

- I have never done this self-assessment before.
- I want a deeper understanding of my current understanding and practice.
- I work better when I take my time and really think things over.
- I have some time to do this self-assessment.

Considered

- I have never done this self-assessment before.
- I have done this self-assessment before.
- I want a comprehensive and full understanding of my current understanding and practice and want to compare that to what I thought before taking the self-assessment.
- I have a decent amount of time to dedicate to completing this self-assessment.

Combined

Fig. 35 How should I approach the self-evaluation questionnaire?

Rate yourself

The final part of the self-evaluation is to rate yourself. This section will ask you to rate your confidence and happiness in each area that has been covered in the questionnaire, with a view to working on these areas for improvement throughout the course of the book. The table below shows how the scale works: the higher the number you allocate yourself, the better you feel you are performing in that area.

Rating	Definition
1	Not at all. I don't. None at all. Not happy. Not confident at all.
2	Rarely. Barely. Very little. Very unconfident.
3	Not often at all. Not much. Quite unconfident.
4	Not particularly. Not really. Not a lot. Mildly unconfident.
5	Neutral. Unsure. Don't know. Indifferent.
6	Sometimes. At times. Moderately. A little bit. Mildly confident.
7	Quite often. A fair bit. Some. A little confident.
8	Most of the time. More often than not. Quite a lot. Quite confident.
9	The majority of the time. A lot. Very confident.
10	Completely. Very much so. A huge amount. Extremely happy. Extremely confident.

Fig. 36 Rate yourself definitions

SEND self-evaluation questionnaire

QUESTION 1: Is the classroom environment conducive to good learning?

Quick response:

_____

_____

_____

_____

Questions for consideration

- Is there a calm and quiet atmosphere?
- Are the walls too busy?
- Are your behaviour rules on show?
- Are there any distractions e.g. Flickering lights, noise from corridor.

Considered response:

_____

_____

_____

_____

_____

_____

_____

_____

_____

_____

Rate yourself

QUESTION 1: How happy are you that you have provided a classroom that is conducive to good learning for all?

1   2   3   4   5   6   7   8   9   10

QUESTION 2: Is the lesson accessible for all children?

Quick response:

_____

_____

_____

_____

Questions for consideration

- Does the child with SEND have their own personal targets?
- Are all your resources ready for the child with SEND e.g. reading ruler, enlarged photocopied work?
- Is the technology set up and ready to go?
- Is the child with SEND included within a group; where is your TA positioned?

Considered response:

_____

_____

_____

_____

_____

_____

_____

_____

_____

_____

_____

_____

_____

Rate yourself

QUESTION 2: Are you confident that all children can access the lesson?

1   2   3   4   5   6   7   8   9   10

QUESTION 3: Do you have personalised resources for your children with SEND?

Quick response:

_____

_____

_____

_____

Questions for consideration

- Have you made adaptations to the PC such as a keyguard or large keys?
- Have you made your PC or iPad switch accessible if needed?
- Have you made alterations to the iPad via the accessibility options?
- Have you installed Clicker 6 or 7, Boardmaker and Writing with Symbols to allow the child to complete their own work?

Considered response:

_____

_____

_____

_____

_____

_____

_____

_____

_____

_____

_____

Rate yourself

QUESTION 3: How happy are you that the child with SEND has equal tech access to your lessons?

1	2	3	4	5	6	7	8	9	10

QUESTION 4: Are the children working quietly?

Quick response:

_____

_____

_____

_____

Questions for consideration

- Are there any distractions from the child with SEND? Are they chatting to their neighbour?
- Is the child with SEND calling out and disrupting your teacher talk time?
- Is the child with SEND discussing things with their TA and distracting others?
- Is group work too noisy?

Considered response:

_____

_____

_____

_____

_____

_____

_____

_____

_____

_____

_____

_____

_____

Rate yourself

QUESTION 4: How happy are you that your children are working quietly in the classroom?

1   2   3   4   5   6   7   8   9   10

QUESTION 5: How are the children behaving?

Quick response:

_____

_____

_____

_____

Questions for consideration

- Is anyone acting up just for attention?
- Is the child with SEND distracting their group by tapping, prodding or talking?
- Is the child with SEND sitting at their table with their peers or moving around?
- Do you have everyone's attention or do you have to continually stop the lesson to get the children to behave?

Considered response:

_____

_____

_____

_____

_____

_____

_____

_____

_____

_____

_____

_____

_____

_____

Rate yourself

QUESTION 5: How happy are you with the behaviour of your class?

1	2	3	4	5	6	7	8	9	10

QUESTION 6: Have you got a plan for dealing with extremely challenging behaviour?

Quick response:

_____

_____

_____

_____

Questions for consideration

- Would you remove the child from the class?
- Would you remove the class and leave the child in the room if necessary?
- Would you use Team-Teach?
- Would you send for SLT?

Considered response:

_____

_____

_____

_____

_____

_____

_____

_____

_____

_____

_____

_____

Rate yourself

QUESTION 6: How happy are you that you can deal with extremely challenging behaviour?

1	2	3	4	5	6	7	8	9	10

QUESTION 7: How consistent are you in your classroom with regard to structure, routine and behaviour?

Quick response:

_____

_____

_____

_____

Questions for consideration

- Do you use visuals every day and for every lesson for those who need them?
- Have you established structure to your day and shared the timetable with the children?
- Do the children understand their behaviour will always result in consistent action from you?
- Have you shared your behaviour management strategies with all staff to ensure consistency?

Considered response:

_____

_____

_____

_____

_____

_____

_____

_____

_____

_____

Rate yourself

QUESTION 7: Are you happy with the level of consistency in your classroom?

1   2   3   4   5   6   7   8   9   10

QUESTION 8: Are you making the best use of specialist SEND activities?

Quick response:

_____

_____

_____

_____

Questions for consideration

- Are you using TACPAC for sensory teaching and for calming children with behaviour difficulties?
- Are you using peer massage as a calming technique and as a sensory teaching experience?
- Have you used the chill-out room or established a 'safe space' within your classroom?
- Have you provided a sensory box with sensory resources relating to your lesson or topic?

Considered response:

_____

_____

_____

_____

_____

_____

_____

_____

_____

_____

Rate yourself

QUESTION 8: How happy are you that your children have access to specialist SEND resources and activities?

| 1 | 2 | 3 | 4 | 5 | 6 | 7 | 8 | 9 | 10 |

QUESTION 9: Do you feel comfortable teaching children with ASC?

Quick response:

_____

_____

_____

_____

Questions for consideration

- Can you make a visual timetable?
- Have you identified their main area of difficulty keeping in mind that children with ASC will display different signs and symptoms?
- Have you got a plan for unstructured times such as lunchtime?
- Do you remember to use visuals such as 'now and next' boards to keep the child on task?

Considered response:

_____

_____

_____

_____

_____

_____

_____

_____

_____

_____

_____

_____

Rate yourself

QUESTION 9: How well do you think you teach children with ASC?

| 1 | 2 | 3 | 4 | 5 | 6 | 7 | 8 | 9 | 10 |

QUESTION 10: Are you comfortable teaching children with LDD?

Quick response:

_____

_____

_____

_____

Questions for consideration

- Have you identified the child's main area of SEND?
- Have you differentiated the work to include personalised, child-friendly targets for the child with LDD?
- Have you made sufficient space in your classroom for all the physical equipment the child may need e.g. standing frame, wheelchair?
- Have you positioned your TA to help the child but not encourage over-reliance?

Considered response:

_____

_____

_____

_____

_____

_____

_____

_____

_____

_____

_____

Rate yourself

QUESTION 10: How happy are you that all children with LDD are included fully in your classroom?

| 1 | 2 | 3 | 4 | 5 | 6 | 7 | 8 | 9 | 10 |

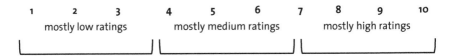

Fig. 37 How did you rate yourself?

Mostly low ratings

You have tried hard but you haven't found it easy to get to grips with all children with SEND. This is no surprise because there are many different conditions and they all manifest themselves in different ways in the classroom. Each child is different and requires their own solution. Try to do some more reading around the different conditions we have covered and get to grips with some of the techniques. Go online and read some of the blogs mentioned and follow the hashtags on Twitter and learn some new things for yourself.

Mostly medium ratings

You have worked hard with some of the techniques and have implemented them in to your daily classroom routine. You can see the benefit of this through the work that the children are producing and the way that your class is calm and quiet. There is more work to do. We can always improve. Keep on reading and trying out the techniques. Aim to introduce a new idea each half term and see the impact on the children. Start to really master some of those techniques that you are finding the most useful. Talk them over with your TA and together you can identify where more work is needed.

Mostly high ratings

You are at an advanced level in your work with children with SEND. Well done! Don't stop there. Keep looking and listening and learning. Now is the time to think properly about sharing your knowledge with others. Is there a local Teaching School who would value your knowledge? Think about who else would benefit from your new skills. Meanwhile, keep perfecting your knowledge of SEND and keep up the good work.

Now what?

It is time now to decide what to do next. The first thing to do is to look at what works best in your classroom. Check your answers to your questionnaire and find your areas of strength and the areas you can improve on. Look for a pattern: is there one emerging? Do you have your behaviour strategies all sorted out but your tech resources let you down – which in turn prevents your lessons from going quite as well as they could do? Is the classroom SEND ready in terms of wall displays, free from distractions for the child with SEND and space for all their equipment but your teaching resources are not as inclusive as they might be? These are all things to consider when evaluating your own practice. Be honest with yourself too. You won't improve your practice if you think you already know all there is to know.

Classroom evaluation

As well as self-evaluating your own practice, it is important to get feedback from others. Most importantly, you want to know first hand from the children themselves what they think about their day-to-day life in school. In addition you can get feedback from colleagues observing your lessons and also you can ask for feedback from children's parents.

The children

The best people to ask about the learning experience is the children themselves. The simplest way to check how your children perceive things are going in your classroom is to use formative assessment consistently throughout your practice. This could be something simple like a 'thumbs up' or 'thumbs down' for a quick and simple way to check children's understanding of the learning objective. Misconceptions can be addressed immediately in this way.
Try out these top strategies for formative assessment:

- Use of mini whiteboards for ongoing assessment during the lesson
- Ask the students for verbal feedback during the lesson
- Paired sharing and teacher circulates and listens to the exchange of information
- Questioning strategies for all children, not just those with hands up
- Quizzes
- Exit ticket – a simple yes or no for understanding on a slip of paper as they leave the room
- Hold a secret vote
- ActivExpressions as suggested by @Sarah_Wright1 - this is a student response device which provides real time feedback on pupil progress www.prometheanworld.com/products/student-response-devices/
- Flags – child flags their understanding on a sticky note
- TOWER tasks – as suggested by @mrwillfox: Talk about topic, Organise visually as a plan, Write first draft, Edit, Redraft
- Feedback and marking during the lesson
- Red circle displayed for lack of understanding of learning objective, green circle for understanding learning objective

- Use of visuals for non-communicating children to show their understanding
- No hands up strategy
- Suggestion box for improvements (anonymous)
- 'Confidence line' – children put their name on a line in terms of where they are with understanding the objective at the start of the lesson and then move their name at the end of the lesson to reflect their new understanding (suggested by @bethben92)
- Socrative questioning – six to ten multiple choice questions based on the lesson and using iPads to answer – allows you to assess pupil learning in real time: www.socrative.com (suggested by @jwscattergood).

> **Top tip: Blog it!**
> Blogging teachers learn from themselves and from each other.

The parents

The next people you could ask are the parents. Try out these questions with parents:

- Is your child telling you they are more settled in school?
- Do you think homework is pitched correctly or is your child struggling?
- Is your child happy when they return home?
- Is your child happy to come to school?
- Most parents are happy to feedback this kind of information. You could ask for individual feedback in their daily planners if you only have one child with special needs in your class. Alternatively, if you want to gauge the views of more parents you could devise a paper questionnaire and send it home with the children. Another possibility is to have a meeting with the parents but we should remember that parents' time is precious and they don't want to spend time in school. A phone call is another, less time-consuming option.

Evaluating the success of your strategies for pupils with ASC and ADHD

As the teacher, it is important that you maintain high expectations for all children including those who have ASC or ADHD. We want them all to feel safe and secure in our classrooms and we want them to reach their full potential. A further requirement is that the learning of the other children is not disturbed.

Parents also have requirements of schools where their children with ASC or ADHD are concerned. I have spoken with many parents and for some their overarching need is to be able to take their child out in to the community and they be able to join in with real social situations rather than sitting on the edge of society. Not all children can achieve academic greatness but hopefully all children can achieve happiness. The wishes of these parents should be kept in mind when we are teaching children at the lower end of the Autistic spectrum.

Use this questionnaire to check your strategies are working for children with ASC or ADHD.

For my ASC and ADHD pupils	Yes	No	Is the strategy helping?
Have I established a daily routine for all children especially those with ASC and ADHD?			
Have I provided visual timetables to show what is the next activity?			
Have I broken the day into small and manageable chunks?			
Am I using behaviour charts and reward systems?			
Are my 'Stop and Go' cards being used effectively?			
Are timers in use in the classroom to enable children to know how long they have left for each activity?			
Are 'Now and Next' cards routinely used?			
Are children making use of the chill-out room?			
Is the environment correct in terms of noise and distractions?			
Are staff wearing plain, non patterned clothes?			
Do I have objects of reference to hand to get a message across very quickly to a child who is highly stressed?			
Am I providing breaks for the children who cannot stay on task for the full lesson?			
Am I using positive, directional language?			
Am I remembering to use social stories to introduce new or stressful routines?			
Am I only picking the battles it is vital to win rather than all battles?			
Am I remembering to allow the child to participate in the running of the lesson, e.g. to operate the IWB to keep them on task?			
Have I provided fidget toys where needed?			
Have I included technology where possible to keep children on task?			

Fig. 38 Questionnaire to evaluate the success of your strategies for children with ASC and ADHD

Any strategies that are not helping should be discarded, leaving you time to concentrate on those that are helping.

Evaluating the success of your strategies for pupils with LDD

As a teacher trying to accommodate children with LDD in the classroom alongside their mainstream peers, you will need to be flexible; flexible with your time, your planning, your resources and the curriculum you provide. Children with LDD will all present with different difficulties and each one is unique. As we know, there are no hard and fast rules. The best advice is to believe that every child can succeed; your job is to find out how. A child with LDD may be non-verbal, unable to move unaided or be wheelchair bound. All of these difficulties may result in further complications such as challenging behaviour as the child becomes increasingly frustrated.Some points to remember:

- Teamwork is essential – enlist the help of parents, TAs, speech and language therapists, physiotherapists and occupational therapists
- Involve the child in decision-making and planning where possible – remember they are the important ones and they should be given a chance to voice their thoughts
- Be prepared to spend time making children in wheelchairs comfortable – their comfort is important for their learning and you may be the only person available.

Use this questionnaire to check if your strategies for helping children with LDD are working.

For children with LDD	Yes	No	Is the strategy helping?
Is the learning objective matched to the child's ability, including P Scales where appropriate?			
Have I provided specialist pens, pencils and writing slopes?			
Am I using sensory resources for those who need it?			
Have I adapted resources and tailored them to the needs of the individual children?			
Is my TA strategically placed to help the child rather than being stuck to their side?			
Have I made the lesson 'hands on' for those who require it?			
Have I included the use of technology for non-communicating children, e.g. BIGMack, specialist keyboards, switch access.			

For children with LDD	Yes	No	Is the strategy helping?
Am I promoting independence skills where appropriate?			
Are visual timetables and visual behaviour strategies in place where needed?			
Am I using writing software to allow for success such as Clicker 6 or 7 and Writing With Symbols?			
Am I remembering to allow plenty of time for the child to answer and ensuring the class is patient?			
Am I encouraging peer friendship groups to avoid the child being permanently in the company of adults?			

Fig. 39 Questionnaire to evaluate the success of your strategies for children with LDD

Any strategies that are not helping should be discarded leaving you time to concentrate on those that are effective.

Evaluating the success of your strategies for pupils with dyslexia

It is our responsibility to ensure that our lessons are differentiated well enough to allow them to be accessible for children with dyslexia. Some of these children may have damaged confidence and low self-esteem due to struggling to read. Much of their time is spent attempting to decode phonics and this slows down their reading. It is our job to unpick this and help them to be the best that they can be.

As we know, it is not just reading that is affected. Organisational skills, directions and understanding instructions are an enormous daily battle for children with dyslexia. Irlen Syndrome, although presenting different problems, is also a major struggle for some.

Use this questionnaire to check if your strategies for helping children with dyslexia are working.

For children with dyslexia	Yes	No	Is the strategy helping?
Is the child near the front of the class, close to the teacher?			
Does the child have a good view of the interactive whiteboard?			
Am I ensuring minimal wandering around the classroom to avoid visual disturbance?			
Am I encouraging the child to speak their answers rather than writing them?			
Am I encouraging paired working so the child can be paired with a good writer?			
Have I provided a visual timetable to help the child with their organisational skills?			
Have I provided a recordable device to prevent the child having to do too much writing?			
Have I provided age-appropriate books with plenty of repetition?			
Have I provided an e-reader if required?			
Have I provided text to speech software?			
Have I remembered to focus learning spellings on key words?			
Have I provided extra time for the child to finish their work?			
Have I remembered to shorten the length of their task?			
Am I only using key words and key instructions in their learning objective?			
Have I remembered to use bullet points to impart instructions and highlight key words?			
Is the child more organised?			
Am I promoting good listening skills and attention skills?			
For Irlen Syndrome, have I provided coloured overlays?			
Am I allowing extra time for the child to process their thoughts?			
Am I giving clear, constructive feedback in my marking?			
Am I encouraging the use of notebooks, checklists and other aids to encourage independence and organisational skills?			
Is my classroom clutter-free to maintain a structured working environment?			

Fig. 40 Questionnaire to evaluate the success of your strategies for children with dyslexia

Any strategies that are not working should be discarded leaving time to concentrate on those that are effective.

Evaluating the success of your strategies for pupils displaying behaviour difficulties

It is your responsibility to understand the cause of the difficult behaviour. This has to be step one or any strategies you put in place will fail. You need to decide if the child is displaying poor behaviour because they do not understand the lesson or whether it is something else. It could be something entirely out of your control such as a problem at home. This will require delicate handling if so.

Another point to remember is that all behaviour management strategies must involve teamwork. There must be whole school buy-in and it is vital that everyone working in one classroom is consistent in their handling of behaviour.

Some points to remember:

- Be aware that a child will repeat a behaviour if it is being rewarded. Therefore look for good behaviour and issue 'time out' as a strategy/reward rather than any form of sanction.
- Be consistent with the child – the same behaviour must result in the same sanction and the child must be aware of this. That said, flexibility is also a consideration. Look at the causes of the behaviour and take this in to consideration when deciding on your sanction.
- Be aware that children who lack attention in their lives will demonstrate poor behaviour in order to gain attention. As teachers we are aware that children prefer negative attention to no attention. Try to pre-empt this and supply some attention. Make the child feel valued and draw them in to the group.
- Remember to teach self-regulation or self-calming skills. We all need these to help us deal with life's trials and tribulations. Teach deep breathing, counting to 10 before speaking and teach children how to control their emotions.

Use this questionnaire to help you check that your strategies are improving the learning for the children who display challenging behaviour.

On behaviour	Yes	No	Is the strategy helping?
Has low-level disruption reduced as a result of my strategies?			
Are the children on task?			
Do the children respond to my reward systems?			
Am I using positive reinforcement techniques and looking for good behaviour to praise?			
Is everyone in their place?			
Is there a behaviour for learning plan in place for those who need it?			
Is the 'chill-out' room (or other 'safe place') created in class working for children who need it?			
Am I checking understanding throughout the lesson to pre-empt any behaviour that may occur from lack of understanding?			
Do specific rewards for the child help?			
Am I targeting specific behaviours?			
Does the child respond better to public or private praise?			
Is my classroom calm and ordered?			
Are pupils courteous towards each other?			
Is my classroom structured and do I provide consistent routines?			
Have I shared the behaviour for learning plan with parents for consistency between home and school?			

Fig. 41 Questionnaire to evaluate the success of your strategies for children with behaviour difficulties

Any strategies that are not helping should be discarded leaving you time to concentrate on those that are effective.

Evaluating the success of your strategies for inclusion

All children have the right to attend the school of their choice or, in some cases, the school their parents have chosen for them. As we know, there is much debate about this but once a child is in a mainstream school the school must cater for the child and overcome any barriers to learning. Every child must have equal access to the curriculum and to individual lessons and it is the responsibility of every teacher to provide this. A teacher should regularly monitor their own inclusion strategy and improve it wherever possible. Use this questionnaire to check if your inclusion strategies are working.

On inclusion	Yes	No	Is the strategy helping?
Is the child seated correctly, near to the teacher and away from passing distractions and noise?			
Does the TA in the classroom sit a discrete distance away from the child?			
Does the TA understand the child's learning objective and where it fits in to the IEP?			
Is the child actively participating in the lesson?			
Do all children remain in the classroom for the entire duration of the lesson irrespective of any problems encountered?			
Do all pupils, including those with SEND understand the learning objective?			
Is the curriculum suited to all children? Is it personalised to suit their needs?			
Do my targets match all the the children's ability?			
Are the tasks differentiated for each child?			
Do I have resources ready for each child to suit their needs, e.g. visuals, overlays, communication aids?			
Is technology set up before the lesson to allow the child to be included fully in the lesson?			
Am I using assessment to find gaps in children's understanding?			
Do all pupils understand the instructions?			
Did I effectively address misconceptions in a way the child understands?			
Are all children participating in the lesson at their own level and with the correct support?			
Do I vary my teaching style to include all children in the way they learn best, e.g. sensory, some dialogue, some visual aids, some real resources?			
Am I remembering to take account of non-academic targets, e.g. finding own PE kit.			
Have I considered how to include all children in educational visits?			
Are the other children encouraged to speak to the child and help them to join in the social aspects of the school day?			

Fig. 42 Questionnaire to evaluate the success of your strategies for inclusion

Any strategies which are not helping should be discarded leaving you time to concentrate on those that are effective.

Evaluating whether you are providing the best classroom experience possible for all children

Try this questionnaire to check if you are providing the best classroom experience possible for all children.

In general	Yes	No	If appropriate, is the strategy helping?
Have I created a positive environment for learning?			
Am I providing the best outcome for each child?			
Do my activities motivate and challenge each child?			
Do my children achieve their learning objectives?			
Have I used the advice of colleagues who have observed my teaching?			
Am I observing others and learning from them?			
Am I following the advice found in blog posts written by other teachers?			
Have I established a positive relationship with each child?			
Do all children feel respected and safe to take risks?			
Have I taken parental views in to account?			

Fig. 43 Questionnaire to evaluate whether you are providing the best classroom experience possible for all children

Create an action plan

Your task now is to create an action plan to help you to move forward with your class and ensure every child is included. You need to plan how you will proceed to ensure you and your TA are ready to share this with the rest of the school staff. Keep in mind that consistency is key. The first thing on your action plan should be working with other teachers. Also consider the SENDCo; can the SENDCo help you to learn more about any of the children in your class? Do they have any extra information to share with you? Add a discussion with the SENDCo to your action plan. Think about all the strategies for the various children and the conditions we have discussed. Could you utilise some of the strategies for a child with LDD for a child with ADHD? A good example of this is communication techniques. Many of the children will benefit from help with communication, not just those with LDD. Add to your action plan to consider all strategies for all children. Think about the child and their needs, not the condition.

- Check your data – are all children making progress?
- Is your classroom happy and purposeful?
- Is everyone working at their own level?
- Are all children included in the wider life of the school such as after school clubs?
- Does every child feel valued?
- Do all staff understand and fully support the school's inclusion policy?

Action to be completed	Reason for action
Work with other teachers.	Ensure everyone is working in the same way in the classroom.
Discuss any inclusion issues with SENDCo.	Do they have any unshared knowledge you would benefit from?
Find out if every child feels valued.	Child needs to feel valued to feel secure.
Check you are consistent in your practice. Ask someone to observe you.	Consistency is key.

Fig. 44 Example action plan

Use this template to create your own action plan.

Strategy	What went well?	Areas for improvement?	How can it be improved?

Fig. 45 Action plan template

Share your action plan with your colleagues in your department. Work collaboratively with other teachers and compile a plan to improve the experience of all children with SEND in your classroom, department and school.

Chapter 7 takeaway

Teaching tip

Keep your goal in sight

Remember you are aiming for full inclusion for all children in all lessons and every aspect of school life. That's your goal. This is no small order. Keep reflecting on your practice. Keep thinking and discussing with others how you can improve things for the children. If the children are happy and progressing you will have a much calmer day. Remember to share your knowledge with your colleagues. Get them to reflect and discuss with you further. Two heads are always better than one.

Pass it on

Be a blogger

There's something very satisfying about blogging. You put your ideas online and others will pass comment. In general the comments made will be helpful and will add to your growing knowledge. Sometimes a debate will start up between teachers with opposing views which again adds to your knowledge and may challenge your thinking. This is all good and helps teaching to progress in a very small way.

CPD book club recommendation

Engaging Learners with Complex Learning Difficulties and Disabilities by B. Carpenter

Bloggers' corner

Jarlath O'Brien is a headteacher at Carwarden House. He is also an associate of @ITLWorldwide and a new author. Follow him on Twitter: @JarlathOBrien and read his blog: jarlathobrien.wordpress.com

TO DO LIST:

- ❑ Think about what you have achieved towards making your classroom inclusive and what you would still like to achieve.
- ❑ Start a blog if you haven't already done so.
- ❑ Read some of Jarlath's posts; they really are recommended.
- ❑ Read *Engaging Learners with Complex Learning Difficulties and Disabilities*.

8

Embedding and developing practice

So far we have learnt many new strategies for improving the learning experience for all children in our classrooms, especially those with ASC, ADHD, LDD, dyslexia and those with challenging behaviours or behaviour difficulties, and I hope to have given you plenty of inspiration for ensuring all children are fully included and valued.We have completed evaluation forms and sought advice from other professionals and from parents and we know which strategies are successful and which are not. We have also completed an action plan to help detail further improvements.

We now need to embed our practice, being consistent throughout the day and throughout our teaching.

Embedding the practice

The main reason for embedding successful strategies in your classroom is to provide a well-structured classroom. We need to provide a classroom where activities within lessons involve and include all children and where all children feel safe to learn. We need to ensure our strategies are embedded at every opportunity and developed further. They need to be internalised by all staff and children to be truly effective. Furthermore the culture of the school needs to incorporate and embed these new skills once they are proven to work. They are based on pedagogical research and practice and they must be allowed to evolve further. Therefore your feedback from other teachers, children and parents proves useful at this point.

Look back at your action plan. The first thing on your action plan should be working with other teachers. As the teacher in your own classroom, your practice must be consistent and you must encourage others, and possibly even insist others implement your strategies when working with your children. All teachers must be using the same strategies for them to be successful. Therefore top of the list must be to ensure there is whole school buy-in.

Working with the SENDCo

The SENDCo has a huge role to play in ensuring that children with SEND are fully accommodated in school and receive all the support they need. The SENDCo should be available to support teachers and TAs and to ensure the school's SEND policy is carried out.

Embedding the practice for children with ASC

Embedding the practice for children with ASC involves taking account of the views of all stakeholders. Consider implementing and embedding these strategies as a matter of urgency.

- Consider a team approach including other professionals, SENDCo, school staff and the family.
- Keep an ongoing dialogue with the parents. Children change as do family circumstances. You need to be aware of any changes affecting the child.
- Tailor your approach to the individual child – remember no two children are the same. There are no generic solutions.
- Have high expectations of all children at all times.
- When using a TA, utilise their skills expertly, e.g. have them teach the child something they can then go on to master on their own.

As we have learned, communication and understanding of the spoken word is part of the difficulty associated with children with ASC. We need to address this urgently as it causes behaviour difficulties. The following strategies should be embedded across the school:

- Teach the other children in class to communicate properly and not to rely on body language as the child with ASC won't understand it.
- Use directional language and ensure the child understands.
- If the child has a high tech or low tech communication aid ensure they have it with them at all times. Without it they cannot tell you if they have a problem.
- Enlist the aid of a speech therapist. Speech therapists are often full of handy behaviour strategies.

In general

- Provide a safe place in the classroom or a 'chill-out room'.
- Be consistent.
- Allow the child time to process your instructions and encourage the rest of the class to do the same.
- Provide structure and make sure children with SEND are warned of any changes to the structure.
- Continue to monitor progress, evaluate and improve your practice.

Embedding the practice for children with ADHD

As a teacher in a mainstream classroom, ensuring a child with ADHD makes maximum progress while not disturbing the learning of the other children is a major task. You must ensure many strategies are in place as we have learned. Consider the value of embedding these strategies as a matter of urgency.

- Teamwork is best – involve the whole school.
- Identify the particular areas for improvement for the individual child.
- Identify how the child learns – this is not the same as a learning style.
- Keep your strategies age-appropriate and relevant to individual needs.

As we have learned, behaviour is a major challenge for children diagnosed with ADHD. This is an area for concern and must be addressed as a matter of priority. Consider embedding the following areas for immediate impact.

- Ensure each child has the means to communicate either through the use of visuals or technology if not verbally.
- Ensure all children with behaviour difficulties have behaviour for learning plans individualised to address their needs.
- Ensure you provide structure and adhere to daily routines.
- Use objects of reference as a means of quickly calming a situation (p 103).
- Allow time for the child to process your instructions.

Embedding the practice for children with LDD

As the teacher in the classroom, embedding good practice for children with LDD is a difficult task. No two children are the same as we know and no two children learn in the same way. Those with LDD require a tailored approach personalised to meet their needs. Embedding the strategies you know to be successful will build the confidence of your children with LDD and help them to feel safe and valued.

Embedding good practice for these children involves taking into account the views of different stakeholders. Have you:

- included the views of the child?
- considered the child's personality and their personal interests?
- used personal observations and knowledge of the child?

- included the views of the parents/carers?
- consulted former teachers?
- considered the expertise of other professionals, such as speech and language therapists, occupational therapists, educational psychologists or physiotherapists to gain a clearer picture of the child and their needs?
- included the views and observations of all staff in the classroom who will work with the child?
- included the views of other members of staff such as lunch time supervisors who are with the child during non-structured time – their input is valuable!

Consider embedding the following good practice to ensure your classroom runs smoothly:

- Individualise your resources for your child with LDD – generic SEND resources will not suffice.
- Check the IEP from the EHC plan – IEPs are still good practice although not statutory, have you addressed the specific targets?
- Check your learning objective for each lesson for each LDD child to check the child can participate meaningfully.
- Have you provided specialised resources such as furniture, writing slopes, pens and pencils?
- Have you provided specialised technology where required, such as AAC, and software programs for helping every child to achieve their potential?
- Remember to embed consistency and routine.

Embedding the practice for children with dyslexia

Children with dyslexia are generally not operating at below National Expectations. Therefore as the teacher in the classroom we need to embed practice that enables our children to remain as independent as possible.

Consider embedding the following strategies as a matter of urgency:

- Provide visual clues in the form of pictures, not huge chunks of text.
- Highlight key words.
- Provide much repetition and practice materials.
- Teach the child how to follow your instructions – this might seem obvious but it is often overlooked.
- Allow extra time for completing work and for thought processing.
- Use ICT to support learning – pay attention to font size and shape.
- Use visual timetables to help with organisational skills.

More top tips provided by and reproduced by kind permission from Drive for Literacy:

Top Ten Tips for Supporting Pupils with Literacy Difficulties including Dyslexia in the Classroom

1. De-clutter the interactive whiteboard - change background (dark blue print on pastel shades)
- keep instructions concise

2. Organise informative and helpful displays around the room - ensure target vocabulary is visible e.g. not too small/too high up and supported by visuals

3. Maximise the readability of worksheets - think layout, font (Arial, Tahoma, Verdana, Comic Sans, Century Gothic) and size 12+
- number paragraphs
- use of colour and helpful visuals

4. Prepare pupils for reading out loud and/or cold calling to minimise stress
- give opportunities to verbalise understanding in pairs or small groups

5. Plan support for writing tasks - writing frames, sentence starts, topic word banks, helpful phrases, checklists
- select the most efficient ways to record information using mindmaps, bullet points, flowcharts, storyboards

6. Reduce copying tasks - can teacher notes be photocopied for and annotated by the weakest readers/writers?

7. Build in regular practise of target spellings - talk about how words work (root word/prefix/suffix/syllables) and what makes them tricky
- provide multisensory experiences to make learning memorable

8. Mark for success – help pupils to see what they have got right - tick over the letter sounds correctly identified in a target spelling
e.g. ✔✔✔
      b e c o z (because)

9. Make use of assistive technology - e.g. Clicker 6/WriteOnline, electronic spellcheckers, voice recognition software, audiobooks, reading pens, Wordshark 4/5

10. Make reasonable adjustments part of normal classroom practice - e.g. extra time in assessments, use of laptop (illegible writing), use of coloured film/reading rulers, use of readers and scribes when needed

Drive for Literacy © 2014

In general, embedding proven strategies for children with dyslexia will have the following effect:

- Independence strategies will help build confidence and allow the child to feel settled.
- Tailoring the resources to suit the individual child with dyslexia will give them a far greater chance of succeeding.
- Avoids any confusion for the child
- Removes any stigma that should not be attached to dyslexia.

Embedding the practice for children displaying behaviour difficulties

As the teacher in the classroom, it is our role to ensure all children are made to feel valued and welcome. The classroom should be a safe haven for all children and there is a need to remind ourselves that some children have appalling home lives. They require a safe and secure place in which to learn and where they can flourish without fear. For these reasons schools need to fully embed approaches across the school that are proven to work. Once again, top of the list is to ensure that there is whole school buy-in to any behaviour strategies. The SENDCo should ensure every member of staff is clear about the behaviour policy and you should review your behaviour policy regularly.

Consider embedding the following strategies as a matter of urgency:

- Use directional language rather than making requests that can be ignored.
- Ensure there is a behaviour for learning plan for those who need it.
- Give thinking time for the child who is struggling to control their behaviour.
- Display your behaviour expectations.
- Make use of visuals such as timetables and stop and go cards.
- Choose your battles carefully – it is not possible to win them all and remain in control of the learning for the class.
- Model the behaviour you expect to see – run a calm and quiet classroom with no raised voices.
- Provide the child with a 'way out' – they often know when they have gone too far but cannot immediately make amends. Be the bigger person and allow time for that apology to arrive.
- Good behaviour must be taught; it does not always just happen.

Twitter tip

Engage with experts. Ask @PaulDix and @tombennett71:

These wise words came from Paul Dix in The Select Committee Report (2011)

'The best schools hang a sign above the door: "This is how we do it here."'

Tom Bennett says: 'Give it time and don't give up.'

Embedding the practice to ensure effective inclusion for all children

As the teacher you need to ensure that you embed your inclusive practices into your classroom. This means:

- Producing personalised accessible resources for all
- Using different teaching methods to ensure all children can access the lesson meaningfully e.g. make it 'hands on'
- Making sure no child is left out of any lesson on the grounds of inaccessibility e.g. PE.
- Keeping up to date with modern technology to ensure your children with SEND have what they need.

Differentiation

An important consideration for children with SEND is differentiation. Differentiation is another hotly debated topic between teachers but in special schools it remains a firm favourite. Without differentiation many children with SEND would make very little progress and there would be no whole class teaching. Every child deserves the right to learn as part of their class; this is inclusion. It therefore follows that not every child within a class will have the same learning objective. A child with SEND may require some modifications to their learning objective to allow them to succeed. As teachers we must maintain the highest expectations of all children at all times. Differentiation is not dumbing down the work; it is carefully personalising the work for the child's individual needs.

Embedding differentiation strategies

In general when we think of differentiation we think of:

1. Differentiation by task – where different groups of children have different tasks according to their ability to enable them to succeed.

2. Differentiation by support – where some children are given extra help from a TA or the teacher.
3. Differentiation by outcome – where children achieve as much as they can on their own level.

For the child with SEND in the mainstream classroom, differentiation is much more. Consider these strategies to help you to embed good differentiation skills across the curriculum.

- Take advice from your SENDCo – they are trained and qualified in this area.
- Take advice from other experts who know the child well.
- Use your data – where is the child working at and how can you set targets to ensure they make progress?
- Observe the child – what do they need to succeed; do your utmost to supply it. This may include sensory resources, visual timetables, smaller amounts of writing and specialised software.
- If phonics is inappropriate for teaching reading, teach using whole words and picture clues.
- Use real life objects where possible – keep it practical especially in maths.
- Use the great outdoors for science teaching.
- Use specially-adapted PE equipment to allow children to achieve success in PE.
- Use cookery for literacy and numeracy at P Levels.
- Provide any means of communication appropriate for the child – pre-programme high tech devices to enable the child to ask questions in history, geography and RE.
- Make use of questioning – a child who cannot write independently may be able to verbalise and show their learning using speech or overlays.

What are the components of good lesson planning for including children with SEND?

Every teacher has their own method of creating lesson plans, although some are restricted and bound by the format of the school. Here are some suggestions to help you include your children with SEND.

- Set your learning objective for the whole class.
- Check the IEPs of the children with SEND – ensure you include any behaviour plan as necessary.
- Check your data, determine their level and set a target – remember you will need an individual objective for each child with SEND; five children with SEND equals five different targets.
- Plan your group work or preferred teaching style for the whole class.
- Build in time for the children with SEND to participate in any discussions using AAC, as is their right.

- Have a range of teaching strategies – not too much talking, reading, writing or group work.
- Have all your resources ready before the lesson begins.
- Include time for independent work, including those with SEND – they should be encouraged to be as independent as possible.
- Place your TA wisely – he or she should not be the constant companion of the child with SEND.
- Plan your assessment for learning to enable all your children to feedback how they found their learning – a simple thumbs up or down may be an option for children with SEND.

When I asked my colleagues on Twitter for their thoughts on what makes a good lesson plan I had some informed responses.

Tweeter	What makes a good lesson plan?	For SEND
@MariaStMarys	Pre-planned questions are good but spontaneous, reactive ones are even better.	Have the communication aids and visuals ready for all to participate. If necessary load some questions on before the lesson begins.
@ASTsupportAAli	Physical constraints of the classroom/space as per activity planned.	Ensure there is enough space for their standing frames/power chairs/wheelchairs to enable them to participate in the lessons fully.
@stevie_caldwell	Accounting for children's different starting points	Remember this may be considerably lower for those with SEND – plan accordingly and build in extra time.
@MariaStMarys	Critical to ensure Quality First Teaching is a secure knowledge of the learners including wider issues that might impact on learning.	Aim to ensure all barriers to learning are removed for each lesson.
@ASTsupportAAli	Issues/triggers that a particular topic might bring up need to be known/considered.	Know your children – for example, those with SEND may not be able to tell you about their home circumstances. Be aware of this and plan sensitively for them.
@funASDteacher	Having precise relevant focus for each student. Topic might be the same but what they learn, different.	Good differentiation required to ensure the child achieves at their level.
@Sablonette	It is important that the teacher ensures students are challenged and persist in face of difficulty	Maintain high expectations of all children.
@reachoutASC	Having the children contribute to the learning objective, owning what they are learning. Allowing different ways to get there.	Value all opinions – go in the direction the children with SEND wish to explore; encourage them and then return to main objective.

Tweeter	What makes a good lesson plan?	For SEND
@Sue_Cowley	A bit where you find out what they know first. Learning Objectives are more a vague map than a blueprint	Vital to recap prior knowledge for children with SEND. They need much repetition. Keep your learning objectives flexible and allow room for success and negotiation in the learning.
@nastyoldmrpike	Good Assessment For Learning at start, have an idea of where I'd ideally like the lesson to go and direct it that way.	AfL is vital for children with SEND. Work out where each child is in their understanding and plan your teaching to address their next steps.
@Historylecturer	Something near the start that makes them expect the whole lesson to be worthwhile.	Very important to grab the attention of all children at the start but more so for children with SEND. This can make or break your lesson.
@cijane02	Spend two–three minutes per lesson linking previous learning to next steps.	Children with SEND like to know what they will be learning and what they can expect in the lesson. On occasions they enter school asking the content of their last lesson of the day.
@Gwenelope	Know your students very well – then lesson planning is easy	All teachers must take the time to know what makes their children tick. Involve yourself in their interests and their home lives and this will help you to plan engaging lessons for them.
@RevErasmus	An objective, few ideas for how it might be met, and a responsive teacher. Like a destination and possible route open to detours.	The 'route open to detours' is perfect for children with SEND. Remember they may not achieve as you expect but may achieve the unexpected.

Fig. 46 What makes a good lesson plan?

> ## Twitter tip
> The above tweet generated a conversation on Twitter that lasted for two days and involved over 30 teachers. Get involved in these conversations and further your own learning!

Remember to keep your plans for children with SEND flexible – they have an entitlement to study the full National Curriculum and it is our duty to remove all barriers to learning. Embed the following practical ideas to your classroom practice:

- Use a multi-sensory approach for those who will benefit.
- Teach some social strategies such as queuing and turn taking – they may not pick them up without help.
- Pair your children up – those with SEND and peers have much to learn from each other.
- Be consistent in everything you do.

The Sutton Trust report

One final thing we need to consider when thinking of embedding best practice for children with SEND is what can be learned from The Sutton Trust Report, 'What makes great teaching?' (2014). In it, Professor Robert Coe et al. reviewed over 200 articles on developing great teachers.

The report listed seven popular teaching practices widely used for all children that they did **NOT** recommend and are unsupported by research. I have picked six out of the seven that are relevant to children with SEND and they are listed below.

Popular teaching practices NOT recommended in the Sutton Trust report	How those with SEND are affected
Discovery learning	In general this will not work with children with SEND – direct instruction is needed except in exceptional circumstances.
Lavishing praise on children	Praise each small achievement to build self-confidence and self-esteem. Beware of the temptation to praise just for completing set work as this is the expectation of all children.
Grouping learners by ability	This will not work with children with SEND – children with SEND need a personalised curriculum, not group teaching.
Presenting information to students based on their 'preferred learning style'	Teach children with SEND the way they learn best – this is not the same as learning styles. For example, some children with ASC are visual learners, possibly due to not mastering reading yet; others are auditory learners. Teach them individually where possible.
Re-reading and highlighting	If a child with SEND has read the text once it is unlikely they will re-read and highlight. Use questioning and use of visual overlays to show understanding.
Making the work hands on and keeping the children active.	In contrast to the report's findings, children with SEND usually benefit from being active. Involve them in their learning and they will remember.

Fig. 47 What we can learn from the Sutton Trust report (2014)

We have learned that excellent teaching involves developing successful, proven strategies based on pedagogy and these strategies need to be consistently embedded across the school by all teachers in order to be successful.

The last word on this section goes to @ChrisSullivanNZ with this tweet.

'Asking yourself "Is my teaching making a difference?" is the wrong question. Instead ask – "How much impact on learning am I making, with who and under what circumstances?"'

Becoming a SENDCo
Whole-school considerations
for the SENDCo

Now that you have read and learned a great deal about children with special educational needs you might even consider taking on the role of SENDCo yourself. Here is how you might become a SENDCo and the role you would play within school.

Special Educational Needs Co-ordinators in mainstream schools and nurseries must be qualified teachers. They must also, if they are new to the role have gained or be working towards the National Award for SEN Co-ordination. This is a Masters level National Award and must be completed within 3 years of taking up the role. SENDCos are responsible for the day to day running of the school's SEND policy. They will co-ordinate any extra support required for the child with SEND and also work with parents, teachers and any other professionals involved with the child. They work with the governing body and the headteacher on the strategic development of the SEND policy. It is recommended that the SENDCo is part of the senior leadership team to ensure they have enough power in school to drive the SEND policy and agenda forward effectively. A further part of the SENDCo role might include updating the school website on matters relating to SEND. A report on the school's SEND policy must be published and should include:

- School's admission arrangements for pupils with SEND
- What measures the school has taken to prevent those with SEND from being treated less favourably than other pupils
- Access facilities for SEND
- For further information see 'What maintained schools must publish online' https://www.gov.uk/guidance/what-maintained-schools-must-publish-online

Consider how you can embed your successes across the school. I posed this question to the teachers on Twitter:

'Why do we embed good teaching strategies across the school?'

Here are the answers most relevant to children with SEND:

- 'So children know what to expect and feel comfortable in the knowledge that the expectation is the same across the school' (@rpd1972) – this is an excellent response from Rachel; she has totally captured embedding good strategies from the child's perspective.
- 'Because all children deserve equality of opportunity etc. herefore needs to be across the school' (@5N_Afzal) – this response from Naureen captures the education profession's thinking on inclusion in 140 characters.
- 'Because it's the best thing for our students and staff' (@kylemarshesq) – Kyle's answer sums it up from the whole school point of view.
- 'To work smarter and not reinvent the wheel, to allow time to focus on developing what is not there.' (@englishcal) – this is a very interesting perspective and one I whole-heartedly agree with.

So, how will you know that your strategies are embedded at every level?

- Begin with your school development plan – does it include conducting training on removing the barriers to learning for all children? Is there CPD in your specialised area for all staff? If not, add it to the school development plan to ensure strategies are embedded across school.
- Departmental meetings – observe the teaching and learning that is occurring in the classroom in your subject. Are the strategies you have suggested embedded in to the lessons? Ask the children for their opinion. Do they feel that they are valued and that they are learning in every lesson? Ask yourself as the subject leader: how is it going? How can my subject improve?
- Classroom level – are all class members of staff fully signed up to your strategies? Are all class staff using them as you intended? Are all resources ready at the start of each lesson?
- Induction of new staff – ask yourself whether you have introduced your strategies to all new staff to ensure they embed them across their lessons. New colleagues need help to learn the ways of the school through a thorough induction programme.

Whole school behaviour policy

Ensure every member of staff is clear about the school behaviour policy and review your behaviour policy regularly.

- Is your behaviour policy still relevant to the cohort of children in your school?
- Does your policy make reference to anti-bullying, cyber-bullying, challenging behaviours, token economy reward systems and sanctions where needed?
- Are your rules for behaviour clear and consistent and visible to all children to ensure there is no mistake about the school's position on behaviour?
- Are the children on board with the behaviour policy?
- Do the children have one page profiles?
- Do the children have the consequences of poor behaviour?
- Are parents aware of the school's behaviour policy and have they signed up to it?

Whole-school inclusion policy

This is the job of the SENDCo. They will check the inclusion policy and ensure it remains relevant and up to date for your school. The policy should:

- Provide curriculum access for all children.
- Ensure all teachers have high expectations for all children.
- Meet the individual needs of all children in a meaningful way.
- Provide opportunities to ensure staff, resources and all interventions lead to the highest possible outcomes for all children.
- Provide a caring environment where all achievements are celebrated.
- Provide a collaborative approach to working with parents.

SENDCo checklist

- Run termly subject meetings to ensure all are signed up to the strategies.
- Run weekly class meetings for all TAs.
- Has everyone signed up to the behaviour policy?
- Does every child who needs it have a behaviour plan to ensure consistency for the child?
- Share your practice with a cluster of other schools in your area.
- Share your practice with a TSA.
- Update website annually.

Chapter 8 takeaway

Teaching tip

Embedding success

That's what you are doing; you are embedding your successful techniques and strategies. You have read around the subject and now you need to see your work embedded. Be proud of what you have achieved and remember there is always room for improvement. Remember to keep on top of the tech; keep an eye on the new PC programs and attend any CPD courses that you can. Your hard work will by now be showing in your inclusive classroom.

Pass it on

Keep sharing beyond your school

Find any means you can to share and pass on your good work. Everyone should benefit from good practice. Visit other schools and pass on your knowledge. Invite teachers from other schools to come and observe you teach. Best of all, share your knowledge with a special school. You have much to learn from each other.

CPD book club recommendation

The Perfect SENCO by Natalie Packer

Bloggers' corner

JordyJax blogs on many issues relating to exclusions, PRUs and inclusion. Always an interesting read. Follow her on Twitter at: @jordyjax and read her blog at: jordyjax.wordpress.com

TO DO LIST:

- ❏ Visit a special school or a mainstream school and share your good practice.
- ❏ Follow #senco on Twitter.
- ❏ Read jordyjax posts for some outstanding blogs.
- ❏ Read *The Perfect SENCO*.

Part 2

Train others

1 Planning and preparing for your training

Everyone connected with education is well aware that there is currently no expectation for teachers to undertake structured CPD. Everyone is also well aware that most teachers do so, often in their own time and sometimes at their own expense. When teachers have been involved in high-quality training, their teaching is improved and we see the impact on the children's learning. The coalition government of 2010-2015 said they were committed to 'closing the achievement gap', and this remains the case with today's government yet it is left to schools to determine the amount of CPD training their teachers and staff need.

In my opinion, there is little more important in schools than planning the CPD. I can't stress how important it is.

The key aim of CPD is to raise the standard of teaching and learning, remove the barriers to learning and close the achievement gap

Priorities should be linked to the school's development plan and high on that agenda for all schools should be SEND. Remember that children with SEND are our collective responsibility and training in this area should be ongoing. SENDCos and inclusion leaders should be prepared to fight hard for children with SEND.

In 2013, NASEN (National Association for Special Educational Needs) launched its 'Every Teacher' campaign (http://www.sec-ed.co.uk/best-practice/sen-training-for-every-teacher). In essence, NASEN called for all schools to commit to one in five INSET days being used solely for training for the one in five children with SEND. Schools who have adopted this approach need to use their time and their budgets wisely.

Why you should do-it-yourself CPD!

One consideration when determining CPD is financial constraints. Schools have very small budgets and as a result, any CPD must have proven impact. One way to ensure the costs are kept to a minimum is to run your own CPD with your own teachers.

I posed this question on Twitter: 'Teachers, what are the benefits of running your own CPD rather than attending external courses?'

These are the thoughts of some of the teachers:

- 'reduce cost, tailoring the CPD specifically for staff/key stages to meet areas for improvement and it also brings staff together' (@garycorbett7).

Unifying the staff is an important consideration. Teachers often spend their time isolated and by working together it saves reinventing the wheel. This is especially important for training for SEND.

- 'when going to internally run CPD I've usually worked with these teachers and developed respect for them and their ideas and it has been fantastic learning from, together etc. From external you have to build up that relationship within that allotted time. Also it is rare that I go to an external trainer and get what I wanted when I signed up.' (@BehaviourTeach).

  @BehaviourTeach has perfectly captured the benefits of using your own teachers to further the learning within your own school. As has been pointed out, there is an element of trust involved and in SEND this is a particular consideration. Teachers who work with the children in your school have no axe to grind; they simply want the best for every child. They are not aiming to sell their own products or resources.

- 'much easier to build a tailored, credible and iterative model that can provide necessary ongoing support to bring about change' (@joeybagstock).

  Phil has emphasised the fact that ongoing support and development of the initiative introduced is key for ensuring change happens. This is a real benefit of completing the training within your own school. For children with SEND new initiatives need time to take effect and further evolve over time to become credible answers to ongoing difficulties.

- 'it enables staff who would not normally do so, to lead sessions and have impact on others. Can also go off at tangents if needed' (@bethben92).

  Beth has highlighted the fact that some teachers rarely lead sessions and running CPD in their chosen area is one way of ensuring that all teachers have a voice. Teachers often have specialisms and these may remain undiscovered if staff are not given the opportunity to use their voice.

- 'the presenter almost puts on a show and within 24 hours you may have forgotten most of the content. Successful CPD is about users actively engaging, taking ownership to achieve their own personal outcomes. You can use this approach with individuals, teams and organisations (@comm_uk).

  This insight was offered by my good friend and ex boss, Eddy Jackson MBE – these are wise words from Eddy.

These are the main benefits of running the training in-house. They are many and varied. The conversation on Twitter lasted for over six hours and over 50 educators gave me their opinion on running in-house training. On the whole, it is a popular method amongst educators, with teachers saying that they listened more to their own colleagues whose practice they respected. Many people also commented that by running the training in-house, you are also in charge of selecting the biscuits. This it seems is a very important consideration and a high priority!

Deciding on the SEND training needs for your school

Senior Leadership Teams (SLT) are usually the ones charged with the responsibility of organising the CPD for their staff. They are the ones who have a clear view of the School Development Plan and are aware of the training needs to bring the plan to fruition. Once the decision has been taken to keep the training in-house there needs to be a clear policy on the training. Where does SEND fit in it? Headteachers and SLT in inclusive mainstream schools work hard to ensure that all children are welcome and all difficulties and disabilities are catered for through thorough staff training. It is through understanding each child that schools can enable good progress to be made.

I asked my headteacher colleagues how they decide on their school's SEND training needs:

- 'diagnosed needs first (priority: medical training) usually for small groups of staff and then more general SEN support – whole team' (@karen_macg). Karen has identified that any medical training must be a priority. This area is of course of the utmost importance. For children with complex medical and neurological conditions there is more to their school life than education.
- 'curriculum review, lesson observations, data, student conversations, highlight areas of need, differentiation always on there. Also we do small group sessions about a need to teach specific students, to share practice, and strategies. Keeping accurate records is key so it can be audited for gaps. Planning around can every learner make progress? Quality first teaching? Differentiation plain/simple hammered in' (@RuthieGolding). Ruth has highlighted general school improvement as a priority and then focused in on how to ensure quality first teaching for SEND is always high on the agenda. I like the phrase 'hammered in' as this means that SEND training is continuous rather than a one off event at an inset session.
- Another headteacher, @virkjay, revealed that she is the SENDCo as well as the headteacher and this allows her to look holistically and build on prior training needs and pupil-specific needs. There is also a strong focus on behaviour in the school to enable all children to feel safe, valued and welcome at school. This is sensible planning and is very unusual. Not many headteachers take on the role of SENDCo but it does give her a full and clear view of everything happening in her school and the training needs of the staff.
- 'We do two SEND audits throughout the year, one in June (when we know our intake) and one in October. Full range of evaluations. We allocate some staff meetings for whole staff training, but also organise specific CPD for

staff running interventions' (@busby_stuart). This is a sensible approach and ensures that the right people are trained in the correct interventions. There is little point in directing your training to staff who will never need it.

Mainstream headteachers have different views on this topic. The Policy Exchange research note by Ralph Hartley (2010) reported that 'all teachers should be equipped with a certain basic understanding of SEN'. This statement remains valid today. I agree with Ralph Hartley when he states that the education of children with SEND is more about the quality of the education they receive than about the place they receive it. I believe if all teachers are adequately trained to deal with many conditions they routinely see in the classroom the children will have a good education. Those with complex, profound and multiple neurological difficulties have different, more specialised and often medical conditions and should be considered on an individual basis.

Assessing your school's SEND CPD needs

It is good practice for the school's SENDCo to be part of the senior leadership team. The reasoning behind this is that if the SENDCo is part of SLT they should have enough power to be able to push through any training that they feel is necessary. SENDCos are usually practising teachers as well as leaders and are in a strong position in terms of ensuring SEND is properly catered for.

Use this checklist to assist you in identifying your school's needs in the area of SEND:

School area of SEND training	Yes	No
Are all governors aware of the new 2014 Code of Practice and does one of them have responsibility for children with SEND? *(Legal requirement)*		
Are all teachers and support staff fully conversant with the 2014 Code of Practice?		
Has the school identified which resources it will use, e.g. IEPs, pupil passports or provision maps?		
Are all staff aware of the philosophy behind one page profiles?		
Are all teachers aware of their responsibilities regarding children with SEND? *(Legal requirement)*		
Have all support staff been trained to help to make the resources mentioned above?		
Has the school informed parents of the changes surrounding statements and EHC plans?		

Is the SENDCo a qualified teacher undertaking the National Award for Special Educational Needs Co-ordinator? *(Legal requirement)*		
Does the school website publish the correct information, e.g. LA 'local offer', school's SEND report including admin arrangements for SEND, the school behaviour policy? *(Legal requirement)*		

FIG. 48 Checklist: assessing your school's SEND CPD needs

We have now identified the legal aspects of training for SEND in mainstream schools.

Focusing on children with SEND

Let's focus on our children with SEND. Children with SEND need specialised teaching. Therefore as teachers we clearly require specialised training.

The most important reason for conducting your own school's CPD is that you and your staff know the children. You know their individual needs and how they learn. External experts and agencies have a role to play, and sometimes there may be no substitute for utilising their expertise. Often the most cost-effective way of achieving training is to send one person on a course who then returns and cascades the information to others.

As the SENDCo it is your role to gather as much information as possible about the children in the school who have SEND, as discussed in Part 1. Talk to:

- Parents – remember they know their child best.
- Other teachers – they had the child before you and will know what makes them tick.
- Headteacher – gain any information they have from background knowledge from any external meetings, if relevant.
- Any medical professionals such as physiotherapists, optometrists, occupational therapists, school nurse – medication can affect a child's responses and moods throughout the day and you need to be aware of this.
- Speech and language therapists – these people are invaluable. Children with ASC or ADHD, for example, often have communication difficulties and this leads to frustration and may result in poor behaviour. Speech therapists can help with articulation or can teach you how to make resources to facilitate communication.
- TAs – these people often know the child with SEND very well. They are the ones who spend much of their time helping the child to cope with their day. Ask their opinion and act on it.
- Educational psychologist – if appropriate.

- Any previous SENDCo – the SENDCo will have access to information about assessment and will help you to review progress. The previous SENDCo will also discuss the statement or EHC plan with you.
- Assessment leader – to help you identify gaps in learning.

Name: Rachel Rossiter

Twitter handle:@rachelrossiter

Who is she? SENDCo

Why to follow her: Follow Rachel Rossiter for passionate and informative tweets from a mainstream SENDCo.

You are now armed with all the information you need to teach your child with SEND. The next step is to train your staff.

Choosing your training

There are several different ways you can choose the training your teachers and TAs require. You need to keep in mind that you may not be blessed with many training sessions for SEND so your time needs to be used wisely. Here are some ideas to help you identify the correct type of training.

- **Do your homework thoroughly**. Have a walk around the school and look and listen to what is happening. Are the children behaving when unsupervised? Where you witness any poor behaviour is it being dealt with appropriately? Are all TAs carrying out their roles effectively in terms of supporting children with SEND? Are visual resources available where needed? You can learn a great deal from just wandering around the corridors.
- **Focused learning walks**. Set a focus for the learning walk – ideally one related to the school development plan. Decide who will take part in the walk, usually three or four people including a member of SLT, and choose which classrooms you are going to visit. The idea is to gain a snapshot of what is happening in the classes by spending around ten minutes in each and gaining an overview relating to your focus.
- **Consult with staff**. What do they require in the area of SEND? Talk to teachers and TAs and gain their views.
- **Conduct an audit of staff needs** (see below).
- **Consider using the expertise within school and training groups according to their needs**. This involves discovering the talents staff already have and requesting that they train other staff in that area. A good example of this is TAs who work with children on one page profiles could train other staff to do this.

- **Cascade the information to others at departmental meetings**. This is good practice and should be encouraged. A quick overview from trained staff will give a taster to other staff who then know who to contact to seek out any further information they may require.

All training for SEND is important. Removing barriers to learning for these children will improve the learning for all children.

Conducting an audit of your staff needs

Use this guide to help you to audit your school's training needs specific to SEND:

Staff/School community	Visuals	Behaviour	E –Safety	AAC/ ICT	IEPs Profiles etc.	Safeguarding
Governors		√	√			√
Headteacher		√	√	√	√	√
SLT		√	√		√	√
Middle leaders	√	√	√	√	√	√
Teachers	√	√	√	√	√	√
HLTAs	√	√	√	√	√	√
TAs	√	√	√	√	√	√
Lunch supervisors	√	√				√
Admin staff		√	√			√
Premises manager, including cleaners		√	√			√

FIG. 49 Audit of staff CPD needs

I have added the premises manager and cleaning staff into some training if they have direct contact with the children in the school. Whole school buy-in is essential for aspects of school training. Similarly, admin staff such as the school secretary or office manager often have direct contact with the children with SEND as they are sent on tasks as rewards or as 'mood changers'. Lunchtime staff should also be fully conversant with behaviour policies due to their direct contact in the playground.

Running CPD sessions

As a teacher working with children with SEND, it is assumed that you have the standard qualifications possessed by all teachers. It is also helpful if you have undertaken postgraduate study and have the SENDCo qualification or possibly a Masters qualification in SEND/Inclusion. All of these qualifications will stand you in good stead when faced with children with SEND. That said, there are some skills that cannot easily be taught. If you are charged with running CPD sessions for teaching children with SEND, before you begin your training session consider asking the teachers these questions to make them think about their own qualities:

- Are you a patient person? (You will need patience in abundance!)
- Are you able to deal with challenging behaviours without losing your cool?
- Do you have good communication skills?
- Do you have good organisational skills?
- Are you able to manage staff? (You may have several TAs who will look to you for direction and training.)
- Are you flexible in your teaching? (When teaching children with SEND things can go in totally the opposite direction from your plans.)
- Are you tolerant? (It is vital that teachers treat all their children equally.)
- Are you innovative and willing to try new things? (You will need to be.)
- Are you confident using technology? (Many children with SEND use technology; you will need to become something of an expert.)
- Do you have a good sense of humour? (You will need this.)
- Do you have empathy with children with special needs. (Practical skills such as planning and assessment can be taught; empathy can't.)

When your teachers have reflected on these attributes you are ready to begin training.

Top 10 tips for running great CPD sessions

Not all CPD is good CPD. Sometimes it falls short of the mark for various reasons. It may be that the trainer was wrong for the school and didn't tailor the training, or it may be too much talk from the trainer. I decided to ask the Tweeting teachers for their top tips for running great CPD sessions for children with SEND.

1. **Don't do anything for Ofsted –** this is my top tip. Train your teachers to put Ofsted out of their minds and concentrate on the children and staff. They are the important ones. If the training is right for them, it's right for Ofsted. This is

particularly true for SEND. Do what you feel is right for the children in front of you and be prepared to explain your actions.

2. **Choose your training time carefully –** twilight sessions prove difficult for teachers especially as the term draws to a close. Teachers and support staff work incredibly hard and it is difficult to maintain concentration after a full day teaching children. A further two hours may be a complete waste of valuable time as staff may be too tired to take in the extra information.

3. **Keep your expectations high for children with SEND** (@clyn40) – sound advice from Carolyn; physical disability, learning disability, illness and conditions such as ADHD are not a reason for lowering your expectations. This advice should be high on the list when running a CPD session for SEND.

4. **Give practical examples of what works; profile known students** (@zaragozalass) – all too often teachers work in isolation. They are often too busy to share their knowledge and their good practice. Following Marie's advice would lighten the load for everyone. Take a student known to the staff and showcase your successful work with them.

5. **Make it interactive –** top CPD sessions should be interactive. This is important. The best way to learn about anything is to do-it-yourself. Experience it through the eyes of a child.

6. **Include safeguarding –** safeguarding, especially staying safe online, should be a thread running through all your training. Young people with special needs are more vulnerable than most, and teachers should regularly revisit this subject with their children. Train your teachers to do this effectively. Look closely at cyber-bullying and exploitation.

7. **Train your teachers how to deal with parents, guardians and carers –** supporting those who are responsible for the children is just as important as supporting the children themselves. Marie (@clyn40) teaches in a further education college and revealed that parents struggle to allow their children to have independence and teachers need training in how to deal with aggrieved parents. Taking this further, you could 'Get expert parents in. They'll have read widely and networked extensively. Probably know up-to-date evidence based practice.' (@StarlightMcKenz). This is a valid point. Parents are experts as they have been coping with their child's particular area of SEND for many years. They have knowledge to share with teachers from a personal perspective and may know more than we as teachers ever could. This is certainly great CPD for SEND.

8. **Tailor your training to the needs of the students within that school rather than generalising** (@BehaviourTeach) – for children with SEND, this is vital. Behaviour needs will not follow a set pattern so train your staff to think about how to help the individual child rather than helping all children with challenging behaviours. They all have different needs and one size does not fit all.

9. **Encourage your teachers to be reflective and to identify their own training needs** – @ChrisChivers2 tweeted that teachers need to be self-developers too. It's not all 'done too'. This should be a cornerstone of great CPD.
10. **Be mindful of the bought in expert** – if you do bring someone in to run training, ask yourself: do they have the correct demeanour, the right voice and is their manner of delivery right for your school? Will the person hold the attention of your teachers and TAs? More top tips can be found at www.chrischiversthinks.weebly.com/blog

---

Top tip
Have a combination of in-house experts and bought-in consultants. Sometimes you have to pay for good training.

Share good practice between SENDCOs from other schools. (Ipec.org. uk/2015/01/26/)

Pass it on! Lorraine Peterson says:

'Organise at least one training day per year for SEND – one-in-five for one-in-five!'

Top tips for CPD for ASC and ADHD

With permission from Lynn McCann, here are her top six strategies. Although these are specifically written for children with ASC they are equally relevant for children with ADHD. These will help you train your staff if you have no budget available.

1. Train your teachers in these four main areas: sensory, communication, social and thinking. Teachers should be aware that children on the autistic spectrum often struggle to understand perspectives and accept change.
2. Use the YouTube video clip 'Autism: Sensory Overload Simulation' (www.youtube.com/watch?v=IcS2VUoe12M) to allow teachers to experience autism as a child might do.
3. Structure the environment, lessons, expectations. Show examples of how things should be done for maximum impact. Explain about the use of visual timetables, less cluttered classrooms and non-busy displays.
4. Make visuals and show teachers how to use them. They are not a bolt-on to make the classroom look decorative.

5. Teach social skills, play games and discuss what skills you could teach from them.
6. Remember that behaviour is logical for children with ASC. Be clear about your instructions. Children on the autistic spectrum take things literally.

The last point made by Lynn is crucial. A teacher at my own school recently provided paints and paper and an assortment of toy cars, bikes, buses and motorbikes. The children were doing a topic on transport and were asked to paint the toys. One child took this literally and painted the actual toys rather than a representation of them (which had been the intention!). Every toy was painted green, his favourite colour. Children with ASC will take instructions literally. Teachers need to be aware of this.

Top tips for CPD for dyslexia awareness

These strategies will help you train your staff on dyslexia if you have no budget available.

1. Train your teachers to help the child to be aware of the difficulties they face and most importantly to ask for help.
2. Train teachers to identify the child's best method of learning.
3. Train teachers to make other children aware of dyslexia and how it affects the child.
4. Train teachers in classroom strategies as discussed in Part 1 of this book, e.g. cream paper, font usage, key words (p 86).
5. Train teachers to use other methods of assessment for a child with dyslexia rather than written methods e.g. oral.
6. Train teachers to communicate with parents effectively about any concerns and also strategies that work.

Top tips for CPD for working with children with LDD

These strategies will help you train your staff to be aware of the needs of children with LDD when you have no budget available.

1. Train teachers and TAs to make sure the classroom is clutter free and a child using a wheelchair or walking frame can access the room.
2. Train teachers to break work into small chunks. Remind staff that children with LDD often take tiny steps in their learning.
3. Train teachers and TAs to ensure that a child with LDD has their communication aid set up if needed to allow them to participate in all lessons.
4. Train teachers and TAs to set up all technology such as clicker grids prior to the start of the lesson to allow maximum independence in the lessons.

5. Train staff to really think about and get to know the child, and provide visual aids in the form of timetables if they will help.
6. Train teachers to think about group work, and about pairing the child with a writer so the child with LDD can talk while the other child writes.

Top tips for CPD when working with children with challenging behaviour

Train your teachers to use these tips for working with children with challenging behaviour with no budget available.

1. Train teachers to use the word 'thank you' at the start of a request. This leaves no room for argument.
2. Teachers need to be trained that consistency is everything. The child should know that the same action will result in the same sanction each time.
3. Train teachers and TAs to provide a way out for the child. Staff should not back them in to a corner, metaphorically speaking, with no way out.
4. Teachers should only promise things they can deliver.
5. Train teachers and TAs to only pick the arguments they need to win. For example, does it really matter if the child with sensory issues has no shoes on? It is more important the child completes their work and doesn't distract the class.
6. Train teachers to have a back up plan in case all else fails. Is it possible to provide a safe space in school for the child to go to when they are distressed?
7. Train teachers and TAs to remember that positive behaviour management strategies such as praise and rewards generally work better. It is easy to lose sight of this in the heat of the moment.

Top tips for CPD for inclusion

Train your teachers to use these tips for inclusion.

1. Train teachers to personalise targets for the individual child by taking account of the information on their IEP. For example, this may mean making adjustments to lesson timings to allow extra time for the child who cannot write easily. It may mean adjusting work to allow the child to complete the work on their own level e.g. Use of iPad for writing.
2. Train teachers to truly know their child. Observe them, decide what they need in terms of physical inclusion in to the school, inclusion in to after school clubs and school trips and non-structured times such as lunch times.

3. Train teachers to look at the PE curriculum when considering inclusion. They should call in an expert if necessary to help ensure all children are included in games such as boccia, cricket and football.
4. Train teachers to know the value of the tech for special children and to buy in the tech. For example, you can purchase headphones to block out background noise and AAC devices to aid speech or writing. Also switch operated cameras and videos can be purchased to aid inclusion.
5. Train teachers to keep it hands on for children with SEND where possible so that all children can be involved. For example, teach shape space and measure in the Summer term to allow children to experiment with water outside rather than use worksheets to learn about measuring.
6. Teachers should be trained to help the children in the class to give the child with SEND plenty of time to answer any questions. Children with SEND often require extra time for thought processing and formulating an answer. This requires great patience from the rest of the class but is important for inclusion.

How to manage a CPD budget (or working without one)

At the same time as more pupils with SEND are being included in mainstream schools, the majority of maintained schools are now facing shrinking budgets and headteachers and CPD leaders in return are faced with the task of choosing the correct CPD for their school and choosing the most cost effective one. Every school wants effective CPD for the sake of their children and above all else it must have an observable impact on the children. Here are some things to think about.

- CPD should primarily be linked to the school's development plan – the needs of the children are the driver for all good training.
- CPD will be far more effective if there is an element of staff interest – this is particularly true when training to work with children with SEND. There is little point in sending a TA on a course for working with children with challenging behaviours if they lack the patience and empathy to work with these children.
- CPD should be relevant for the needs of the children in school – a member of staff may express a desire to attend training to work with children with visual impairments, but if there are no VI children currently in school you have to consider whether the training is cost effective: could the money be better spent elsewhere? If the answer is yes, it is difficult to justify the training.

> **Top tip**
>
> CPD must have proven impact on raising standards and removing barriers to learning.

Financial support for all children with and without disabilities in mainstream schools is provided by the LA through the school's budget. There are several elements of funding available.

1. **Age-weighted pupil unit** – this is provided for all children in the school and is dependent on their age. This funds a suitable curriculum for all and some of this is allocated for supporting those with SEND.
2. **Deprivation factor** – this funding is dependent on the area the school serves; if it is in a socially deprived area there will be increased funding to support those who may make lower than expected grades.

The two types of funding above should enable all schools to support those with SEND. If there are more complex needs, then a third fund is available.

3. **High needs top-up funding** – this funding stream is designed to support those with complex needs. The amount of funding, and for how long, is decided by professionals who know the child. In addition, the government introduced 'Pupil premium'.
4. **Pupil premium** – this funding is designed to 'close the gap' and remove barriers to learning for children on free school meals from Reception to Year 11. Schools can spend this money how they see fit and it may be used to give extra training for working with those with SEND.

The SEND budget is dependent on the number of children with special needs in the school. The primary use of a SEND budget must be to provide evidence-based interventions that work to remove barriers to attainment. Leaders and subject leaders should think carefully about the best use of the money allocated to them for SEND. Value for money is imperative. Think carefully about any training needed. Do you have the expertise already in school? Do your TAs have undiscovered skills? Audit their skill sets – can they provide training for no financial outlay?

> Top tip
>
> Develop a whole school action plan for SEND spending and use it wisely.

Use your SEND CPD budget to:

- **Support early identification of SEND** – this is inexpensive and can save money in the long term. Train staff to observe children at work and at play and gain an overview of their progress.
- **Raise standards for children with SEND** – the best way to do this is to develop the school's own expertise. Share your knowledge with other colleagues and departments. Pool your resources. Identify the needs of the child and correctly match the intervention. Remember, there are no generic answers to teaching children with SEND.
- **Develop your own resources and teaching materials** – this saves money for buying in the external trainer when needed.
- **Train your teachers in the art of tracking progress and looking for patterns where there may be problems** – this will help you to target specific interventions where training is needed. You can use your funding to buy in the interventions, if necessary.
- **Buy in outside expertise for specialist training** – such as for ASC, visually impaired, hearing impaired and EAL.

Think of Quality First teaching. What should your teachers and support staff provide for every child in their care during every lesson? How can you support your staff to provide this? Audit their needs and plan accordingly. Develop staff through peer mentoring and coaching.

> Top tip
>
> Sustain the CPD over at least two terms in order to embed the practice.

Supporting and mentoring other teachers

Most of us are used to having a mentor at some point in our careers. Mentors are usually wise, experienced teachers who want to pass on their knowledge and be supportive of others who are just learning their craft. Mentors are particularly important for those who are learning to teach children with special needs. As we have discussed in Part 1, there is very little training out there for teaching SEND. There is a shortage of expertise within this area and this will reach crisis point if it is not addressed successfully.

A good mentor needs to spend as much time with their mentee as possible. This sounds obvious but is not easy to achieve. Let's assume you are the SENDCo and you are the mentor. Have the trainee SEND teacher accompany you to all lessons and explain your strategies for working with the children as you go. Take the time to explain about the different conditions; don't assume the teacher already knows as they may not. Recall how you felt on your first day in a special school or during your first encounter with children with SEND and use this to help you to empathise with the teacher just encountering SEND.

Top tips for mentoring teachers who will be teaching children with SEND

- **Begin with the basics** – discuss a specific child in your school as a case study. Show their statement/EHC plan and discuss their medical, learning or behavioural challenges until your mentee has a clear picture of the child.
- **Observe** – introduce your mentee to the child to allow them to see how the child manages in school. Give them time to see their surroundings through the eyes of the child.
- **Demonstrate all the resources you routinely use** – visuals, timers, stop and go cards, communication books and charts. Also show them any special adaptations there are for the specific child within the school and classroom. Show them anything you regularly use as an aid to their learning such as PC apps, writing implements, etc.
- **Teach them how to write a SMART target** (specific, measurable, attainable, realistic and time-bound) – decide exactly what is to be achieved, how and when you want to achieve it and what are the barriers to achieving it. Keep it specific, measurable, attainable, relevant and time bound.
- **Teach them how to use your assessment tool** – special schools use many different tools for tracking and assessing their children's learning. As the SENDCo you will have adopted one of these tools; teach your mentee to use it.
- **Teach them to differentiate** – this is not having three different levels of worksheets, but real, useful differentiation that allows children with SEND to move on at their own level.
- **Have them spend time with your TAs** – TAs are the unsung heroes where children with SEND are concerned. They spend much time with them and often know the children best. Allow your mentee to observe how the child trusts the TA, but how the TA encourages independence by making sure they are not glued to their side.
- **Have them observe you** – even if they have been qualified for some time, teaching children with SEND is completely different to anything they will have

done before. They need to learn to balance their time with all children while spending time with the child who needs their expertise the most.

- **Explain why you are using certain strategies** – it may seem obvious to you that a child needs to spend time in the chill-out room every 30 minutes even though they are showing no signs of misbehaving or discomfort, but it won't be obvious to a newcomer. They will be unaware of the fact that you are aiming to keep the behaviour of the child on track by giving them regular breaks in routine.
- **Demonstrate and teach them how to handle a behaviour crisis** – a child with challenging behaviours needs careful handling. The child is looking to you for consistency and routine. They trust you and it is your duty to pass on your knowledge to a trainee in order that they may gain that trust.
- **Start with some team-teaching** – this is a powerful way of learning and developing skills before giving your mentee the responsibility for a whole class including several children with SEND.
- **Be encouraging but also truthful** – it is important to build their confidence; we all need that, but if they are storing up trouble for the future you must be honest with them. They may have avoided a child's shutdown by the skin of their teeth and you should point this out.
- **Encourage them to ask questions** – be prepared for a barrage of questions relating to ASC/ADHD and other special conditions. Do share your expertise freely. Also, learn from them. A good mentor picks up tips from anywhere and everywhere.

Coaching

Coaching and mentoring are similar in nature, but coaching is based on asking questions rather than merely providing answers. It's much quicker to simply supply answers but the teacher doesn't learn as much as when they have thought it through for themselves. In the area of SEND, this is a powerful way for a teacher to learn. There has to be an element of trust between the two parties and the coach need not be an expert in teaching SEND. In fact, it is helpful if the coach is not an expert and therefore there is no danger of them influencing the thoughts of the teacher.

The 'Achievement for All' (AfA) schools programme (2009) (afaeducation.org/ programme_schools) used by many special schools uses an achievement coach who is an experienced senior leader and a teacher in their own right. The coach helps schools to devise an action plan to help the school to improve and close the achievement gap. Using the 'structured conversation' coaching technique, questions are used to find out more about SEND pupils and discuss with parents what they could do to help the child. Many special schools, academies and mainstream schools have found this approach to be successful.

Self-assessment using videos

Another method of sharing best practice between teachers of SEND is through the use of videos. They can be used just for the teacher to reflect on their own teaching and see how to improve, or they can be shared with colleagues and management. Teachers of children with SEND often report that watching videos of others teaching is a powerful way to pick up tried and tested techniques that would be difficult to learn from a book.

Working with other schools

Our greatest resource in raising standards in schools is teachers and support staff. We know that good collaborative practice between mainstream schools is the key to success. However, when mainstream schools and special schools work together, there are amazing results. Key benefits include assuring parental confidence, better inclusion and improved standards. Mainstream schools benefit through developing pupil-centred planning and sharing resources with special schools. SEND teachers are able to advise their mainstream colleagues and also work with pupils in both schools.

One of my colleagues, Brian Walton (@Oldprimaryhead1) is headteacher of a primary school with a co-located special school. He is a firm advocate of the benefits of special and mainstream schools working together. He says he now understands how inclusion works as a result of the two schools being co-located. He has been able to develop the practice so that both provisions grow. Brian also reported some logistical difficulties such as ensuring staff meetings and CPD cover everyone's needs.

As you can see, Brian is an advocate of special schools and mainstream schools working collaboratively. He has found many areas where the situation is advantageous for both schools. During the same conversation Katie, a CPD leader, also pointed out the opportunities for saving money through conducting shared CPD. There would also be the opportunity to check the combined 'in-house' expertise when working with two schools together.

As a specialist leader of education (SLE) allied to the Fylde Coast teaching school, my fellow colleagues and I work collaboratively with many mainstream schools. As an SLE for SEND I have delivered the following training:

- Training for TAs working with children with ASC. This is a twilight course for mainstream teachers working with children with ASC in mainstream classrooms.

- How to best use your TA. This is a course consisting of three two-hourly sessions designed for TAs working with children in mainstream schools. A section of this course deals with children with SEND.
- The best use of social media for improving attainment for children with SEND in mainstream schools.

During the training, SLEs for SEND are also on hand to meet with mainstream teachers and to give advice on assessment, behaviour, feeding, speech and language and any other information needed.

This inter-schools collaboration works well. Special schools have much to offer mainstream schools and it is a two-way process. By forging close links with other schools, our collective knowledge will grow and we will be in a better position to improve the lives of children with SEND.

Special schools gather together to externally moderate the work of our children. There are eight special schools in the Lancashire cluster and we share our knowledge and expertise of assessment. We regularly meet and discuss assessment and other issues relating to SEND. The next step is to invite some mainstream colleagues who have children with SEND in their classes to join our group. This sharing of knowledge would be a truly powerful combination.

TeachMeets

One effective way of boosting your learning in an area of your own choosing is to attend a TeachMeet. I cannot recommend these highly enough.

A TeachMeet is an informal gathering of teachers who wish to share proven good practice in their area of expertise. TeachMeets are very popular and there is no hierarchy involved in presenting at one. They are a very real alternative to other more formal types of external CPD.

External CPD

Sometimes you find you have to call in the outside experts. This might be for a variety of reasons, for example, children with ADHD can display extremely challenging behaviours and an outside expert can help you to put effective solutions in place. Similarly, those with LDD need specialist support and as good as SENDCos are they cannot provide all the answers all of the time.

CPD in the form of external courses is very expensive. Therefore we need to get the best value for money possible. We need to be as sure as we possibly can be that all external courses accessed by staff are quality assured.

Top tips for finding good quality external CPD:

1. **Word of mouth** – there is no finer recommendation than talking with people who have been on a course and who will tell you it is exactly what you need to move your school forward in the area of SEND.
2. **Knowing the trainer** – it is always a bonus if the school knows the person doing the training, e.g. it may be a previous or trusted colleague. If the trainer is known and there is a relationship established already, then achieving good CPD is easier.
3. **Choosing a trainer who knows the school and knows the cohort of children** – in this scenario the trainer will be aware of the challenges and difficulties faced by the children and will be able to tailor their training according to the school's needs.

Once you have identified the course that will be useful for your staff, you need to decide on how you will achieve value for money. You may have many members of staff who request the training but your funds will not stretch that far. As mentioned previously, a popular way to address this is to send one person on the course and ask them to disseminate the information to all staff on their return to school. This is effective CPD and is very cost-effective. They can feed back to the rest of the staff in a number of ways:

- Run a twilight session for the rest of the staff – perhaps selecting only the staff who require or need the training in the particular area of SEND and focusing on them.
- Blog about it – this is my favourite method of feeding back from a course. I highly recommend blogging as a fast and effective way of spreading our message far and wide. Blogging has the added advantage that it will impact on many teachers and schools, not just your own.
- There is also the 'all staff' email – if the training focuses on an aspect of SEND that all staff need refreshing on it is possible to swiftly train everyone in the basic points with an email.
- Feeding back in a weekly fifteen-minute briefing session – ongoing bite-sized chunks is ideal for keeping staff updated on a regular basis.
- Scan the handout from training and save in iBooks on the iPad.

However you choose to feedback from an external course, the most important part is evaluating the impact of the training and considering how it is linked to the school development plan. This can be done initially through a quality written form. The key is to ensure staff fill in the form and treat this as a useful piece of evidence rather than a paper exercise.

This is an example of part of the evaluation form I use for Schools Direct trainees who are experiencing SEND training as part of their course (reproduced with kind permission from Fylde Coast Teaching School Alliance):

Evaluation

1. How would you describe your knowledge of SEND before the training?

\
\

2. How would you rate your knowledge of SEND after the training?

\
\

3. Were the aims and objectives of the day clearly explained?

\
\

4. Was the trainer knowledgeable?

\
\

5. Was the day well structured?

\
\

6. Was there ample opportunity to ask questions?

\
\

7. Do you think the training will help you to teach children with SEND?

_____

_____

8. How can the training be improved?

_____

_____

9. What was the most important thing you learned from the training?

_____

_____

10. Is there anything else you would like to add?

_____

_____

Fig. 50 Example evaluation form

Another method of evaluating the impact of external courses is through observing. This does not mean lesson observations. This means observing the effectiveness of the training on the day-to-day running of the school or classroom. For example, if the training was for behaviour, there should be a noticeable and immediate impact on the behaviour of the children around the vicinity of the school. The task is to then ensure that the training is sustained over a period of time.

Medical training for TAs

Important point! Training should be provided by a qualified health care professional and should be regularly reviewed. This is one area of training for which you will most likely have to look externally. Much of the training listed below, such as gastro feeding is free as it is vital for the child's health.

One of the most important aspects for inclusion for children with complex medical needs is ensuring their medical needs are met. Who will care for the child with SEND while they are at school?

Remember! Schools have a legal duty to support pupils with medical conditions.

Consider the following areas. Do your TAs need extra training to enable children with complex medical needs to be included in your school? (Some teachers may also wish to be trained in these areas.)

- External gastric feeding
- Administration of oxygen
- Moving and handling
- First aid/Early Years first aid training
- Administration of drugs
- Use of an EpiPen®
- Diabetes awareness
- Coping with bereavement
- Care and diet plans specific to diseases such as cystic fibrosis
- Hydrotherapy training/lifeguard training
- Speech and language training specific to individual children
- Specialist AAC resources for communication aids
- Design and make specialist resources for children with LDD
- Feeding children with complex medical needs
- Anaphylactic shock and choking prevention and treatment.

Schools must ensure staff are properly trained to provide medical support for their pupils. The DfE document, 'Supporting pupils at school with medical conditions' states that schools should develop a policy to identify how they will support children's medical needs and who is responsible for providing this support.

Any member of staff can be asked to support children's medical needs and this includes administering medicines and drugs. Teachers may be asked but are not required to undertake this duty unless they choose to do so as it falls outside of their contractual duties. TAs are often employed to carry out this role. Governing bodies and SLT must ensure that staff are competent before they undertake this responsibility.

Use the following table to help you decide which of your TAs should be trained in each area:

Who should be trained?	Training required
Higher Level Teaching Assistants (HLTAs) or those with special responsibilities	• Coping with bereavement • Specialist AAC resources for communication aids • Lifeguard • Administration of drugs • Mini-bus driving (MIDAS)
All TAs	• Health care plans • Diet plans • Feeding children with complex needs • Moving and handling • Care of children with specific illnesses and conditions
Year group/Key Stage TAs	• Design and make specialist resources for children with LDD
Class TAs	• Design and make visuals for classroom use • First aid • Early Years first aid
1:1 support TAs	• EpiPen® • Epilepsy • Diabetes • Speech and language specific to individual child • Gastric feeding • Administration of oxygen • Anaphylactic shock

Fig. 51 Medical training for TAs

For each of the above areas the length of time necessary for training will be dependent on the:

- number of children requiring medical care
- number of specialised areas to be included in the training
- number of staff requiring training.

Top eight activities for training others in the area of SEND

I asked the tweeting teachers for their top tips for training others in the area of SEND and these were the top answers:

1. Use a sorting/diamond 9 activity (@warwick_beth)
This is an activity to get people talking and drawing their own conclusions and thinking about their own priorities. The idea is that people rank their ideas on a certain subject with the top idea going at the top of the diamond. Then the next

two items, then the next three and so on until the least important idea is reached at the bottom. Beth says that teachers need to have ownership of their training and should be encouraged to be reflective practitioners. By using Beth's method the training tends to stay with the teachers for longer.

2. Create activities to put the adults in the child's shoes (@MikeArmiger)
This is a favourite activity of mine. I have spent time being blind-folded to understand how a child with visual impairment interprets their surroundings. I have also worn ear defenders to understand how a child who is hearing-impaired understands their world. I have spent time in a wheelchair – which quite frankly was sometimes terrifying as staff pushed me too close to cars on the roads and adults ignored me and spoke to the person pushing me. Similarly, when training teachers to use PECS, the teacher could be the child – the idea is that you have to say as little as possible and stick to an agreed format. This gives teachers a greater understanding of what the child is experiencing and how hard it is for a child who cannot communicate verbally.

3. Assessment task
I have found one way to help teachers to understand assessment is to give them several pieces of work assessed at various P Scales. Sit as a group and moderate together to develop their understanding.

4. Paired observations of pupil interactions within the classroom, looking at particular needs (@SimonKnight100)
This is a valuable suggestion as two people's collective thoughts are more useful than one person's opinion. Between the two people observing they can reach conclusions concerning strategies for working with the child in question.

5. Look at data (@DavidBartram)
Train teachers when listening to a child with reading difficulties to look at reading and spelling tests and learn what they can from the data. By doing this they will develop a greater understanding of what the scores really mean. This real hands-on learning involving the children is better than any other training.

6. Think about an activity @MariaStMarys)
Take one activity and challenge all teachers to consider their approach to it to meet the needs of a particular area of SEND, e.g. a pupil with hearing or vision impairment. Ask the teachers to consider how they might teach fractions to that child. They should reflect on how they would facilitate independent access where possible. Come together as a group and discuss the suggested practice. This is powerful practice and would result in deep learning.

7. Go and watch others teach (@betsysalt)
This effective CPD is to go and work alongside a teacher in a subject of your choosing who has a proven track record at getting results. This is good practice and is more effective than being trained at INSET without the children.

8. Invite others in to watch you teach
This is the ultimate form of training. Gather your knowledge and pass on your learning.

Getting started

Achieving effective CPD for mainstream teachers with SEND in their classes is difficult. There are many demands on the time allowed for CPD and SENDCos, or the person charged with organising CPD needs to be creative with the small amount of time allotted to them.

Keep in mind that CPD for teachers need not always be formal, structured work. New methods of training which are less formal are just as popular and are generally free. This includes: peer mentoring, coaching, observations, teacher discussions in staffrooms and in the corridors, and feedback from learning walks. TeachMeets are increasingly popular and are outside of the working day. Members of staff fund these themselves and choose the workshops they wish to attend; all very civilized and incredibly informative with up-to-the-minute teaching techniques.

How to plan and run a whole term/year CPD programme

Let's consider our six areas of need identified in part 1 as:

1. ASC
2. ADHD
3. LDD
4. Dyslexia
5. Behaviour for learning
6. Inclusion

Behaviour for learning is ongoing and should be revisited regularly. Members of staff need to be at the top of their game in this area. Consider the amount of time you need to dedicate to staff training. I recommend a regular update from the behaviour leader once per half term as a minimum to ensure the whole school buy-in to the strategies continues to be in place.

Inclusion should be at the heart of everything you do. The philosophy of inclusion should be evident as soon as you enter the school: the atmosphere, the staff and the environment should all promote the school's commitment to full inclusion. In the best schools, where all staff truly believe in equality for all, there is less need to constantly re-visit inclusion in staff training.

For the remaining areas of SEND, which for the purposes of this book have been ASC, ADHD, LDD and dyslexia – but these will vary according to the specific needs of the children in your school, a good model for training within a year could be to have working groups for each of the areas identified. Choose your staff carefully from those who have an interest and those who are working with the children who have the particular difficulty. Give the groups a twilight session each to update their strategies and resources.

If you only have one INSET day allocated for the year, you need to use your time wisely. Split the day into four time slots and have all staff visit each working group and update their skills. Using this strategy your staff will be updated throughout the year in all areas of need and the impact will show in improved behaviour and improved teaching and learning. Staff will also have increased confidence as they will be newly trained in the latest techniques. Your staff will also have ownership of the training as they will have played a key part.

Some things to consider:

- The role of the school CPD leader is to identify the person who can best lead the training – for SEND that may be an external speaker. Keep an open mind.
- CPD time is precious, especially for SEND. Don't waste it.
- Avoid forcing staff to be trained in certain areas if they have no interest whatsoever.

When I asked the tweeting teachers for their thoughts on CPD, a great number of them said that the best CPD was always subject-specific or tailored to their individual needs. Many were not in favour of CPD being forced upon them as a whole-school initiative if it had little relevance to them. This is something to keep in mind when planning your CPD; if you want good feedback ask staff what they need.

When planning formal training, SENDCos or CPD leaders need to consider several aspects relating to their training:

- **Aim to have a theme to your training** – just because the remit is 'SEND' you still need to have a focus for the session.
- **Do not try to cram everything relating to SEND in your training** –irrespective of the length of time slot you have been allocated.
- **Plan in time for staff to discuss the new strategies and techniques** – the best training will have time planned in for teamwork, for making new resources and discussing implementing them.

Keep in mind that not all of the training for SEND is relevant to all staff. Those who are not involved with the particular aspect of SEND will resent their precious time being squandered by training they do not need. Others may already be fully up-to-date with the training and therefore do not need it. They too will resent their time being wasted. Choose your delegates carefully.

Here are a few things to consider:

- How will I introduce the topic and get people engaged?
- How much time do I have to train staff?
- How much time do I have to plan the training?
- What resources will I need?
- What is my budget?
- What could possibly go wrong and how can I solve the difficulty?
- Any specific planning advice?
- Can I produce training plans for staff to use?

Things that can go wrong during CPD training sessions

Use this table to address some of the issues listed above.

Problem	Suggested by	Solutions
There are mismatched expectations, or not knowing your audience's starting point.	@PeteJeffreys	A quick online survey to all participants beforehand helps even if you don't get one hundred percent response rate.
You leave the memory stick at home complete with the presentation.	@reachoutASC	If you don't have a helpful family member who would be able to bring it in, I suggest you go cloud based; learn to use Dropbox or Google Drive.
Someone answers a call during the training session and talks over you.	@reachoutASC	Ask for all phones to be turned off or at least on silent prior to beginning the session.
A delegate tells you that she doesn't want the training, doesn't need it and doesn't want to be there.	@mjlongstaffe	Encourage active participation right from the start. Direct questions to the reluctant person and encourage them to share their expertise. Use their knowledge to good effect.
You find that you have led the CPD with a presentation and therefore talked for the duration of the CPD; some trainees look a bit bored.	@r_brooks1	Introduce some activities to keep people interested. Aim to talk for no more than 10 minutes before introducing an activity or you will see eyes glazing over.

Problem	Suggested by	Solutions
Halfway through the training, a member of SLT announces 'this is not what we want.'	@michhayw	Send an email outlining your plan for the training session to the headteacher or CPD leader prior to the training.
A delegate gives feedback at the end of the training that they have had no opportunity to reflect, discuss and decide how it might work for them and how to take it forward.	@hannahtyreman	Allow time during the session for discussion. This is often when the best ideas are exchanged.
You receive feedback that doesn't help to work out how to improve the training for next time.	@hannahtyreman	Ask people if they have any complaints before you give out the feedback form. You may be able to resolve some issues by asking.

Fig. 52 Things that can go wrong in CPD training sessions

Top training tip

'At the start of the session I always give out some large pads of sticky notes and ask delegates to write what they want from the session. I write their key points to be covered on the flip chart and refer to them as I go through the training. At the end of the session they put their feedback to the questions and session on their sticky note and that is the feedback completed.' (@MaryMyatt)

Another hurdle to overcome is the fact that staff cannot easily be released from their teaching duties during the working day. Children are obviously the priority. With this in mind let's look at the different time slots available for CPD for teachers working with children with SEND.

2 Training plans

This section of the book provides you with training plans for a range of different time slots:

- Time slot 1: No time at all
- Time slot 2: 15 minutes
- Time slot 3: A two-hour twilight session
- Time slot 4: An INSET day
- Time slot 5: Half a term of training
- Time slot 6: A full term of training
- Time slot 7: A year's worth of training.

The training has been split into different time slots to help you to organise your CPD around all the variations of timings allowed for training. You may have no time at all, you may have a whole year's worth of slots or you may have a variation of these. These different plans will help you to plan your session whatever its length.

Time Slot 1: No time at all

Overview

Sometimes it is vital that SEND training happens immediately and you may have no time at all to do it. An example of this might be that a new child, with a severe, less well known condition is due to arrive at your school. You are aware that staff may have no knowledge of this condition but it will have an impact on their lesson so you need to provide some training instantly.

Tips for this time slot

- The best way to communicate with all staff is via email
- Follow up your email by checking that key staff have read it and understand the information
- Provide a time when staff can come and discuss their concerns with you
- Meet key staff at the end of the first day to brainstorm ideas and strategies.

Example scenario

As SENDCo you have been notified that a child who is new to the area will be joining your school the following week. The child has Asperger's syndrome and is therefore on the autistic spectrum, and this is combined with Oppositional Defiant Disorder (ODD). One in ten children with Asperger's syndrome may also have the added complication of ODD at some point in their lives and this makes them angry and confrontational towards those perceived to be in authority. You and your staff are completely unaware of how to plan for and how to teach this child. All members of staff will need training in educating this child and or coping with any adverse behaviour exhibited. A plan of action is required as there is clearly no time to draft in an external expert at this stage.

Use this training plan to help you.

Time slot 1 training plan

Training focus	Prepare all staff for a new SEND pupil arriving at the school. • Send email to all members of staff who will have immediate contact with child • Compile a document with brief, salient bullet points
Who will be trained?	• All members of staff who will be in contact with the child, including class teacher, TAs, subject leaders, lunchtime supervisors
Own research time required?	• One evening for dedicated research on the Internet to avail yourself of the facts
Resources required	• Internet, PC, printer
Budget required	• None
Problems that may arise	• Email fails to reach all staff • Staff members do not read the email • Staff members don't understand the information given • Staff members prefer to make up their own minds on how to educate the child and ignore the advice given
Solutions to problems	• Follow up with a briefing the following morning • Give handout to all members of staff concerned and discuss the handout in the briefing • Discuss the importance of a consistent approach especially while the child becomes accustomed to a new environment
Any specific planning advice	• Concentrate on particular behaviours and medical difficulties that will need immediate attention
Advantage of this training	• Information can be disseminated quickly • Gives the reader chance to digest the information at leisure • As the email is followed by a handout you, the trainer, will know that everyone has the basic information required to welcome the child on the first day
Disadvantages of this training	• Only basic information can be disseminated via email • Cannot be sure everyone has read the email, you may be relying on the staff briefing.
Evaluation	• You will be able to evaluate the impact of this brief training by gathering information about the number of requests for information you received • Further evaluation will be seen by informal observation of how the child settles in school and informal observation of how members of staff cope with the child

Fig. 53 Time slot 1 training plan

Your handout and email should contain these points.

Time slot 1 Handout

Autism, Asperger's syndrome and ODD

What we know about the child:

- Disruptive behaviour at home and at school
- Intolerant and disobedient
- Extreme tantrums have been present for more than six months
- Child will be hostile and defiant with those in authority
- Child will continually be negative with those around them.

These behaviours will manifest in the following ways:

- Unable to form friendships
- Extreme anger and frustration
- Difficulty with work
- Aggression towards others
- Frequent tantrums
- Refusal to follow requests
- A strong desire to irritate, annoy or upset others.

Ways to cope in the classroom:

1. Have clear and consistent rules.
2. Seek out and praise good behaviour.
3. Keep calm while facing opposition.
4. Give acceptable choices so that the child feels they have some control over the situation.
5. Avoid the power struggles without giving in by using effective strategies within the classroom.
6. Schedule 'time out' in the daily routine to allow the child a chance to calm themselves.
7. Remind yourself and the child that you are objecting to the behaviour and not the child.
8. Begin again after each tantrum, remind the child of expected behaviours and move on.
9. Model the behaviour you expect to see, e.g. no raised voices, calm composure.

Fig. 54 Handout on autism, Asperger's syndrome and ODD

This brief handout will be a helpful starting point for introducing training with no planning time at all. The key thing is to remain calm. With a bullet point handout your staff can be quickly informed of the main facts and how to work with this child.

Adapting this training plan

This training plan is easy to adapt to any training you need to introduce at speed.

Consider adapting this plan for:

- Reinforcing staff knowledge of any SEND condition where they may need a reminder
- Training staff to make visual timetables
- Training staff to make 'Now and Next' cards
- Training staff to use technology such as Talking Tins
- Reminding staff how to make Clicker 7 grids

Time Slot 2: 15 minutes

Overview

A 15-minute time slot does not sound like a very long time; however, it can be very useful as a meeting time to impart important information before the children arrive at school in the morning. For example, you may have received notification that morning from a parent that a child is dealing with the death of a much-loved pet the previous evening. Hold a 15-minute meeting with class staff and discuss how to help the child deal with their emotions. Other uses of this time slot might include a series of short training sessions on certain SEND issues.

Tips for this time slot

- A 15-minute time slot is not too onerous for teachers or TAs who have many demands on their time.
- The 15-minute time slot before the children arrive in the morning is a good time to choose as all key staff will be present. Later in the day some may be on break or lunch.
- This time slot is good for keeping discussion focused due to the 15-minute deadline.
- You can hold a further 15-minute meeting later in the day or the next morning to check any further action required.

Example scenario

As SENDCo you have been allotted a regular 15-minute session for the whole school year to work with the whole school on any aspect of CPD for SEND. You need to use this time wisely; 15 minutes, although a relatively short space of time, can be useful.

When considering this 15-minute session consult your school development plan and check the whole school priority for SEND. Are you still in agreement with this document? Has it been updated recently to include any new SEND training that your staff has undertaken?

Let's imagine you have decided there is an urgent need for more behaviour training. Use this training plan to help you to address this issue in a weekly 15-minute session that can involve as many staff as required.

Time slot 2 overview training plan

Training focus	Series of 15-minute training sessions to improve the behaviour of children with SEND across the whole school
	• In the first instant, members of staff to work in departmental teams to brainstorm ideas
	• Teams will then take it in turns to present their ideas to the other groups over a rolling programme of 15-minute sessions
Who will be trained?	• All staff from all departments who teach children with SEND: potentially all teachers, all TAs, SLT and lunchtime supervisors
Own research time required?	• Own time to seek out strategies proven to work as seen in other schools
	• Extra time to research further around new theories concerning behaviour
Resources required	• Flip charts, sticky notes, highlighter pens in different colours, tables, chairs
Budget required	• None
Problems that may arise	• Staff may be unreceptive to new ideas
	• Staff may be reluctant to speak up in front of such a large audience
Solutions to problems	• Point out the benefits of change to staff, e.g. their daily classroom experience will be improved for all through having a quieter environment, all children on task, fewer behaviour difficulties, less stress
	• Address the cause of the reluctance to change, e.g. not wanting to tackle poor behaviour, no time to make new resources or possibly no time to engage with new working practices
	• Encourage the reluctant speaker to maintain eye contact with you and promise to smile at them reassuringly – encourage them to read from their notes to calm their nerves

Any specific planning advice	• Ensure you provide enough thinking time • As with all training, avoid running over the allotted time as this causes anxiety with staff
Advantage of this training	Ability to train large groups of people in just 15 minutes in basic theories. • Fast and efficient • Encourages interaction from staff who may otherwise be reluctant to speak out • People learn best when involved rather than being passive • All new strategies can be addressed at length during a longer training session such as a full INSET or over the course of a term
Disadvantages of this training	• Cannot easily address brand new, untried strategies in such a short time
Evaluation	• The new training can be evaluated by informal observation of whole school strategies for behaviour • There should be a calmer atmosphere around school as new ways of working take effect • There should be fewer incidents of challenging behaviour as staff become more able to deal with challenging behaviour

Fig. 55 Time slot 2 overview training plan

Session 1 training plan

Focus	Activities	Timing
Introduce the idea of sharing best practice for dealing with behaviour issues in children with SEND	• Gather all members of staff together in an adequate-sized room and seat them in departmental teams	

	• Introduce the new weekly 15-minute training sessions:
	  ○ Each departmental team to share their strengths and areas for development in relation to the behaviour of their children with SEND
	  ○ Each week you will ask a different team to feed back their thoughts to everyone
	  ○ You will encourage all staff to share best practice and strategies and any areas in which they require further training
	  ○ This will then form the basis for your behaviour training over the coming months	

	• Allow time for teams to process the information they have received and discuss the training between themselves	

Fig. 56 Session 1 training plan

Session 2 training plan

Focus	Activities	Timing
Begin brainstorming within departmental teams best practice and strategies for improving behaviour of children with SEND	• Set the teams off deciding on one behaviour they would like to see improved and use this to focus their thoughts.	
	• Each departmental team will write down their ideas, strategies and solutions on their own flip charts.	
	• At the end of the 15-minute session gather all the flipcharts together to make notes of suggested strategies.	

Fig. 57 Session 2 training plan

Session 3 training plan

Focus	Activities	Timing
To train staff in the use of positive language	• Work through the 'Using positive language in the classroom' handout to show teachers how to introduce a behaviour strategy for using positive language in the classroom in a 15-minute training session.	
	• Give the handout to your teachers after the session to take away.	

Fig. 58 Session 4 training plan

Session 4 and each subsequent session training plan

Following the model of session 3 above, choose a member of staff from each of the departmental teams in turn to deliver a short session to everyone on one of their highlighted strategies or solutions.

Adapting this training plan

This regular 15-minute session can be applied to any training, as required. You could apply this format for any areas of SEND, such as those looked at in detail in this book (ASC, ADHD, LDD, dyslexia, behaviour for learning, inclusion), for a quick and easy gain in the classroom.

A good use of a 15-minute session would be to update your behaviour for learning plans. Staff can work in class groups and suggest adjustments to the plans as they see the child's behaviour improving as the term continues.

Using positive language in the classroom

Reasons for introducing 'positive language' in the classroom:

- To help children to become aware of behavioural expectations
- To teach children basic manners and a respect for others
- To build an effective relationship between child and teacher
- To remove the element of choice from your language
- To build a positive working environment free from confrontation with children.

Examples of ineffective language:

- Can you please sit down?
- Why are you not working?
- Can you stop talking?
- Can you line up quietly?
- Will you stop prodding the child next to you?

What we want to achieve:

- Model the behaviour and the language you wish to see.
- Teach children social skills they may not be seeing at home.
- Show the children that you truly believe they are capable of working and behaving well.

Examples of 'positive language':

- Well done for sitting down promptly in your seat.
- I'm pleased to see you are on task and working well.
- Well done for stopping talking and listening to the lesson.
- I'm pleased to see that my class is able to line up correctly with minimal chatter.
- I'm very pleased that you are behaving sensibly and working well with your partner.

Use of positive language will have the following effects:

- Helps children to know that their teachers believe in them and will encourage them to choose positive behaviour
- Shows the children the expected behaviour through your choice of words
- Helps children to become confident and believe in themselves.

Always use clear language, short sentences and avoid sarcasm.

Fig. 59 Using positive language in the classroom handout

An added benefit of brainstorming using this 15-minute training session is that, if you are the CPD lead or SENDCo, you will have a ready-made list of areas identified by staff as needing extra training. These lists can form the basis of your CPD training for the coming months.

Time slot 3: A two-hour twilight session

Overview

All those who work in schools are aware that the two-hour after-school twilight sessions, although exhausting for staff, are the backbone of the school's CPD. As the name suggests, twilights occur at the end of a long hard day when staff struggle to take on board training aimed at improving the school experience for the children and staff alike.

Top tips for this time slot

My main advice for twilights is to ensure that they do not overrun the prescribed time. Staff become very grumpy and stop listening to what is happening. Also, make them fun if at all possible. Keep them relevant to the staff. If the whole school does not need the training don't waste everyone's time asking them to attend. The feedback from others on Twitter is:

- Keep the session interactive and hands-on – get the participants up and moving around the room and have them writing and completing activities. These are the things that make the training fly by and these are the things which staff find easier to retain at the end of a long day.
- Ensure there's time for discussion – an overwhelming number of tweeters requested time for discussion. This was cited as one of the main problems with SEND training: members of staff are trained and sent away to implement the new initiative and are allowed no time for discussion. Keep this in mind when planning your activities and allow discussion time.
- Role play is not popular – avoid unless you know you have a receptive audience.

Example scenarios

In this section, the following scenarios have been addressed in twilight session training plans:

1. Beginning to train your staff in SEND
   1: Paperwork
      Session 1: one page profiles and pupil passports
      Session 2: IEPs and provision maps.
   2: Training your TAs to work with children with SEND
   3: Training your teachers to work with children with SEND

2. Behaviour for learning (p 229)
   Session 1: Using visual aids to improve behaviour in children with SEND
   Session 2: Understanding behaviour in children with SEND
3. Differentiation for children with SEND (p 244)
4. Technology training (p 248)
5. Assessment training (p 253)
6. Training on a specific area of SEND: Introduction to dyslexia (p 255)

1. Beginning to train your staff in SEND

This first set of twilight sessions works as a cluster of sessions to help you make a start training your teachers and TAs with the basics of working with children with SEND.

1. Paperwork

As we have seen in Part 1, there is a brand new Code of Practice in place for children with SEND from September 2014. Schools, both mainstream and special are at different points in adapting to all the changes. You should keep this in mind when training your staff and look primarily at what works best for your cohort of children with SEND. Choose only the resources that you need.

For example, not all schools will continue to use IEPs; some will, some will not. It is good practice to have some form of IEP even if an alternative name for them is used. Similarly some schools will use provision maps, pupil passports and all will use one page profiles. Schools will design their own versions of all the paperwork and will choose their own names for it. Only train your staff to use the paperwork your school has chosen.

Top tip

Always remember that every child is different; personalise your approach and your resources to the child in front of you.

To train your staff to make a selection of the paperwork required for SEND you should allow 2 twilight sessions.

You will need a whole twilight session to train staff how to make a one page profile or a pupil passport (depending on the name chosen) as these are quite detailed. A further one will be required to train your staff to make IEPs (or the alternative to these) and also provision maps or their alternative.

Training focus	To train staff to make a selection of the paperwork required for SEND
Who will be trained?	Teachers and TAs
Own research time required?	Allow 1 hour to recap on different aspects of paperwork
Resources required	Paper, ink, printer
Budget required	None
Problems that may arise	Teachers may feel they should be able to give this job to TAs.
Solutions to problems	Remind teachers that SEND is everyone's responsibility.
Any specific planning advice	Staff to make an actual resource
Advantage of this training	Can do it in house
Disadvantages of this training	None
Evaluation	Can staff all make the required resources?

Fig. 60 Beginning to train your staff in SEND

Session 1: Train staff to make a one page profile or a pupil passport

Focus	Activities	Timing
To train staff to make a one page profile or a pupil passport	• Recap with staff how to make a one page profile e.g. Child centred.	15 minutes
	• Collect a photograph of the child and any information the child might not know about themselves. This might include their age, family members, food allergies. Include their likes and dislikes.	30 minutes
	• Train your staff to identify strengths and needs of the children in their classroom – work through the handout 'How to create a one page profile'.	45 minutes
	• Remind staff to keep it child centred by encouraging the child to take a lead in giving the information.	30 minutes

Fig. 61 Session 1: Train staff to make a one page profile or a pupil passport

One page profile

Children with SEND benefit from a one page profile (see part 1, chapter 2 for an example of a completed one page profile p 37). A one page profile forms the basis of the 'All about me' section on the EHC plan and it is therefore important that information is gathered through direct discussions with the child. A profile is also an opportunity for family, friends and teachers to share their collective knowledge of the child. The following handout may be useful when training your teachers to create a one page profile.

How to create a one page profile

A good profile is made up of three elements:
1. What people like and admire about the child – this could be their talents and gifted areas.
2. What is important to the child from the child's point of view.
3. The support required from those close to them including family, friends and teachers.

To create a one page profile:
1. Brainstorm the topics below with the child. Work on a one to one basis in a quiet area of the classroom. Either you or your TA can complete this task with the child. Remember you may need to use communication charts or AAC.
   - Who is in their family? (Include pets)
   - Do they have a personal assistant at home?
   - Who are their friends?
   - What is important to the child? This includes places they like to visit, favourite toys, family members and friends.
2. Discuss the layout of the profile with the child including favourite colours and shapes. Remember the profile is child centred and should reflect the child's own thoughts: therefore their input is needed.
3. Include on the profile the child's name, age, class and year group as well as a photo of the child.
4. Send home a letter to ask the parents or carers what people like and admire about the child. If no information comes in from home, then the teacher or TA should use their own ideas.
5. Ask parents for their input regarding routines at home. What support do parents want in place to keep their child happy and content?
6. When you have gathered all the content you need, work with the child to include the information they have specified, using the background colours and shapes they have specified.

Fig. 62 Handout: How to create a one page profile

Pupil passports

An alternative to a one page profile is a pupil passport (see p 38). These contain similar information to one page profiles. They are child-centred, generally contained on one page and much of the content is created through conversations with the child. Again, they are not statutory but they are good practice. They should be used to inform Quality First Teaching and consulting with the child is the best way of achieving this.

Pupil passports should be written in the first person in consultation with the child where possible. Here is a summary of what should be contained in a pupil passport:

- Child's photograph and name
- Areas the child struggles with, identified by the child
- Strategies the child finds helpful
- Topics and areas of interest including motivators
- Things that are important to the child.

A pupil passport looks similar to the one page profile in design and schools usually design their own template.

Session 2: Train your staff to use IEPs and provision maps

Focus	Activities	Timing
To train staff to use IEPs and provision maps	• Discuss IEPs with staff and remind them that they are not statutory and may be called by a different name. • Show an example IEP or similar document with new name.	15 minutes
	• Staff to select school template for IEP. • Staff to gather main information from statement or EHCP. This will include level child is working at and details of SMART targets and strategies to achieve the targets. • Staff to work in class groups and produce an IEP for a specified child.	45 minutes
	• Discuss provision map with staff and remind them that they are not statutory and may be called a different name. • Show an example provision or similar document with new name.	15 minutes
	• Staff to work in class groups and identify through discussion all the extra provision and interventions provided for children with SEND that is different from the provision provided for other children through the school's curriculum. • Staff to make a provision map detailing all the provision provided.	45 minutes

Fig. 63 Session 2: Train your staff to use IEPs and provision maps

Individual Education Plans (IEPs)

The SEND Code of Practice 2014 does not specifically refer to IEPs; rather it leaves schools to design their own format for identifying personalised targets, strengths and needs. Many schools are continuing to use IEPS although they may be calling them an alternative name.

If you choose to use IEPs in your school, you need to make sure teachers are aware of this introductory information:

- The IEP is designed to help teachers and all school staff to work on specific targets arising from the child's statement (if they still have one) or EHC plan.
- The targets and strategies for achieving them are different from or additional to those required by all children.
- There should be no more than four targets; they should be SMART targets, and they should be short-term and reviewed regularly.

Here is an example IEP to help with staff training.

Individual Education Plan			
Name of child:	**Date of birth:**	**Academic year:**	**Class:**
Targets	**Strategies**	**Assessment**	**Resources required**
English P4 comprehension. Points to the character/object when being asked about it.	Daily 1:1 reading session. Use hand over hand and model pointing to objects of interest around the room.	To do this successfully once per day after initial structured teaching.	• A book that will engage the child. • Toys and objects strategically placed around the room.
Maths P4 Relates familiar objects i.e. gloves for hands, shoes for feet.	Remove shoes and socks of two children. Jumble all together. Encourage child to try on shoes and socks and try to identify which are theirs. Move on to include gloves. Finally, mix all items together and expect child to identify body parts they belong to.	Structure teaching to include 1:1 to begin to identify own clothing. Reduce support over time. Child to do this successfully independently on three occasions.	• Gloves • Shoes • Slippers • Socks
PSHE P4 Responds when informed it is lunchtime.	Child to collect own object of reference card at the sound of the lunch bell. 1:1 teaching to begin with. Slowly withdraw support.	Child to complete this successfully once per day to show understanding of the transition to lunch.	• Attach a real knife and fork to some card along with a photograph of the dining hall.

Fig. 64 Example IEP

Provision maps

Again, the 2014 Code of Practice does not make provision maps statutory but they are considered good practice in both mainstream and special schools. Provision maps help schools to reduce barriers to learning, match provision to need and inform all staff of the interventions in place to help children with SEND.

Train staff to make a provision map:

- Gather all information about your children with SEND, including data, past interventions, previous successes
- Identify any new areas of need for your children
- Determine which staff will work with the children
- Remember – Paragraph 6.76 of the Code of Practice states that provision maps are an efficient way of showing all the provision that the school makes which is additional to and different from that which is offered through the school's curriculum.

Here is a template you can use to train your staff with some examples of support provided.

Provision map						
Name (List all children who receive this intervention)	Year group	Intervention provided	Staffing	Pupil premium	Cost	Impact seen
		Behaviour support, lunchtime/ break time				
		Daily booster phonics group for SEND				
		SATs/ external exam support				
		Occupational therapy for hand-writing				
		ICT support for loading specialist software				
		AAC support for creating specialist resources				
		Speech and language support				
		1:1 TA class support				

Fig. 65 Example provision map

By providing the above resources, all staff who are in close contact with the child with SEND will know their targets and will be able to include them in their overall lesson plans.

2. Training TAs to work with children with SEND

If used wisely, TAs can be the most valuable resource a teacher will have access to. TAs often work closely with the children, although it should be remembered that the class teacher maintains overall responsibility for every child in their class.

Consider inviting teachers to your TA training session, to ensure they are aware of the key areas the TA has been trained in and the advice they have received.

Focus	Activities	Timing
To train TAs to work with children with SEND	• Group TAs in class/departmental groups. Have them review the class behaviour policies. Swap with other classes to ensure all TAs are aware how to work with all children with challenging behaviour.	30 minutes
	• PC Training. Group TAs in class groups. Review the use of Clicker7 and Writing With Symbols PC programs. Ensure all are aware of how to support children who cannot write.	30 minutes
	• Phonics and numeracy training. TAs who run phonics interventions groups should have their training updated regularly.	30 minutes
	• PE Training. PE leader or outside consultant to train TAs how to include children with physical disabilities in PE lessons.	30 minutes

Fig. 66 Session plan 2: Training TAs to work with children with SEND

When I asked the tweeting mainstream teachers how they used their TAs to work with children with SEND I had some interesting and informative answers. These are the ones I considered to be using best practice:

(@bethben92) said:
- for specific interventions, e.g. fit to learn, music interaction, sensory diet activities, socially speaking
- to repeat instructions and break down instructions for the child
- to set timed targets within independent work
- to be someone for the child to speak their ideas to before writing
- to provide encouragement.

@bethben92 also said that as deputy head and SENDCo she has made it a non-negotiable for their teachers to work with children with SEND as it was embarrassing if TAs knew the child better than the teacher during discussions and at annual reviews.

- @isright said: 'I use my TA as a personal teacher for SEND kids – not 1:1 but someone that gives them small step achievable targets daily. Between us we work 3/5 or 2/5 days each week alternating. Usually means I get SEND 2 or 3 times every day in my group'
- @MrHeadComputing @jwscattergood @MacJude all agreed that the best use of a TA is to work with the class which in turn frees up the teacher's time to enable them to devote specialist attention to the children with SEND.

Properly trained TAs are worth their weight in gold. As a special school teacher and leader I know many highly trained TAs. It must be remembered that as good as they are they should not be used as substitute teachers for children with SEND or those with lower cognitive ability. TAs should complement the work of the teacher rather than replace them. They should promote independence skills and help the child to stay on task.

Basic tips for TAs working with children with SEND
The role of the TA is to support children with SEND with all aspects of work, care and social issues.
The TA should feed back to the teacher on how the work was achieved and what level of support was given to the child.
The TA should listen to the teacher's instructions and break the instructions down into 'now' and 'next' chunks.
The TA should encourage independent reading and writing.
The TA should help to differentiate the work. (See twilight training plan 4: Differentiation for children with SEND p 244)
The TA should contribute ideas to the lesson plan.
The TA should think about their questioning skills: • avoid leading questions • keep questions clear and specific • encourage the child to answer • use a mixture of open and closed questions and find a balance that allows the child to succeed and build confidence.
The TA should have a good grasp of behaviour strategies used by the class teacher and should model the behaviour they want to see, e.g. quiet voices and moving around the room in a calm and orderly fashion.
Reminder: TAs are part of the Ofsted framework and will be inspected; they need to be aware of their responsibilities.
The TA needs to find out as much information about the difficulties the child is living with in order to be the best possible assistance to the child. Ask the SENDCo for relevant reading material or seek out experts on Twitter.
The TA must complete safeguarding training. Remember many children with SEND are vulnerable and as staff working with children with SEND, teachers and TAs are vulnerable too.

Fig. 67 Handout: Basic tips for TAs working with children with SEND

Top tip

TAs should form positive relationships with children with SEND as this is beneficial to whole school improvement, and in some cases can be the most positive relationship the child gets. (@alanlee and @jwscattergood)

This point is vital for many children, not just those with SEND. In some cases the teacher and the TA are the most steadying and possibly the most influential and caring person a child encounters in their young life. This point should be added to any training for school staff.

3. Training your teachers to work with children with SEND

Teaching children with SEND requires different skills from working with children in mainstream classrooms. The teacher could be faced with children with behaviour difficulties, medical difficulties, physical difficulties or learning difficulties. As we have seen in part one different teaching skills will also be required. As the SENDCo it is important to provide training for your teachers.

Focus	Activities	Timing
Train teachers to work with children with SEND in the areas of assessment, planning and visuals.	• Train your teachers to assess below the National Curriculum using P Scales. • Group your teachers in departments. Give out some work completed by children with SEND. Have the teachers assess and moderate the work together to ensure agreement on assessment.	1 hour
	• Give your teachers a topic and ask them to plan a series of lessons that will successfully include a child with a visual impairment. Compare strategies.	30 minutes
	• Train teachers in the use of visual timetables and 'now and next' cards.	30 minutes

Fig. 68 Session plan 3: Training your teachers to work with children with SEND

Share this guide with your teaching staff.

Basic tips for teachers working with children with SEND
Plan in extra time to enable you to discuss objectives and targets for children with SEND with your TA. They need an overall picture of your aims.
Ignore any diagnostic labels; they may help to gain finances and resources through the statement/EHC plan, but will not help with teaching.
Personalise each learning objective for each child with SEND.
Build time into your lesson for the child with SEND to answer your questions. AAC users need time to navigate their communication system and the class should be encouraged to allow them time.
Keep instructions short and focused and give no more than two instructions at a time.
Repeat your instructions and provide them in pictures, if appropriate.
Give immediate feedback and praise where appropriate.
Provide sensory objects to aid their understanding, e.g. things they can touch and feel and smell.

Fig. 69 Handout: Basic tips for teachers working with children with SEND

2. Behaviour for learning

This is an important area to consider when aiming to achieve inclusion for all. From a quick survey on Twitter most behaviour training is reviewed and updated at the start of each new academic year. The most effective approach for behaviour is to train the whole school together during an INSET day. I have included a training plan for a full INSET day (p 258), but here I have selected two areas of behaviour for learning to provide as example twilight session training plans.

Use these points to introduce your behaviour for learning training:

- Begin by reminding all staff about the school behaviour policy – has everyone read it?
- Have all new staff understood how it relates to children with SEND and internalised it?
- Remind staff that good behaviour should be part of the culture and ethos of the school – it is an expectation that children will behave appropriately, including those with challenging behaviours, with the correct support.
- Does everyone know how and where to seek help if required?

- Is there a whole school reward system for behaviour? Consider the use of class dojo (p 124) this makes use of animations and is appealing to children with special needs.
- Do all teachers make class rules with their classes to give the children ownership? Are children with SEND given input to the rules?
- Do all children, including those with SEND, make a learning agreement at the start of each new year? Provide support if necessary.
- Are token economy systems in place (p 124) and do they include all children? Does the token economy system take account of the personal interests and preferences of those with special needs? Is it relevant to them and do they understand it?

Session 1: Using visual aids to improve behaviour in children with SEND

Communication is often at the heart of many behaviour issues for children with ADHD, ASC and LDD. School staff working with children with SEND require specialised training to overcome this barrier to learning.

In part 1 of the book we saw the value of the use of visual supports for children with special needs. One area where this support is paramount is communication. This training plan is to train your staff to make use of visual supports for children with SEND.

Training focus	To improve behaviour using visual aids
Who will be trained?	All teachers and TAs
Own research time required?	None
Resources required	Paper, laminator, PC symbols or pictures
Budget required	None
Problems that may arise	Boardmaker not available on PC
Solutions to problems	Use photographs
Any specific planning advice	Consistent use of pictures or symbols
Advantage of this training	Will improve behaviour through consistent use
Evaluation	Can everyone make visuals?

Fig. 70 Overview: Using visual aids to improve behaviour in children with SEND

Session plan: Using visual aids to improve behaviour in children with SEND

Focus	Activities	Timing
To use visual supports to improve behaviour	• Choose 3 areas of behaviour you wish to improve, for example: 　1. A timetable for the morning's activities. 　2. Sitting at the table sensibly and not calling out or annoying the child next to you. 　3. Leaving a favourite activity to move on to another activity.	30 minutes
	• Choose your pictures, make your visuals (the pages that follow include examples or a variety of visuals).	1 hour
	• Work with staff as a class group to ensure everyone knows how to use them.	30 minutes

Fig. 71 Session 1: Using visual aids to improve behaviour in children with SEND

Introduce your training by telling staff of the benefits of using visuals:

Benefits of using visuals:

- They will help with communication barriers and therefore improve behaviour
- They are simple to make
- With the correct training a teacher or TA can make one quickly to support any new situation
- They may be laminated for ease of cleaning
- They are portable
- They build self-esteem and self-confidence
- Allays most anxiety
- Teaches sequencing and next steps.

Use these steps to train all your teachers and TAs to make a visual timetable for a child with SEND to help them cope with a whole day in school.

Creating a visual timetable

1. Decide on the layout of your board – horizontal or vertical – the National Autistic Society recommends vertical as this resembles a list which can be ticked off.
2. Create individual word or picture cards or a combination of both; this will be determined by the cognitive ability of the child – can they read or are pictures a better alternative?
3. Use clear words or pictures that convey information at a glance and be consistent in their use, e.g. the same picture should always be used to denote a reading lesson.
4. Split the day into chunks of time – this should include individual lessons, break times and lunchtime.
5. Include other time slots such as returning the register, lunchtime club or other extra-curricular activities.
6. If a whole day is too much for the child to cope with, split the day into manageable time slots.
7. Personalise the board to the child, e.g. for a child who enjoys collecting bugs at lunchtimes, add a picture of a bug on the lunch break picture.
8. Attach Velcro in strips to your board and to your pictures.
9. Add a 'finished' pocket so that your child can remove the chunks of time as they are completed.

Fig. 72 Handout: Creating a visual timetable

Top tip

Think about the colour of your visuals. Some children cannot cope with bright eye-catching colours and others will prefer them. Choose pastel colours of pale blue or pale green for visuals for ASC children. It is also worth remembering that for some children the noise of the Velcro ripping may also be a trigger for a sensory shutdown. If this is the case you can cover the Velcro in duct tape to silence the Velcro.

This example of a vertical timetable has been kindly supplied by Lynn McCann (@ReachoutASC) who is my number one 'go to' person for all things relating to children with ASC.

Fig. 73 Visual timetable example

The next step is to train your staff in the use of a visual timetable. Discuss the following key points:

- It is good practice for teachers to display one for whole class use
- Refer to it at the start of each new activity
- Teach the children how to sequence by using the visual timetable
- At the start of each day the teacher should remind the class of the activities they will enjoy that day – this ensures the child with SEND is included fully and, although they are in possession of their own visual timetable, they do not stand out from the crowd
- Train staff that children will use them in different ways: some will remove the picture as the activity is completed, while others will take the picture with them to the activity
- Use hand over hand support to teach the sequence of activities and how to remove the picture as it is finished
- Teach the child to check their timetable for news of the next activity
- Teachers and TAs should withdraw their support over time if possible.

Top tip
Teach the child how to use the visual timetable.

How to make a quick and easy morning routine timetable

Here is a quick and easy visual timetable that you could make in your training session. It may be attached to a piece of card. It is ideal for children who will only be able to cope with activities until break. Therefore your timetable might only consist of three or four picture symbols.

For example, the morning routine might consist of completion of the register and the date, followed by maths and coats on for break time. The visual for this would be similar to the example below:

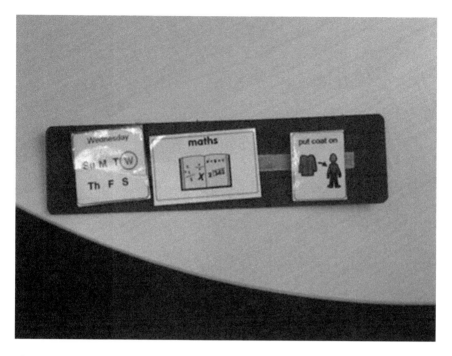

Fig. 74 Morning routine timetable

Now you have trained your staff in the art of making visual supports teach them to think outside the box. How can these visuals best help teachers and TAs to run a calm and ordered classroom? Here are some other examples to use in your twilight session.

How to make 'now' and 'next' cards

Children who lack organisational and sequencing skills are often confused and may not be able to convey their lack of understanding of what is required of them. This may manifest itself in a behaviour tantrum. These children will benefit from a 'now' and 'next' card. This is very quick to make and does exactly what it says; it informs the child what is happening now and what activity they will be moving on to next. These visuals are particularly helpful for children in mainstream schools, as the environment and atmosphere is far busier in special schools. These children are seeking comfort and reassurance for what is coming next.

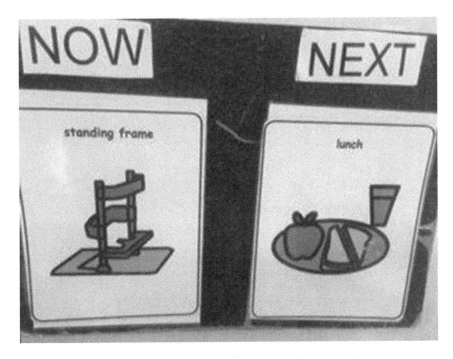

Fig. 75 Now and next card The Picture Communication Symbols 1981-2011 by Mayer-Johnson LLC. All rights reserved Worldwide. Used with permission. Boardmaker is a trademark of Mayer-Johnson LLC.

Top tip

By providing this type of structure for the child you are helping them to overcome anxiety and fear of the unknown. You are communicating with them without using words that they may not understand. You are pre-empting their problems before they arise.

How to add a visual timetable to a ruler

Train your staff to add a visual timetable to a ruler for older children to use. The principle is the same but is more discrete.

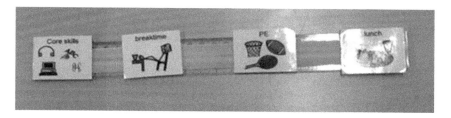

Fig. 76 Visual timetable on a ruler

As the teacher you can choose whether the whole class would benefit from having class rules displayed or if they should be confined to the child's work area.

Session 2: Understanding behaviour in children with SEND

Children with SEND can cause many problems for mainstream teachers. Teachers need to alter the way they think about behaviour. Children with SEND react very differently to their mainstream peers.

A common problem identified in a mainstream classroom is the child who cannot cope and who subsequently displays some challenging and aggressive behaviours. Almost all behaviour is a form of communication. This particular type of communication is undesirable and may disrupt the learning of their peers and valuable learning time is lost as a result.

This twilight training session is intended to help teachers understand more about behaviour in children with SEND.

Training focus	To understand the behaviour of children with SEND
Who will be trained?	All teachers and TAs
Own research time required?	Allow time to research reward systems if school uses them
Resources required	Whole school behaviour policy
Budget required	None
Problems that may arise	Staff who do not want to change their strategies
Solutions to problems	Give examples of how new strategies have worked; convince reluctant staff by showing them successful methods
Any specific planning advice	Take on board all ideas to ensure it is a whole school training session
Advantage of this training	Consistency of behaviour management
Disadvantages of this training	Staff may prefer own methods
Evaluation	What is the impact; has the behaviour improved?

Fig. 77 Overview training plan: Understanding behaviour in children with SEND

Focus	Activities	Timing
To understand behaviour in children with SEND	All teachers and TAs review whole school behaviour policy. Does it reflect current practice at the school? Discuss whole school strategies, for example: – low voices from staff – model the behaviour you wish to see. Discuss class rules: do they reflect the whole school behaviour policy?	30 minutes
	• Train staff how to recognise and handle a sensory shutdown.	30 minutes
	• Staff to review all the behaviour for learning plans for each child. Are they current; does everyone understand the need for consistency?	30 minutes
	• Ask for questions from staff. Is everyone clear on the policies? Are all staff happy with the behaviour strategy at the school.	30 minutes

Fig. 78 Session 2: **Understanding behaviour in children with SEND**

Sensory shutdowns and temper tantrums

Some children with ASC and other sensory processing conditions may have a sensory shutdown. Step one is to train your teachers to know the difference between a temper tantrum and a sensory shutdown. A sensory shutdown looks like a temper tantrum to the untrained eye but in reality is completely different.

Use these points to train your staff to determine whether the behaviour is a shutdown or a tantrum. Consider this first list of triggers.

Triggers	Yes or no?
Loud noises	
Sudden noises	
Chaotic environment	
Bright lights	
Pens clicking	
Constant tapping	
Many different voices in the area of the child	
Child next to them prodding them	
Fluorescent lighting	
Someone touching child's arm, shoulder or face	

Fig. 79 Sensory shutdown indicators

If you have answered 'yes' to most of the above, it is likely the child is having a sensory shutdown. A sensory shutdown may be caused by any one of the above list, or a combination. The shutdown occurs when there is too much sensory information for the child to process. Most sensory shutdowns trigger the 'fight or flight' response, which makes it very difficult to cope with. A good example of this might be your school's Christmas fair.

Encourage your staff to close their eyes and picture the annual Christmas fair.

The child is faced with loud music, crowds, noise, people dressed up, bright lights and music. This may be too much sensory information for a child with ASC to cope with. The inevitable happens and the child screams, cries, hits out, kicks or runs off. A sensory shutdown will not disappear by giving the child their own way or by rewarding them. The amount of sensory input needs to be reduced.

Consider this second list of triggers.

Triggers	Yes or no?
Not having their own way	
Non-compliance with instructions	
Attention-seeking	
Refusal to take turns	

Fig. 80 Tantrum indicators

If you have answered 'yes' to most of the above, it is likely the child is having a temper tantrum rather than a sensory overload. The resulting behaviour will be similar and will manifest itself in crying, screaming, kicking and hitting others. All of these behaviours are highly inappropriate in any situation. The tantrum will stop when the child receives the attention they desire or they get their own way.

The main thing your staff should remember is that a child having a tantrum is in control of their actions. A child having a sensory shutdown is not in control of their actions.

Top tip
A sensory shutdown should not be treated as poor behaviour.

Work through the ideas in the following handout to train the staff how to deal with a sensory shutdown and a temper tantrum.

How to deal with a sensory shutdown

1. Give the child time and space.
2. For a child who is on the floor, avoid standing over them; sit on the floor with them.
3. Remind other children to give the child some space and not to crowd round to see what is happening.
4. Reduce the amount of sensory input by taking the child away from the situation that is causing sensory overload.
5. Resist the temptation to talk to the child – remember you are aiming to reduce the sensory input.
6. If appropriate for the child, apply deep pressure over the child's body in the form of a weighted blanket or a weighted cushion. If none is available, seek permission to give a tight hug. This often helps.
7. Give the child time to come round.
8. Avoid taking it personally if the child is physically or verbally aggressive. Aggression of this nature is due to panic and fear and members of staff should not try to restrain the child.

Prevention is always better than cure

- Learn and look for the signs of sensory overload with each child. Stimming is self stimulatory behaviour and is usually seen in the form of rocking, hand flapping, walking in circles or similar. An increase in the child's preferred stimming is often an indicator that all is not well. Take action!
- Use your safe place in the classroom or in another room for the child to have peace and quiet.
- Provide noise-blocking headphones.
- Avoid trying to 'normalise' the child – if the child is deeply unhappy in assembly due to noise, lights and movement, do not force them to go to assembly.

How to deal with a tantrum

1. Avoid attempting to reason with the child while they are in the middle of a tantrum.
2. Direct the child to a different activity to remove them from the situation.
3. Make it clear that the undesirable behaviour will not result in the child having what they desire.
4. Don't give in to temptation and reward the child by giving them attention.
5. Show the child the correct way to gain attention.
6. If the tantrum continues, tell the child to 'stop'. Simple advice but often forgotten.
7. Take the child to the calming area or chill-out room.
8. If all else fails and the child will not be removed, remove the audience – take the class to a safe place.

Fig. 81 Handout: How to deal with sensory shutdowns and tantrums

Calm to angry chart

Train your staff to make a visual similar to the one below to help with behavioural difficulties. This is a 'calm to angry' chart, which is a communication tool that can be used in a number of different ways: children can tell staff how they are feeling and staff can help the child to understand how to calm down in stages. Children with ASC are not always aware of what calm is, so the base line is important.

This chart and the instructions were made and supplied by Lynn McCann @reachoutASC.

Visit www.reachoutasc.com for top resources for children with ASC.

Fig. 82 Calm to angry chart

This visual supplied by @reachoutASC supports a child with staying on task.

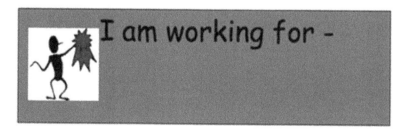

Fig. 83: Example visuals

> **Top tip**
>
> Visit www.5pointscale.com for information on how to teach social and emotional concepts to children with ASC.

3. Differentiation for children with SEND

Differentiation for children with SEND has been debated over the years and some teachers claim there is no need to differentiate. The fact is that we all differentiate the work whether we are aware of it or not. Differentiation is any way in which the work is modified to help the child to learn. This could be something simple such as moving a child with visual problems to the front of the class, or it could be something far more complicated.

> **Top tip**
>
> Remember! Differentiation is not low expectations.

This twilight training session is intended to help teachers to master the art of differentiation for children with SEND.

Training focus	Teachers and TAs to be able to differentiate
Who will be trained?	Teachers and TAs
Own research time required?	An hour to research PC programs
Resources required	Examples of AAC, iPad/tablet, chunky pencils, writing slopes
Budget required	None
Problems that may arise	Teacher thinks TA should differentiate for child with SEND
Solutions to problems	Remind them that all teachers are teachers of SEND
Any specific planning advice	Allow time for staff to try the resources
Advantage of this training	Equips teachers with the confidence to teach all children with SEND
Disadvantages of this training	None
Evaluation	Can all children access the lesson?

Fig. 84 Overview training plan: Understanding behaviour in children with SEND

Focus	Activities	Timing
To train teachers and TAs to differentiate to include all children.	• Give an overview of iPad/tablet/PC apps the school has to improve all aspects of the curriculum. Allow staff time to try some of them out so they have first hand experience of how they can help the child.	45 minutes
	• Train staff to use AAC. Have an array of Talking Tin Lids and BIGmacks and train staff how to record on them to allow the child to join in question and answer sessions.	30 minutes
	• Provide a lesson plan and ask teachers and TAs to differentiate all aspects of the lesson for a child working at P Levels. This would include questioning techniques, written work and support for reading.	30 minutes
	• Allow staff to experience working with all the practical resources such as chunky pencils, writing slopes, e-readers.	15 minutes

Fig. 85 Session plan: **Understanding behaviour in children with SEND**

Remind your teachers that there are three main types of differentiation:

1. Differentiation by task – where different groups of children have different tasks according to their ability to enable them to succeed.
2. Differentiation by support – where some children are given extra help from a TA or the teacher.
3. Differentiation by outcome – where children achieve as much as they can on their own level.

I am not a fan of differentiation by outcome. This is where there is no extra or personalised target setting for the child. Good planning and individualised target setting as in differentiation by task are better forms of differentiation and allow the child to succeed.

However, a combination of the above three methods is the solution to good differentiation. For children with SEND, a personalised approach is needed. They may need one method for one subject and another method for another subject. No two lessons will be the same and a number of factors will affect the outcome.

Here are some quick and easy tips to use when training teachers about differentiation for children with SEND. Details of all of the resources mentioned are given in Part 1.

Quick and easy differentiation tips when working with children with SEND

1. Break the work into small chunks.
2. Write down instructions for the child to refer to.
3. Use visuals to support the learning.
4. Build in some 'time out' for a child who struggles to stay on task.
5. Use questioning at different levels.
6. Provide key words to scaffold writing.
7. Teach only what is necessary.
8. Use ICT in the form of apps such as 'Book creator' (itunes.apple.com/gb/app/book-creator-for-ipad-create/id442378070?mt=8).
9. Consider whether the work needs to be enlarged for children with visual impairments.
10. Consider grouping the child with a more able peer.
11. Use Clicker 6 or 7 to support non-writers.
12. Use AAC for non-communicating children.
13. Use real objects whenever possible.
14. Use symbols to aid understanding.
15. Use simplified worksheets.
16. Have a one-to-one teaching session with the child to introduce a new topic.
17. Include multi-sensory approach to learning, if required.
18. Offer different ways to record work, e.g. orally – matching labels to pictures or diagrams.
19. Think about using QR Codes to avoid writing tasks.
20. Provide practical resources such as chunky pencils, writing slopes, adapted scissors, weighted blankets, fidget toys.

Remember: withdrawal from the classroom to work is not differentiation.

How to approach differentiation

1. Have high expectations of all children at all times – a diagnosis of an illness or a behaviour difficulty is not an excuse.
2. Always prepare the child with SEND for any change in routine or anything they are not expecting.
3. Take the time to teach the child how to behave: explain social norms such as queuing with other children; explain how to be polite rather than voicing their true feelings or speaking their mind.
4. Build in rest breaks for those who struggle to stay on task.

5. Avoid damaging confidence by correcting every single mistake.
6. Encourage a child with LDD or ASC to try new experiences by supporting and scaffolding.
7. Consider flexible grouping or working in pairs.
8. Be clear about rules: children with ASC become very upset if anyone in the room breaks the rules – that includes the teacher and TA.
9. Use lists – children with SEND like to tick off their day; they often enjoy the structure of this action.
10. Good differentiation involves finding the interests of the child and using them to your advantage.
11. Use role play rather than asking questions.
12. Ad lib your way through classic books – children with SEND enjoy the story but cannot understand the language of the author.

Fig. 86: Handout: Differentiation tips when working with children with SEND

Top tip

'The key thing is to remember that the TA/LSA is not the differentiation, nor is it their responsibility to differentiate the work.' (@funASDteacher) Follow @funASDteacher for top tips on differentiation.

Fiona's folders

When I asked teachers on Twitter for their tactics for differentiation, I received a wonderful solution from @FKRitson. Like many teachers, Fiona is unhappy that she is unable to spend as much time as she would like with her children with SEND. This is her solution.

Fiona has devised a folder for every unit, for every year group and for each lesson. All are designed for the child to work with a TA or independently if possible. 'All folders have the same layout to encourage the child to be as independent as possible. There are differentiated resources or different, simpler questions, sentence starters, broken down grids, simplified model answers, etc. all linked to the lesson'. (@FKRitson)

A folder containing resources such as these would be time-consuming, but it would be worth training your staff to use Fiona's idea. This is excellent differentiation and encourages inclusion for all.

4. Technology training

The iPad and other mobile devices are not popular with all mainstream teachers for a variety of reasons. However, for children with ASC, ADHD and LDD there are many benefits and staff should be made aware of these.

This twilight training session is intended to train teachers and TAs to make the best use of technology.

Training focus	Train staff to make the best use of technology
Who will be trained?	Teachers and TAs
Own research time required?	Allow several hours to find favourite apps
Resources required	iPads/tablet PCs
Budget required	None if apps are available
Problems that may arise	Staff are not receptive to technology
Solutions to problems	Show them how to use the technology with a particular child in mind
Any specific planning advice	Give staff time to try out the apps
Advantage of this training	Will have good knowledge of how to use many different apps to enhance lessons
Disadvantages of this training	None
Evaluation	Has the technology added value to your lesson?

Fig. 87 Overview training plan: Understanding behaviour in children with SEND

Focus	Activities	Timing
To train staff to make the best use of technology for children with SEND	• Train staff to use Proloquo2go and then have them practise entering a child's daily news.	30 minutes
	• Give staff a list of useful apps for numeracy and literacy and allow time to find their favourite ones for a particular child with SEND.	30 minutes
	• Train staff to use Book Creator and have them make a book.	1 hour

Fig. 88 Session plan: Technology training

There are many benefits to using technology for children with SEND. Sometimes it is the only way in which a child can access the lesson. For example, a child without a voice needs some form of technology to provide them with a voice. A child with limited use of their hands who cannot write needs a form of technology to record their work. These are a few of my own ideas concerning technology. Teachers will have their ideas depending on the children they teach and their own experiences.

Benefits of iPads and mobile devices:

- Lightweight and portable
- A robust cover can be purchased for the iPad which limits damage if dropped
- Touchscreen is easier to use than a mouse for those with co-ordination difficulties
- Can be used to support communication
- Many apps available
- Promotes independence
- Children are motivated to learn through the use of brightly-coloured images and animations
- Helps teach new skills
- Access to the Internet which provides many free apps and programs.

Disadvantages:

- Cost – they are expensive
- May be thrown by children during a sensory shutdown or temper tantrum
- Children become attached to them and reluctant to let them go and return to lesson.
- Some children do not like the bright colours and may refuse to use the technology.

Best apps for children with SEND

I asked my colleagues on Twitter for their favourite apps for children with SEND. Some of these are recommended for literacy, maths, other curriculum areas, sensory learners, mood changing apps, rewards and to support any other lesson. You could encourage your staff to research these apps as a useful starting point. Prices and apps were correct at the time of publication. New apps are being released daily so it is worth keeping up to speed with new releases.

App name	Weblink	Curriculum area	Description	Cost
Book Creator	https://itunes.apple.com/gb/app/book-creator-for-ipad-create/id442378070?mt=8	Literacy; PSHE	Create own ibooks	£3.99
Autism iHelp	https://itunes.apple.com/gb/app/autism-ihelp-play/id521485216?mt=8	Speech and language	Language intervention tool	Free
Proloquo2go	http://www.assistiveware.com/product/proloquo2go	Speech and language	Language development app	£199.99

App name	Weblink	Curriculum area	Description	Cost
iTrace	http://itraceapp.com/	Writing	Writing, spelling and letter identification	£2.99
Maths Drills Lite	https://itunes.apple.com/gb/app/math-drills-lite/id302881372?mt=8	Maths	Basic maths skills	Free
Mathmateer™	https://itunes.apple.com/gb/app/mathmateer-free/id408770902?mt=8	Maths	Teaches the 4 basic operations through rocket launch	Free
Maths Puppy – Bingo Challenge	https://itunes.apple.com/gb/app/math-puppy-bingo-challenge/id450482382?mt=8	Maths	Basic maths skills	Free
Time Timer	https://itunes.apple.com/gb/app/time-timer/id332520417?mt=8	Stay on task	Teaches time	£2.29
ChoreMonster	https://www.amazon.co.uk/ChoreMonster-Inc/dp/B00L2QZZQU?ie=UTF8&*Version*=1&*entries*=0	Rewards	Teaches household tasks and rewards	Free
Calm Counter – Social Story and Anger Management Tool	https://itunes.apple.com/gb/app/calm-counter-social-story/id470369893?mt=8	General anger management	Calming techniques and anger management	£2.29
Choose It Maker	http://www.inclusive.co.uk/chooseit-maker-3-p6708	Language and literacy	For teachers to create personalized teaching materials	£55.00 for 3 month subscription
See. Touch. Learn	https://itunes.apple.com/gb/app/see.touch.learn./id406826506?mt=8	Teaching	For teachers to make visual resources for SEND and ASC	Free
Talk Assist	http://appsforaac.net/app/talk-assist	Speech and language	Converts text in to language	Free
Talking Rex	http://talking-rex-the-dinosaur.soft112.com/	Speech and language	Helps with speech and language by encouraging children to hear their own voices through the dinosaur	Free
Talking Tom Cat 2	https://itunes.apple.com/gb/app/talking-tom-cat-2/id421997825?mt=8	Speech and language	Voice recording and games with reward	Free

App name	Weblink	Curriculum area	Description	Cost
ABC Pocket Phonics Lite	https://itunes.apple.com/gb/app/abc-pocketphonics-lite/id302689971?mt=8	Literacy	Phonics	Free
Math vs Zombies	https://itunes.apple.com/gb/app/math-vs-zombies-2/id888205622?mt=8	Maths	General maths skills	£3.99
Mental Maths	http://www.topmarks.co.uk/maths-games/7-11-years/mental-maths	Maths	Ordering and sequencing numbers	Free
Kid Maths	https://itunes.apple.com/gb/app/math-kid/id465213584?mt=8	Maths	Basic maths	Free
AB Maths	https://itunes.apple.com/gb/app/ab-maths-fun-games-for-kids/id412827941?mt=8	Maths	Teaches the 4 operations through games	£1.49
Zoom Maths app	https://itunes.apple.com/gb/app/motion-math-zoom/id451793073?mt=8	Maths	Decimals	£2.29
Animal Sounds	https://itunes.apple.com/gb/app/animal-sounds-fun-toddler/id445259736?mt=8	Sensory	Teaches animal sounds to very young children or SEND	Free
Puppet Pals	https://itunes.apple.com/gb/app/puppet-pals-hd/id342076546?mt=8	Literacy/ speech and language	Improves speech and language	Free
Kids can match	https://itunes.apple.com/gb/app/kids-can-match-animals-vocal/id403443510?mt=8	Literacy	Improves speech and language and memory	Free
Bluster!	https://itunes.apple.com/gb/app/bluster!/id416160693?mt=8	Literacy	Vocabulary building	Free
Chicktionary Lite	https://itunes.apple.com/us/app/chicktionary-game-scrambled/id365374807?mt=8	Literacy	Aids vocabulary and spelling	Free
Futaba Word Games	https://itunes.apple.com/gb/app/word-games-for-kids-futaba/id426517722?mt=8	Literacy	Aids vocabulary	Free

App name	Weblink	Curriculum area	Description	Cost
ABC Sight Words	https://itunes.apple.com/gb/app/abc-sight-words-writing-free/id379874412?mt=8	Literacy	Aids writing	Free
Dragon Dictate	https://itunes.apple.com/gb/app/dragon-dictation/id341446764?mt=8	Literacy/ dyslexia	Voice recognition to aid writing	Free
Make Sentences	https://itunes.apple.com/gb/app/make-sentences-age-5-35/id587265511?mt=8	Literacy	Interactive language app	Free
WritePad	https://itunes.apple.com/gb/app/writepad-for-ipad-handwriting/id363618389?mt=8	Literacy	Aids writing	£3.99
Times Table Clock	https://itunes.apple.com/gb/app/times-table-clock/id366282531?mt=8	Maths/ sequencing	Fun way to learn times tables	£1.49
Starfall	https://itunes.apple.com/gb/app/starfall-free/id707189889?mt=8	Literacy	Letter recognition	Free
Dyslexia Quest	https://itunes.apple.com/gb/app/dyslexia-quest/id448166369?mt=8	Literacy/ dyslexia	Aids memory and tests learning skills	£2.99
Dinosaur Letters Lite	https://itunes.apple.com/gb/app/dinosaur-letters-lite/id693840398?mt=8	Literacy/ dyslexia	Aids learning letters	Free
Hairy Letters	https://itunes.apple.com/gb/app/hairy-letters/id410276288?mt=8	Literacy/ dyslexia	Aids reading by teaching letters and sounds	£2.99
DD's Dictionary	https://itunes.apple.com/gb/app/dds-dictionary-dyslexics-dictionary/id590239077?mt=8	Literacy/ dyslexia	Aids spelling	Free
Ginger Page	http://www.gingersoftware.com/ios-writing-app#.VycuG6MrLow	Literacy/ dyslexia	Writing app for ios	Free

Fig. 89 Apps for SEND

Top tip

For excellent Scratch activities to help you to teach computing to children with SEND see Sheffield eLearning team
www.sheffieldclc.net/sen-scratch-activities

5. Assessment training

This twilight session will cover assessment for children working below the level of the National Curriculum.

Training focus	To train teachers to work on assessment for children working at P Levels/scales
Who will be trained?	Teachers
Own research time required?	Allow an hour to recap your own knowledge
Resources required	P Scales document
Budget required	None
Problems that may arise	Teachers may not have experienced work as low as P3
Solutions to problems	Give some examples of work at this level
Any specific planning advice	Show lots of work at different P Levels from P1-P8
Advantage of this training	Gives teachers a thorough understanding of assessment for all children
Disadvantages of this training	Teachers may not have children at this level this year and may resent training time.
Evaluation	Can all teachers assess below the NC?

Fig. 90 Overview training plan: Assessment

Focus	Activities	Timing
To train all teachers in the use of P Levels/scales.	• Show some work in a chosen subject such as literacy assessed at P3 P5 and P7. Teachers to discuss why it is that level using the P Scale document.	30 minutes
	• Give teachers an example lesson plan and ask them to plan a piece of work to be produced at P3 P5 P7. How would the work look at this level?	1 hour
	• Swap the work around between the teachers. Have discussions to see if everyone agrees what the work looks like at those 3 levels.	30 minutes

Fig. 91 Session plan: Assessment training

P scales and performance descriptors

The P scales are used to assess the progress made by children in Key Stages 1-3 who have SEND and who are working below the level of the National Curriculum. All schools have to use the P scales; they are not confined to special schools. The term P Scales is often used interchangeably with the term P levels.

- 'This document supplements the National Curriculum by specifying performance attainment targets (P scales) and performance descriptors for pupils aged 5-16 with special educational needs (SEN) who cannot access the National Curriculum.'
- 'The use of P scales is statutory for reporting teacher assessment in English, mathematics and science to the Department for Education at the end of key stages 1 and 2.'
- In KS4, P scales are non- statutory.
- P scales measure below the National Curriculum and should only be used for children with SEND. It should not be used for those who are currently working below age related expectations but who do not have special needs.
- P scales should not be used as a curriculum.
- 'The performance descriptors for P1–P3 are the same across English, mathematics and science.'
- Schools can choose to continue to use EYFS profile, rather than P scales up to the end of Year 1.
- P scales are used in target setting and for tracking progress.
- Currently there is a gap in assessing attainment for children who are working above the P scales but below the level of the national tests.

Overview of assessment software packages

Here are some of the current software packages for assessing attainment and progress for children with SEND:

- B Squared (www.bsquared.co.uk)
  B Squared has developed a system to work alongside the new National Curriculum and uses levels or end of year outcomes. B Squared offers assessment in tiny steps for low P scales/levels, National Curriculum, Foundation and pre-entry levels and entry levels. B Squared is also cloud-based and may be used on an iPad for ease of access.

- Pivats (www3.lancashire.gov.uk)
  Pivats is a system devised by Lancashire LA 'to inform target setting for pupils of all ages whose performance is outside national expectations'. Pivats uses the P scales and allows schools to show progress in English, maths, science, computing and PSHE. Progress is shown individually or for cohorts.

- MAPP (www.thedalesschool.org)
  MAPP was developed by The Dales School in North Yorkshire for planning, assessment and recording for learners with SEND.

- CASPA (caspaonline.co.uk)
  Comparison and Analysis of Special Pupil Attainment (CASPA) is a tool that
  enables schools to benchmark attainment and progress for individuals and
  cohorts. CASPA includes the DfE progression materials to allow a national
  comparison of data for Ofsted, school improvement officers and other
  external agencies.

The most important thing your staff needs to be aware of is the need to match
interventions to individual needs. Generic interventions will not work, as every
learner with SEND is different, despite sharing a diagnosis with others.

Look for patterns in their progress and use this to inform your next steps for
planning. Use the school's assessment tool wisely and it will reflect progress.
REMEMBER: children with special educational needs often have spiky profiles.

Top tip

Some children with profound and complex neurological conditions will
make lateral progress. This is acceptable and should be celebrated.

---

6. Training on a specific area of SEND: introduction to dyslexia

I am going to use the subject of dyslexia for this two-hour twilight session. This
is intended to serve as an introduction to dyslexia, or a reminder session for
teachers who have children with dyslexia in their class. Training should be more
specialised, but this will be a starting point and will be of benefit to student
teachers or mainstream teachers who need a refresher.

Training focus	To introduce the topic of dyselxia or reintroduce it as a useful reminder for all staff working with children with dyslexia
Who will be trained?	Invite teachers and TAs working with children with dyslexia. Any who are more experienced can share their knowledge with the group. Invite student teachers and NQTs.
Own research time required	Allow time to gather your information using part 1 of this book and the presentation provided which summarises the information in an easily accessible manner.
Resources required	Flip chart, IWB for presentation, handout of presentation slides. PC for demonstration.
Budget required	None
Problems that may arise	Technical issues, presentation not working.

Solutions to problems	Provide handout of presentation slides as a backup plan.
Any specific planning advice	Stick to the time allotted. Dyslexia is a complex topic and staff may struggle with the varied concepts of the condition.
Advantage of this training.	No financial outlay. Can train and refresh the skills of several staff in a single twilight session.
Disadvantages of this training.	Staff may not be receptive to the information. Some may continue to believe that dyslexia can be 'cured' with the correct teaching.
Evaluation	Children will be on task and producing better work. This will be evident in the marking in their books. Children will be happier in school.

Fig. 92 Overview training plan: Introduction to dyslexia

Focus	Activities	Timing
To update staff on working with children with dyslexia	• Starter activity: Ask staff to draw a well known National Rail sign. They will struggle despite seeing it daily. Explain this is how dyslexia feels to a child (suggested by @MariaStMarys)	15 minutes
	• Introduce the topic of dyslexia. Ask staff what their understanding of dyslexia is. Have staff brainstorm their understanding of dyslexia, making notes on a flip chart or sticky notes. Allow time for discussion in groups.	30 minutes
	• Ask staff for their thoughts on how to spot a child with dyslexia. Answers should include: reads slowly, takes excessive time to write or complete tasks, avoids reading, lack of phonics ability.	15 minutes
	• How does dyslexia look in the classroom? Answers should include: child takes an excessive amount of time to carry out instructions, needs extra help with tasks that require organisation, struggles with reading, may show word finding difficulties (see handout).	30 minutes
	• Making the classroom dyslexia-friendly. Work through the presentation/handout.	30 minutes

Fig. 93 Session plan: Introduction to dyslexia

Starter activity

Start your training with an activity that will help your staff to think about how children with dyslexia see the world around them and how they face challenges with many everyday activities.

This activity was suggested by @MariaStMarys and is her preferred training activity and is provided by driveforliteracy.co.uk.

Ask your staff to draw a well known National Rail sign or something similar they have seen hundreds of times previously. They will struggle to do this despite being familiar with the sign. They can liken this challenge to how a child with dyslexia feels and the confusion and distress this causes.

When you have completed your basic training as above you will have made all staff think about dyslexia and how children are affected in the classroom.

Now show this PowerPoint presentation: 'What is Dyslexia' from YouTube by Kelli Sandman-Hurley: https://www.youtube.com/watch?v=zafiGBrFkRM.

Making the classroom dyslexia-friendly

Use this handout to accompany your training.

Making the classroom dyslexia-friendly

How the child presents in the classroom

- No drop in cognitive ability
- Lack of organisational skills
- Some lack of confidence and self-esteem due to struggling academically
- Struggles with sequencing and following instructions
- Difficulty decoding words
- Usually has a poor short-term memory.

Teaching strategies

- Give a written overview of the lesson using bullet points
- Keep your language succinct
- Break tasks into small, manageable chunks
- Write instructions for homework in their book for parents
- Avoid asking the child to read aloud
- Give lots of time for practising reading, writing and spelling
- Use coloured film if the child finds it aids reading
- Provide audio books to develop a love of reading
- Provide age-appropriate books that provide repetition
- Introduce mnemonics to help the child to remember things
- Stick to a daily routine so the child will be able to become more organised
- Encourage paired working so the partner can do the writing
- Display key words around the room
- Provide word banks, starter sentences and spelling lists
- De-clutter the classroom.

Computer strategies

- Clear font, e.g. Arial, Comic Sans or Verdana
- Font no smaller than 12 point
- Double line spacing
- Number your paragraphs
- Use blue markers on whiteboard
- Use no more than two font colours.

Fig. 94 Handout: Making the classroom dyslexia-friendly

Adapting this training plan

You could adapt this twilight session for any of the areas covered in part one. Choose your area to train your teachers from the list of ASC, ADHD, dyslexia, LDD, behaviour and inclusion. Go to Chapter 5 and look at the quick tips lists in your chosen area. Also, revisit Chapter 6 and extract information from the checklist tables. Using the information mentioned you can create a twilight session for any of the areas we have looked at in detail.

Time slot 4: A full day's INSET

Overview

Tips for this time slot

- Spend a short time re-visiting the condition you have chosen to address.
- Keep your activities hands-on where possible to keep staff engaged for the entire day.
- Allow time for staff to make resources in the area you have addressed. There is never enough time to make resources.
- Allow time for Q and A session with SENDCo to clear up any misapprehensions and to be sure any new staff are fully on board with the training.

Example scenario

As SENDCo you are in the wonderful position of being granted a full INSET day for training for SEND. This is a rare occurrence as there are so many other demands for CPD time from other members of staff. The whole school development plan has identified that there is to be a focus on children with LDD. You have a whole day to improve the education for children with LDD – this must be carefully planned.

In advance of the session

As a CPD leader and SENDCo, I would always conduct a questionnaire in advance to ask people how advanced they feel their knowledge is. Which areas would they like training in and which areas require a refresher. If the staff feel that they have requested the training, they have ownership over it and are more likely to retain and use the knowledge.

Send this questionnaire to all staff several weeks in advance to help you plan your training.

Thinking about children with LDD, do you require training in the following areas?	Yes or no?
What are learning disabilities and difficulties (LDD) and how are children affected?	
Are you aware of how to modify your teaching to ensure those with LDD are included?	
Are you aware of the AAC available to help children with LDD?	
Is your classroom modified to enable full inclusion of children with LDD?	
Are you confident with behaviour management for those with LDD?	
Are you making full use of visuals to help the child with LDD?	
Are you making the best use of your TA?	
Are you using multi-sensory resources?	
Are you encouraging independence?	

Fig. 95 LDD CPD questionnaire

From the answers you receive to the questionnaire you can plan your day's activities. You may also have access to staff appraisal information in which members of staff have previously identified their training needs. Use this information to help you plan your activities.

Training focus	How to teach children with LDD
Who will be trained?	Invite all teachers and TAs to this particular training as children with LDD can arrive in any class at any time, not just at the start of the term. Everyone needs to be prepared and ready to accept the child and do their utmost for the child with LDD.
Own research time required?	Allow yourself time to find out how much knowledge staff already have.

Training focus	How to teach children with LDD
Resources required	Flip charts to make notes. Practical equipment such as wheelchair.
Budget required	None
Problems that may arise	I once did a session where the delegates were coming from a spread of experience from trainee to HT, meeting needs of all was tough. (@SimonKnight100)
	The TA might be the one with the most knowledge, rather than the teacher. TAs are sometimes the ones who know the children best and they are often the ones differentiating the resources. This needs delicate handling.
Solutions to problems	Get hold of the delegate list in advance of the training. You can then grant permission for those with prior knowledge to drop in and out. As the SENDCo I would strongly advise all staff take part in Objective 4 and experience life as a wheelchair user. Only by doing this can an able-bodied person glean any understanding of how it is to spend your life in a wheelchair.
Any specific planning advice	Ensure that TAs and teachers are in mixed groups – more TAs than teachers in each group if possible. TAs may then feel empowered to share their knowledge with the group and the teacher could feed back to the whole group.
Advantage of this training	All staff will work co-operatively
Disadvantages of this training	None
Evaluation	Are all staff comfortable with teaching children with LDD?

Fig. 96 Overview training plan: INSET day training on LDD

Top tip

Remember, staff training works best if you split it into manageable chunks.

Teachers and TAs are like everyone else and they require some time on task, some time completing activities and some time off task to ponder the information they have received.

A whole day of training for LDD might look like this.

Time	Session	Focus	Activities
9–9.15	1	Aims and objectives for the day.	• Introduction and welcome to the day. • Split staff into unfamiliar working groups to allow delegates to swap ideas with new and unfamiliar staff.
9.15–10.30	2	Objective 1: to understand LDD and how it affects the child.	• Ask the question: What is LDD and how does it affect the child? Give all staff sticky notes to write their answers on. Stick them on the walls and encourage staff to wander round and read them all. • Correct any misconceptions there may be around the diagnosis. • Discuss how children are affected, e.g. no two children are affected in the same way, all require different modifications, how to set up your classroom for full inclusion (see handout).
10.30–10.45		Coffee break	• Provide good biscuits!
10.45–12.30	3	Objective 2: to be aware of and know how to make best use of technical devices and AAC.	• Provide an array of low tech devices. Low tech does not need much training and does not require a battery. • Staff work in pairs to try to communicate using these methods – the idea is to give them an understanding of how it is for the child. • Provide an array of high tech devices. • Allow all staff to attempt to communicate with each other using only the AAC devices. • Discuss problems experienced.
12.30–1.30		Lunch	• Provide lunch – if finances available.
1.30–2.30	4	Objective 3: to be able to modify the curriculum and the environment for children with LDD.	• Have staff think about their actual teaching and classroom layout. Share ideas on: differentiation, computer programs, how to persevere with teaching reading, ideas to help access the curriculum. • Ask the staff to work in groups to identify how they endeavour to remove barriers to learning. • Discuss classroom environment. • Choose a spokesperson to feed back the views of each group.
2.30–3.45	5	Objective 4: to be aware of the environment through the eyes of a child with LDD.	• Many children with LDD are in wheelchairs and may have associated difficulties with hearing and sight. Staff work in pairs and take turns to be the child in the wheelchair. Add a blindfold for good measure. • Feed each other if time allows and experience how the child feels. • All these activities will cause great hilarity but will deliver a powerful message.

Time	Session	Focus	Activities
3.45–4.00	6	Q and A and evaluation.	• Conduct a Q&A session. Be prepared to offer to make enquiries if you are unable to answer all questions posed. • Give out an evaluation sheet. Allow time for all staff to fill in an evaluation sheet to help to improve subsequent training. • Give all members of staff a copy of the fact sheet handout to retain for future reference.

Fig. 97 Session plan: INSET day training on LDD

Prepare a fact sheet handout relating to your day's training. This is helpful for any staff who may have missed the session and will serve as an aide memoire for staff who were present.

LDD INSET day fact sheet

Objective 1: to understand LDD and how it affects the child

- LDD is a generic term.
- No two children with LDD are alike.
- Some may have a condition affecting movement and co-ordination.
- Most will have learning disability.
- Some will have associated conditions such as ADHD or ASC.
- Some will require help with communication.
- Some will need help with feeding and dressing.
- Some will have associated behaviour challenges.
- Some will not be able to walk unaided.
- Most will need a modified curriculum.
- Most will struggle to stay on task and stay focused.

Objective 2: to be aware of and know how to make best use of technical devices and AAC
Low tech:

- Communication charts
- Communication books
- Symbols
- Objects of reference
- Photographs

- High tech:
  - Tablets
  - BIG mack
  - Eyegaze
  - iPod touch
  - Dynavox
  - PC adaptations
  - PC programs such as Clicker 6

Objective 3: to be able to modify the curriculum and the environment for children with LDD

- Check child's position in the classroom – away from distractions.
- Can the child see and hear properly?
- Are they included with a group?
- Have they got everything they need to begin work, e.g. writing slope, adapted specialised pens?
- Are you keeping it tactile for those on low P levels?
- Is the technology prepared and ready for use?
- Are you making good use of visuals to help with communication?
- Are you using sensory resources if required?
- Is your classroom free from clutter to avoid distractions and to ensure the safety of all children?
- Have you got positive behaviour management strategies in place?
- Are you using positive language?

Objective 4: to be aware of the environment through the eyes of a child with LDD

- Encourage worst-case scenarios – members of staff to treat their partner as they might the child, e.g.
  - whisk them off in a wheelchair with no warning and no information of reason or destination
  - going too fast and not warning of bumps on the ground
  - talk over the top of the child, do not involve them in a conversation
  - experience how it feels to be hoisted out of a wheelchair to perform an intimate bathroom function while members of staff discuss their night out
  - when attempting to feed each other from a spoon, allow the food to remain all over the face while you feed them.
- Show how to set up the classroom for full inclusion including wheelchair access.

Fig. 98 Handout: LDD INSET day fact sheet

Adapting this training plan

This one day training plan could be adapted for other SEND training days. Choose your area in which to train your staff from the areas we have looked at. Once you have chosen your area of training work your way through the advice offered in part 1 of this book. Train your staff about the signs and symptoms of the condition, how to work with children who have the condition and the strategies to use. Have your staff imagine they are that child and let them experience how the classroom and the environment feels for that particular child. Putting yourself in the place of the child is powerful training and truly helps staff to understand how the child is feeling and helps you understand any behaviour they may exhibit.

Time slot 5: A half term's training for SEND

Overview

If you have been granted a full half term's worth of training for an aspect of SEND, you need to choose your topic wisely. This should be an area of high priority and ideally should involve all school staff for maximum impact. A whole half term is a gift and should be planned with care.

Top tips for this time slot

- Ask the teachers what training they would like. Ask them if they would like to share any of their own expertise.

Example scenario

You have a child who is new to the area arriving at your school very soon. The child is a powered wheelchair user and also uses an iPad mounted on their chair with which to communicate. You have only a week to prepare the school environment and the staff to fully include this child. Think about how you will do this and the areas you need to cover in staff training.

I would suggest that inclusion is an ideal topic for such a length of time and it is at the heart of all mainstream schools, and rightly so. After following the half term's training on inclusion your staff should feel ready and well-equipped to include all children in their classes and feel confident to teach, track progress and assess them.

Split your half term into six twilight sessions – one per week. This amounts to 12 hours in total. Plan your areas that you need to cover in each session. For inclusion I would recommend that you cover the basics and be sure that all staff are clear on the right for every child to be included.

Training focus	To ensure all staff are clear on the right of every child to be fully included
Who will be trained?	All teachers and all TAs
Own research time required?	Allow time to brush up your own knowledge in the different areas
Resources required	Part one of this book
Budget required	None
Problems that may arise	Teachers may not accept the fact that all children have the right to a mainstream education
Solutions to problems	Remind them of the CoP 2014: 'All teachers are teachers of SEND'
Any specific planning advice	Ensure any staff who don't attend have a copy of the handout so the whole school is trained
Advantage of this training	Staff will feel empowered to include all children
Disadvantages of this training	None
Evaluation	Are all staff aware of the need to fully include all children?

Fig. 99 Overview training plan: Inclusion half term's training

Here are the basic facts to be covered in each session.

Session 1: Background to inclusion

- New SEND Code of Practice
- Every teacher is a teacher of SEND
- SEND is not the responsibility of the TA
- The graduated response and SEND support
- Four categories of SEND
- EHC plans brief overview
- IEPs and writing relevant SMART targets

Session 2: What is inclusion?

- What does inclusion look like in the classroom?
- Removing the barriers to achievement
- Teaching strategies
- Differentiation
- Making good use of your TA

Session 3: Understanding behaviour

- All behaviour is communication
- Specific behaviour strategies for the child with SEND
- Resources for behaviour management
- Token economy
- Positive behaviour management
- Modelling the behaviour

Session 4: Including all children

- Don't label the children
- Think outside the box
- No two children are alike
- The best educational quote
- Grouping children
- Position your TA

Session 5: Some special needs you may encounter in mainstream schools

- ASC brief overview
- ADHD brief overview
- LDD brief overview
- Dyslexia brief overview
- Challenging behaviours – some strategies

Session 6: Understanding assessment

- History of assessment for SEND
- P scales
- Pivats
- B Squared
- CASPA
- National comparative data
- Ofsted and SEND

Fig. 100 Inclusion CPD: half term plan

Now we have established a weekly plan of action let's see what training is to be included within each twilight session, and most importantly how it could be tackled.

As with all training sessions, you should provide a handout as a reference for the training and also ensure it is given to those who were absent from the day. Your handout will also add to staff CPD files and should therefore include as much information about the day as possible.

Week 1

Time	Focus	Activities
	Aims and objectives for the session	For all teachers to be aware of the contents of the Code of Practice 2014.
15 minutes	**Objective 1:** to be aware of the SEN Code of Practice 2014	Give out the SEND Code of Practice 2014. Ask teachers to go through with a highlighter and mark the most salient points. Find the big changes for example, the change from statements to EHCPs.
15 minutes	**Objective 2:** to understand that every teacher is a teacher of SEND **Objective 3:** to understand that SEND is not the responsibility of the TA	Teachers and TAs to find the part that relates to all teachers being teachers of SEND. Use a different coloured highlighter for this section.
20 minutes	**Objective 4:** to understand the graduated response and SEND support	Teachers and TAs to work in class groups and devise a flow chart to show how they would implement the SEN Support. This should include four parts: assess, plan, do, review.
30 minutes	**Objective 5:** to know the four categories of SEND	Divide your staff members into four groups. Hand out some ready-made lesson plans and ask groups to differentiate each lesson plan for a child in each of the four categories of SEND.
15 minutes	**Objective 6:** to give a brief overview on EHC plans	Staff to brainstorm and produce a quick overview on what an EHCP contains.
25 minutes	**Objective 7:** How to write IEPs and relevant SMART targets	Give staff some targets and request that they turn them in to SMART targets.

Fig. 101 Session plan: Week 1 inclusion

Week 1 on your half term's training is quite heavy on facts. Mainstream teachers need to be aware of the new Code of Practice and how if affects them within their classrooms. Keep in mind that teachers have been working all day and will not appreciate a heavy session where they are 'talked at' for two whole hours. Inject a little fun in your training. Objectives 1–4 can be covered very quickly with a brief read through of the facts and a quick discussion between staff.

Tackle objective 5 in a light-hearted manner whilst also being aware of the serious message involved. For example, ask how would you differentiate a maths lesson on 'quantity' using water for a child with challenging behaviour? Tell each group that their lesson must be a practical lesson where the child is allowed to use water. Staff will be creative with their answers and enjoy the challenge.

For Objective 7, SMART targets are difficult to set and need careful consideration. Several years ago I saw this target written for a child with SEND in a mainstream school: 'to engage with the Literacy Strategy and be able to read age-appropriate books'. I hope the person who set this target was able to access some training!

A SMART target for reading could read like this: 'to correctly sound out four of five specified CVC words by the end of the half term'.

During your first week's training session, get members of staff to set some SMART targets for each other. I have been involved in training of this nature and it really does make you think. Setting targets for each other can be entertaining, whilst also being very educational.

Fact sheet for Week 1

Aims and objectives of this session: For all staff to be aware of the SEND Code of Practice 2014

Objective 1: to be aware of the SEN Code of Practice 2014
New SEND Code of Practice 2014 in brief:

- Involves all children and young people with SEND from 0–25 years.
- Is child-centred.
- An EHC plan replaces statement of SEN and learning difficulties for those with SEND.
- There will be a focus on outcomes that will predict the level of support needed for transition through to adult life.
- Parents and carers can challenge a decision not to carry out an assessment and not to create an EHC plan. They may also challenge the special educational support in the plan or the named school.
- There may be a personal budget available for those with an EHC plan.
- The child must have a greater difficulty with learning than those of a similar age.
- Not all children with a disability have SEND, and not all with SEND have a disability.
- There will be a published 'Local Offer' giving details to children and young people with SEND about what is on offer in their local area.
- All children may have the choice of a mainstream school.
- For those with most complex needs, the EHC plan will put emphasis on personal goals and list the support the child requires from various agencies to help the child achieve their goals.

Objective 2: to understand that every teacher is a teacher of SEND

This is clearly highlighted in the new Code of Practice. All teachers should have knowledge and be capable of including all children in their lessons. SENDCo will liaise with teacher to provide Quality First teaching, differentiated for individual pupils.

Objective 3: to understand that SEND is not the responsibility of the TA

- Historically some teachers handed over their children with SEND to the class TA – the reality was that the TA sometimes had responsibility for those who needed a qualified teacher the most.
- Parents also requested a statement, especially in mainstream schools, in the hope that their child would receive a one-to-one TA.
- The new Code of Practice advocates a move away from this system.

Objective 4: to understand the graduated response and SEN support

- There will be early identification of those with SEND in order to give all children the best possible life chances.
- School Action, School Action+ and statements are all removed and replaced by SEN support. There are four types of action to put effective support in place: assess, plan, do, review. This is the graduated response known as SEN support. Class work should be differentiated to allow every child to be included on their own level. Remember that the way the teacher delivers the lesson can determine whether or not the child understands the lesson.
- The aim is for high expectations for all children. The key test for the need for action is whether the child is making adequate progress. This is determined in a number of ways including checking to see whether the attainment gap is closing or widening.

Objective 5: to know the four categories of SEND

These are:

1. Communication and interaction
2. Cognition and learning
3. Behaviour, emotional and social development
4. Sensory and/or physical.

The Code of Practice states that every child is unique and that these are very broad categories and there will often be some overlap. Schools should not categorise children and should teach according to the needs of the child.

Objective 6: to give a brief overview on EHC plans

- An EHC plan is a legal document that states a child's needs in terms of what they can and cannot do. This includes education and health care.
- The EHC plan also states what needs to be done to meet the needs of the child through joint working between education, health and social care.
- Professionals and parents together consider what outcomes are required by the child and what is needed to achieve those outcomes.
- The EHC plan is protected in law.

Objective 7: How to write IEPs and relevant SMART targets

- IEPs (or any name the school chooses) should be used to record short term targets that are different to or additional to those in place for other children.
- These targets should be SMART: specific, measurable, attainable, relevant and timely.

Fig. 102 Handout: Week 1 inclusion fact sheet

Week 2

Week 2 of your half term's training covers the facts about inclusion. It will serve as a reminder for your teachers and TAs of the reasons why they need to adapt their teaching to include all children.

Time	Focus	Activities
	Aims and objectives for the session	For all teachers and TAs to be aware of the right to full inclusion for every child.
15 minutes	**Objective 1**: to understand full inclusion	Teachers and TAs to brainstorm their thoughts on a flipchart to say what is full inclusion. What does it mean for the child?
15 minutes	**Objective 2**: to know what inclusion looks like in the classroom	Give staff some time to sit in a wheelchair and experience moving around the room in it. What are the obstacles?
30 minutes	**Objective 3**: to work towards removing the barriers to achievement	Provide any AAC you have in school to assist children who have no voice. Set staff the following task: imagine you have no voice; use one piece of AAC to record your thoughts on your teacher and class staff.
15 minutes	**Objective 4**: to develop some teaching strategies	Give out a literacy lesson plan and set teachers and TAs the task of seeking sensory resources to deliver the lesson with.

Time	Focus	Activities
30 minutes	**Objective 5:** to understand effective differentiation	Set the members of staff the following task: Imagine you are a child who uses a Roller Ball to access the computer. Use 'SwitchIt Maker 2' from Inclusive Technology Limited to make a book about your school day.
15 minutes	**Objective 6:** to be able to make good use of your TA	Discuss in class groups the best position for TA. Should they be 1:1 or support the whole group. Record ideas and keep for reference for classroom.
	Evaluation: Discuss one aspect of inclusion: the environment	Staff to give a practical demonstration of how they found life in a wheelchair. Show how they managed getting around the room without assistance.

Fig. 103 Session plan: Week 2 inclusion

In the differentiation task (objective 5), encourage staff members to put themselves in the position of a child with profound and multiple difficulties and attempt to make a book or a presentation just as the child would do. They will then understand how it feels to be that child. I am a big fan of this type of practical learning experience.

Fact sheet for week 2

Aims and objectives for this session: For all teachers and TAs to understand full inclusion.

Objective 1: to understand full inclusion

The principle of inclusion is that children with SEND have the right to be educated in a mainstream school within their local area with their local peers. This right is now protected by law.

Objective 2: to know what inclusion looks like in the classroom

- Keep the classroom clutter-free.
- Provide space for a child with a disability to move around.
- Consider all the equipment they may need, e.g. wheelchair, standing frame, acheeva (tilting bed), adapted furniture.
- Have all adapted equipment ready for the child, including writing slopes, specialised writing tools, fidget toys, etc.

Objective 3: to work towards removing the barriers to achievement

This is the government's vision for SEND, and it has its foundations in the firm belief that all children should be able to fulfil their potential and have the right to a good education at a school of their or their parent's choosing. Teachers in mainstream schools must be trained to teach children with SEND and must develop effective skills and strategies. This involves 'Quality First Teaching'. The essence of QFT is to maintain high expectations of all children, adapt your teaching environment to include all children and plan appropriate, individualised lessons for inclusion for all.

Objective 4: to develop some teaching strategies

- Create a safe learning environment where all children feel free to voice their ideas.
- Break learning into small chunks.
- Have consistent routines so all children know what to expect.
- Include sensory resources.
- Involve the children's lives in their learning to maintain interest.
- Mind your language – keep it clear and easy to understand.
- Provide lots of opportunities for success in order to build confidence.

Objective 5: to understand effective differentiation

Differentiation is not simply 3 different levels of work sheets for the different ability groups. Differentiation is any adaptations you make to your teaching and your classroom to allow every child to access the lesson.

For example, instead of a child writing their understanding of a comprehension passage the child could use a microphone and PC Program 'Switch it maker' and make a simple book to show their understanding.

Objective 6: to be able to make good use of your TA

- A child with SEND should not be glued at all times to a TA.
- Position your TA to work with higher ability groups of children leaving you free to work with lower ability ones and SEND.

Fig. 104 Handout: Week 2 inclusion fact sheet

Week 3

In the third session in your half term's training addressing inclusion, focus on the behaviour aspect.

Time	Focus	Activities
	Aims and objectives for the session	Introduce your behaviour training with the following video from YouTube: www.youtube.com/watch?v=tQTx26ELkSs
15 minutes	**Objective 1:** to get to grips with challenging behaviour	Discuss with staff the key message from the video. Discuss and define challenging behaviour as a school. These are the behaviours you are looking at during your training.
30 minutes	**Objective 2:** to know that all behaviour is communication	Remind staff that all behaviour is communication. Have teachers and TAs work in class groups and try to get a key message across using only AAC and visual resources.
15 minutes	**Objective 3:** to learn some specific behaviour strategies for a child with SEND	Staff work in pairs and brainstorm favourite behaviour management strategies. Swap groups and add to each list to pull together as many ideas as possible.
30 minutes	**Objective 4:** to develop resources to aid behaviour management	Staff to make some resources for behaviour management e.g. Traffic lights, Now and Next cards, visual timetables.
15 minutes	**Objective 5:** to make the best use of Token Economy	Staff work in class groups and devise their own brand new behaviour certificate or Token Economy reward system based on the age and interest of the children in the class.
15 minutes	**Objective 6:** to be able to adopt positive behaviour management strategies and **Objective 7:** model the behaviour you wish to see.	Question and answers to round off the session. Staff to give their best examples of positive behaviour management strategies. This might include positive language, providing clear boundaries and writing class rules.

Fig. 105 Session plan: Week 3 inclusion

Fact sheet for Week 3

Aims and objectives for this session:

Objective 1: to get to grips with challenging behaviour

Begin with defining 'behaviour', e.g. for this training I am referring to challenging behaviour that is more than a temper tantrum. Many children are prone to poor behaviour in times of stress or confusion, but challenging behaviour is that which puts others or the child themselves in danger. Examples include: self-harming, biting, kicking, throwing furniture and other forms of aggression.

Objective 2: to know that all behaviour is communication

In many cases, challenging behaviour results from an inability to communicate effectively. The child is unable to express their feelings, their likes or dislikes or have their message understood by peers, parents and teachers. The challenge for teachers is to unlock the child's potential to communicate and give them the means to express themselves.

Objective 3: to learn some specific behaviour strategies for a child with SEND

- Unpick the behaviour – what happened immediately prior to the shutdown?
- What was the adult's response? Did the adult unwittingly inflame the situation?
- Check the environment – is there a sensory overload contributing to the child's distress?
- Provide as many aids to communication as the child needs, e.g. visuals, objects of reference, AAC aids.
- Have clear structure and routine in your classroom – everyone feels safer when they know what to expect.
- If there is to be a change in routine, prepare the child in advance.
- Respond calmly to challenging behaviour.
- Provide a chill-out room or a place of safety for the child to visit, if necessary.
- Choose your battles carefully – only choose the battles you need to win.

Objective 4: to develop resources to aid behaviour management

- Provide an array of certificates, stickers, charts and badges for children who respond to these
- Provide prompt cards to show a child how to deal with their anger

- Use behaviour management cards in red, green and amber to reward children, or to remind them when they are beginning to misbehave
- Similarly, use the traffic light system – all members of staff should wear these traffic light cards on a lanyard and produce them regularly to keep a child out of trouble
- Provide class rules, made with the children to give them ownership – display the rules and refer to them regularly
- Make phone calls home to parents to discuss good behaviour
- If your school uses ClassDojo then award points for good behaviour – alert parents to the fact you are using ClassDojo. If your school is not using ClassDojo discuss with SLT the benefits of it.

Objective 5: to make the best use of token economy

This provides positive reinforcement for children by providing tokens or rewards for behaving in a certain way. Not all teachers approve of token economy but it can be effective for those with challenging behaviour. There are many different token economy strategies and teachers could create ones to suit the children in their classes.

Objective 6: to be able to adopt positive behaviour management strategies

This is based on giving regular praise and feedback to children for working and behaving in the manner you require.

- Establish your ground rules and stick to them
- Use positive language
- Actually teach children how to behave; this sounds obvious but is often forgotten in the array of good advice given
- Do not forget the ones who always work hard; they also require praise and encouragement

Objective 7: to understand the need to model the behaviour expected

- Be a positive role model for the children
- Model the behaviour you expect to see, e.g. use a calm, clear voice and be polite at all times
- Avoid holding grudges or labelling the child
- Every lesson is a fresh start – the child needs to know and understand that their behaviour will not be carried forward to the next lesson

Fig. 106 Handout: Week 3 inclusion fact sheet

When I asked my tweeting teacher colleagues about the best form of CPD they had experienced they were adamant that it should be solution-based.

Top tip

'It is fine to voice problems, but also suggest solutions.' (@thosethatcan)

With this in mind, keep your training focused on providing answers. Once you have run through the fact sheet on behaviour, allow members of staff time to work in pairs and come up with suggestions for improving behaviour.

Next, give them time to design and make new resources. Members of staff often voice their complaints that they never have time to make resources. This week's training is an opportunity to rectify that. You could introduce a competitive element to your training by providing a prize for the best behaviour management resource made within the timescale of this week's session. Staff enjoy a good competition and will rise to the challenge.

Week 4

We are halfway through our training on inclusion for all children. In week 4 there is an opportunity to discuss the children with SEND and how you can best include them in your classroom.

Time	Focus	Activities
	Aims and objectives for the session	To understand the paperwork for CoP 2014. To devise a behaviour for learning plan for a child and a social story.
15 minutes	**Objective 1:** to understand the need for including all children	Begin with a question and answer session regarding paperwork, for example, one page profile, pupil passport, IEP, provision map or whatever paperwork school is using. Discuss their importance. Discuss Quality First Teaching.
15 minutes	**Objective 2:** to be able to ignore labels	Give staff a scenario of a five year child who destroys other children's work. Child has undiagnosed condition therefore no label and no advice how to teach them. Discuss in class groups how you would approach this.
45 minutes	**Objective 3:** to be able to think outside the box and to know that no two children are alike	Teachers and TAs to work in class groups and devise a behaviour for learning plan for the child. Teachers and TAs to write a social story to teach the child why this behaviour is not acceptable.
15 minutes	**Objective 4:** to sum up your training in one quote	As a whole staff group discuss how you can adapt this training for other children with other behaviour difficulties. Discuss the educational quote which sums up how we should change our teaching to adapt to different children.

Time	Focus	Activities
15 minutes	**Objective 5:** to understand the reasons for grouping children with SEND	Discuss groupwork. Brainstorm in departmental groups the various ways you can group children and which is best for the child with SEND, for example, group with a more able child, group on a table of less able and allow TA to work with group, teacher to work 1:1 with child and ask TA to supervise class, child to work 1:1 with TA. Other variations on this.
15 minutes	**Objective 6:** to evaluate your training	Question and answer session to finish the session. Discuss the social stories, can they be improved?

Fig. 107 Session plan: Week 4 inclusion

Fact sheet for Week 4

Aims and objectives for this session: To be able to include every child in every lesson.

Objective 1: to understand the need for including all children

- Ensuring that all children have access to the best possible education.
- Discuss what this means for the teacher and other children in mainstream classes.
- Run a five-minute recap on graduated response and Quality First Teaching.
- Answer any questions relating to new Code of Practice.

Objective 2: to be able to ignore labels

Labelling a child is unhelpful and achieves little. It may sometimes serve to secure extra funding if certain accommodations or medical interventions are required, but labels should be avoided because staff may become familiar with the diagnosis and begin to treat all children with that diagnosis in exactly the same manner. This is unacceptable as every child will display different signs and symptoms. A stigma may also be created when a teacher is informed they have a child on the spectrum in their class. The teacher immediately begins to think of all the children and adults they have met who are on the spectrum without having any actual knowledge of where the child is on that spectrum.

Objective 3: to be able to think outside the box

This is about thinking about the individual child; what works for one child may not work for another. Think outside the box. How can you get your message across to the child who prefers to sit under the table rather than on a chair?

- Think flexibly.
- Try approaches that you have never tried before.
- Think about using social stories to introduce new scenarios for the child.
- Think of simple things that may be overlooked, such as pointing to a picture of a pencil on the child's desk if they are a constant pencil tapper – this avoids constant confrontations and plays down attention seeking behaviour.

Objective 4: to understand that no two children are alike. To enhance your training with an appropriate educational quote.

Every child is unique and should be educated as such. A diagnosis of ADHD will look very different in two different children. There will be some similarities but it is wrong to assume they will all have the same signs, symptoms and severity of ADHD.

Share this best educational quote; it beautifully sums up all your training to date for children with SEND:

'If a child can't learn the way we teach, maybe we should teach the way they learn.' (Ignacio Estrada)

This is exactly how we would like teachers to teach all children, especially those with SEND.

Objective 5: to understand the reasons for grouping children with SEND and to be able to position your TA effectively.

As everyone knows, the class TA is no longer expected to work in a one-to-one situation with a child. Best practice is to position your child with SEND within a group of other children. They will benefit from being with a good mix of children rather than those who are cognitively less able.

Think about the dynamics of the group you are proposing to place the child in. Will they dominate the group, will they chat too much and be a distraction, will they prod and pester other children? Alternatively, will they be overcome by being with children who are far more able than themselves? All of this can be overcome by choosing the correct group for the child and the teacher and TA take turns in working with that group.

TAs are generally experienced and well-qualified individuals and many classes would struggle to run without them. Position your TA cleverly. You can use your TA to work with the class while you work with the group where the child with SEND is positioned. Remember, your TA is a valued part of the team. Quite often they are the ones who make and implement Token Economy systems for behaviour management. Spend time with your TA and discuss behaviour management systems. Ensure you and your TA, as the class team, have the same approach.

Objective 6: To discuss the impact of and evaluate your training.

End your session by sharing some of the social stories written. Which will work best? Can they be improved?

Fig. 108 Handout: Week 4 inclusion fact sheet

Once you have gone through the basic facts as above, your staff will appreciate some discussion time. Have your teachers and TAs working in class groups to encourage teamwork.

Top tip
Follow @maximisingTAs to see some fantastic work being done on making the most of TAs.

Activity for Week 4, Objective 2

Provide the class teams with the following scenario:.

You have a child who is new to your class and they are showing some challenging behaviour that is causing you some distress and preventing the other children from working. Behaviours seen include:

- Destroying other children's work
- Destroying own work
- Talking over the teacher
- Prodding the child next to them
- Hitting other children
- Ripping down displays.

Challenge the teams to think of creative ways of managing this behaviour and creating a safer environment in which everyone is happy.

Answers should include:

- Devise a Behaviour for Learning plan showing all the undesirable behaviours.
- TA and teacher work together to decide what instigated the behaviour.
- Strategies to prevent the behaviour, such as
    a. giving the child some paper to screw up rather than ripping down displays
    b. avoid highly colourful and busy displays
    c. provide visuals so the child can show you when they are becoming irritable or are not coping in the lesson
    d. provide regular time out that is scheduled so the child knows when to expect it and does not play up to be achieve time out
    e. ignore behaviour that is doing no real harm and save your energy for the main difficulties
    f. use now and next cards to keep the child on task and show them what is happening next.

- Devise a Token Economy system that utilises their interests. Begin with small chunks of time. Staying on task for two minutes will result in one dinosaur sticker (or whatever is the child's motivator). Use a timer to show how long two minutes is. Build up the time you expect the child to stay on task without any behaviour lapses.
- Build the child's confidence by showing you trust them. Send them out independently on tasks around the school and make them feel important. They will return; you just need to be brave!

When all teams have completed this activity, pass the ideas around and share them with your colleagues. Once the activity is completed there should be some wonderful new strategies for helping children with behaviour difficulties to be more settled in school.

Week 5

Time	Focus	Activities
	Aims and objectives for the session	To learn basic information about some of the most frequently seen SEND conditions in school.
10 minutes	**Objective 1:** to learn the basic facts about some special needs you may encounter in mainstream schools	Discuss the ones seen in your particular school. Discuss the need to be flexible in your approach for all the conditions.
20 minutes	**Objective 2:** to gain a brief overview of ASC	Staff to write on sticky notes their view on how ASC looks in the classroom. Compare and complete a full list of staff ideas.

Time	Focus	Activities
20 minutes	**Objective 3:** to gain a brief overview of ADHD	Choose one set of class staff to write their ideas of how ADHD looks in the classroom on a flipchart. Whole school staff to contribute their ideas.
20 minutes	**Objective 4:** to gain a brief overview of LDD	Give each class group of staff a scenario of a child with LDD e.g. cerebral palsy; ask them to write how they might need to adapt their classroom and their teaching to accommodate this child. Devise a class list to share with whole group.
20 minutes	**Objective 5:** to gain a brief overview of dyslexia	Teachers and TAs to brainstorm signs and symptoms of dyslexia. In class groups compile a list of strategies to overcome difficulties experienced in the classroom, e.g. electronic dictionaries, writing programs.
10 minutes	**Objective 6:** to gain a brief overview of challenging behaviours	Whole staff list of positive behaviour management strategies, what works and what does not.
5 minutes	**Evaluation**	Are staff comfortable with their knowledge of SEND? What further information is required?

Fig. 109 Session plan: Week 5 inclusion

Fact sheet for Week 5

Aims and objectives for this session: To train staff how to include all children in every lesson.

Objective 1: to learn the basic facts about some special needs you may encounter in mainstream schools

Remind staff that children are all unique irrespective of the school they attend and whichever label or diagnosis is attached to them. Children with SEND always require a personalised approach and a tailored curriculum.

Objective 2: to gain a brief overview of ASC

ASC is a developmental disorder that affects behaviour, communication, development, learning and socialisation. The term ASC is an umbrella term and includes Asperger's syndrome. Included in the signs of ASC are:

- repetitive behaviours
- difficulty understanding the emotions of others
- possible challenging behaviours
- delayed language development
- a desire to stick to rigid routines.

Not all signs will be present in every child with ASC and every child will present differently.

Objective 3: to gain a brief overview of ADHD

ADHD is a group of behaviours and presents with trouble staying on task, poor concentration and hyperactivity.
Further difficulties are seen with:

- organisational skills
- following instructions
- acting on impulse
- challenging or poor behaviour.

Again, all children with ADHD will present differently and will not display all the signs and symptoms.

Objective 4: to gain a brief overview of LDD

LDD takes many different forms and various signs and symptoms will be seen in different children. Some difficulties seen could include:

- poor gross/fine motor co-ordination
- lack of cognitive ability
- difficulty learning new things
- under-developed speech
- poor social skills
- poor behaviour
- inability to walk unaided or sit without support
- lack of social skills.

As with all conditions, every child will have different signs and symptoms; every child will need a personalised curriculum.

Objective 5: to gain a brief overview of dyslexia

Dyslexia is a specific learning difficulty leading to problems with reading, writing and spelling. The cognitive ability of the child remains unimpaired.

Other problems are:

- lack of organisational skills
- lack of sequencing skills
- difficulty following instructions
- trouble with planning tasks.

> **Objective 6**: to gain a brief overview of challenging behaviours
>
> Children who display challenging behaviours may have an associated learning difficulty that is a trigger for the behaviour. All behaviour is a form of communication. Our job is to find out what the behaviour is telling us. Look for triggers; determine what the child is trying to tell you. Use pictures, visuals, clear and easy language and anything else that helps the child to communicate.

Fig. 110 Handout: Week 5 inclusion fact sheet

Use the week 5 fact sheet to remind your staff of the basic facts about what the children are coping with on a daily basis. Staff should always try to empathise with the children and develop a greater understanding of what the child is experiencing.

Once you have reminded your teachers of the facts surrounding the various special educational needs they may encounter you need to provide an activity to cement their learning.

A colleague from Twitter @FBanham informed me that one of her most favoured and most effective CPD activities is a word search. I whole-heartedly agree with her on this as there are obvious benefits to completing word searches:

- They are fun to do and make you think.
- They are stress-free.
- They appeal to most people.
- They enable you to practice a new skill.

With these benefits in mind, I recommend you produce a word search relating to one of the areas mentioned in your training. For example, you can compile a list of words relating to dyslexia which would include: organisation, sequencing, memory, reading, writing, spelling, intelligence, ability, cognition, books, epens, kindle, ereader, eBooks, filters, behaviour, frustration, visuals, structure and routine.

Pop the words in the word search generator and you will have a ready-made training resource. These are the apps that were recommended to me.

Word search maker	Recommended by	Free/not free?
Crossword compiler	@vallesco	£39 (charge correct at the time of publication.)
Puzzlemaker	@dannynic	Free
Just Word Search	@dannynic	Free
Printables	@jmpneale	Free

Fig 111 Word search generator apps

Week 6

In week 6, the focus is on assessment. This is a tricky area for all teachers at the moment since the demise of levels. Each school is forming their own assessment answer and the story is no different for children with special needs. However, all teachers, including mainstream teachers, need to have some understanding of assessment for children with SEND.

This session will take you through the basic facts on assessment for SEND. The Rochford Review chaired by Diane Rochford, published an interim report in December 2015 for the assessment of children working below the standard of test at Key Stage one and two. The essence of the interim report as previously mentioned is:

1. the introduction of pre key stage standards
2. 'pupil can' statements
3. one extra pre key stage standard was created for the gap between P Scales and Key Stage 1 standard
4. three extra pre key stage standards created for the gap between P Scales and Key Stage 2 standard
5. these standards will be included in whole school relative progress measure in the future
6. Rochford Review to review if change is required to P Scales in light of new curriculum.

Time	Focus	Activities
	Aims and objectives for the session	To train teachers about assessment for children with SEND
15 minutes	**Objective 1:** to begin to understand the current situation with assessment for SEND	• Talk staff through the demise of levels for all children, both mainstream and SEND. • Discuss P Scales. What are they? What happens in the gap above the P Scales but below the NC? Discuss the interim report from the Rochford Review.
1 hour	**Objective 2:** to understand the P scales	Train teachers that P Scales are similar to a ladder leading up to the National Curriculum. Give out some work where the standard is P3 P5 and P7 and task teachers to level the work correctly.
45 minutes	**Objective 3:** to understand how commercial assessment packages work in relation to tracking progress for SEND	• Talk teachers through some of the commercial packages such as B Squared, MAPP. Demonstrate the small steps of progress. • Ask teachers to work in groups and to plan a writing task for children at P3 P5 and P7. Swap groups and ask the next group to moderate the work using the P Scale document as a reference.

Fig. 112 Session plan: Week 6

Fact sheet week 6

Aims and objectives of this session: to train all teachers to understand assessment for SEND

Objective 1: to begin to understand assessment for SEND

The National Curriculum for England previously began at Level 1 when levels were in force for assessment. All children working below the level of the National Curriculum were awarded a 'W' which meant 'Working towards Level 1'. This did not depend on age or challenge faced by the child. So, a child who entered school at age 4 years and was facing profound and multiple difficulties began on 'W' and was likely to leave school at age 16 still working on level' W'. The child had apparently made no progress whatsoever for their whole school career. This was distressing for all concerned.

Objective 2: to understand the P scales

To address the situation, the government introduced the P scales in 1998 beginning with English, maths and PSD. These were far from ideal as the divisions were still too wide and it still looked as though no progress had been made. In 1999, the Qualifications and Curriculum Authority (QCA) produced booklets covering every subject to help teachers of special children.

Assessment was now P1–8 plus the eight mainstream levels. P1–3 were generic across all subjects and P4 and above became subject-specific. By 2001, teachers had a statutory duty to set targets for children on P scales in English, maths and science. Many mainstream schools ignored this and continued to use 'W'. By 2007 the collection of P scale data at Key Stage 1-3 was compulsory.

Objective 3: to understand that B Squared, (http://www.bsquared.co.uk/) Pivats, (http://www3.lancashire.gov.uk/corporate/web/?PIVATS/14588) MAPP (http://www.thedalesschool.org/article/assessment-progression-mapp/275) and Routes for learning (http://complexneeds.org.uk/modules/Module-2.4-Assessment-monitoring-and-evaluation/All/mo8po1oc.html) are all planning, assessment and recording tools for children working below the NC. These materials and assessment packages allow teachers to show progress for those working below the level of the National Curriculum.

Objective 5: to be able to understand CASPA (http://www.caspaonline.co.uk/)

CASPA is a tool which allows staff to benchmark attainment and progress for individual pupils and for groups of pupils with SEND. It also includes the DfE Progression Materials to allow a national comparison of data for Ofsted and for school improvement purposes.

Fig. 113 Handout: Week 6 inclusion fact sheet

Understanding P scales

The best way to understand anything is to actually take part in it. Give out the information relating to the P scales and show some examples of levelled work. Give teachers time to discuss this information.

Next, produce several pieces of work from children who are working at P1–P3, P4–P6 and P7–P8. Divide your staff into three groups and hand out the work. Give each group five minutes to discuss and reach an agreement on the level of the work in front of them. Swap the work around a further two times until all groups have assessed all the work. Comparisons can be made and conclusions drawn about the success of your training.

As with all training there are things that can go wrong and we must be prepared. For example @warwick_beth informed me that when she was providing training the video she was playing froze. Luckily she had a back up plan and all was well but this is something to keep in mind: have an alternative plan

Adapting this training plan

This training can be adapted for any area where you feel your staff would benefit from some extra, extensive training. Inclusion always requires revisiting and is ideal for half a term's training. Focus on teaching and learning strategies, differentiation, inclusion in PE lessons, inclusion for children in wheelchairs in the school environment and inclusion during non structured times such as lunchtimes.

A full term's training

Overview

If you have a full term to train your staff in one aspect of SEND it needs to be a whole school, high priority initiative.

Top tips for this time slot

- Be realistic, limit your training to an hour each session to keep staff motivated and on task.

Example scenario

One whole school issue that I recommend looking at is positive behaviour management for SEND. Behaviour management constantly requires updating to ensure all staff are singing from the same hymn sheet.

Deliver your training in ten sessions lasting for one hour each. An hour is a good timespan after a full day's teaching. Start at the beginning with the policy, and work your way through to strategies for behaviour management.

Training focus	To focus on positive behaviour management strategies for children with SEND.
Who will be trained?	Invite all staff including SLT, teachers, lunchtime staff, TAs, school secretaries, site supervisor and anyone who has dealings with the children.
Own research time required?	Allow an evening for own research
Resources required	<ul><li>Laminating paper</li><li>Velcro™</li><li>Computer and monitor to show YouTube video clips</li></ul>
Budget required	None - all of the suggested behaviour training is free. You can complete this training for the whole staff team yourself using YouTube, your own knowledge and some stationery (see above). If you require further specialised training for behaviour, I would consider calling in the experts.

Problems that may arise	Internet not working. Staff not receptive to behaviour management for SEND.
Solutions to problems	Have some notes on a memory stick in case the internet is down. Remind staff that SEND is everyone's responsibility.
Any specific planning advice	Listen to the views of TAs; they often know the children best.
Advantage of this training	Most of it can be done in house, free of charge.
Disadvantages of this training	Staff know the children very well and may have their own ideas about what works. Not necessarily open to new ideas.
Evaluation	There should be an improvement in the behaviour of your children with SEND.

Fig. 114 Overview training plan: Full term on behaviour CPD for SEND.

Here is a suggestion for how to structure your ten sessions. I suggest you read all the way through the ten objectives from start to finish before beginning your training. You will then have a clear picture of the focus for each week and your overall aim for the entire 10 sessions.

Week	Training	Activities
Week 1	**Objective 1:** to remind staff of the whole school behaviour policy.	• Group your staff in to departments. Give each group a copy of the whole school behaviour policy. Task each department to highlight two areas especially pertinent for SEND. Feedback to the rest of the groups. • Staff to highlight areas they are unsure of and these will form the basis of the training; reiterate the need for consistency throughout.
Answers to include: • consistency • no raised voices • class rules which feed in to whole school behaviour policy • token economy reward systems for all children with SEND • specific rules on the use of 'time out' and rules on the use of chill out spaces.		
Week 2	**Objective 2:** to be able to write behaviour for learning plans	• Group your staff in class groups so that they are discussing their own children with SEND. Class teams are the experts on their own children. • Show all staff a behaviour for learning plan. • All staff to write on flip charts what should be included on the plan. • Staff to visit other group's flipcharts and check for ideas. • Each class to produce new behaviour plans for SEND. • Choose a spokesperson from each team to feed back the contents of one of the behaviour for learning plans.
	• What to add on a behaviour for learning plan • Triggers for the behavior, for example sensory issues, work is too difficult, lesson not accessible for the child leading to boredom.	

Week	Training	Activities
		• Support required to prevent the behaviour for example, structure and routine, personalise the work to make sure the child can access the lesson, have all resources ready before the lesson starts, explain lesson to the child to avoid communication difficulties. • Strategies for dealing with the behaviour for example time out, loss of choosing or reward time, other sanctions.
Week 3	**Objective 3:** to be able to manage classroom behaviour effectively	• Assemble all staff and have them read this from @ tombennett71 www.tes.com/news/school-news/breaking-views/new-behaviour-tsar-tom-bennetts-top-ten-tips-maintaining-classroom (with kind permission from TES and @tombennett71) • Group your staff in to class groups. Give out the post and using highlighters groups to highlight the points they think are vital for children with SEND and why. • Choose a spokesperson from each group to read a point they have chosen. • As a whole school team discuss the points that are right for your school and for your children with SEND.
		Answers should include: (points refer to those in Tom Bennett's article) • Point 2. Have a seating plan. Think carefully where your children with SEND will sit, away from distractions and in a group where they will participate and not take over or disturb the other children. • Point 4. Rule breaking. This is vital for children with SEND. Consistency and structure always. • Point 6. Remember you are part of a team. Have a plan, what will you do if it all goes wrong? A consistent plan is vital for SEND. • Point 7. Involve the parents. Consistency of discipline at home and at school is a good plan. All children are happiest in a routine and SEND need that structure. • Point 8. Keep calm. It will not help you or the child with SEND to raise your voice. All you are doing is teaching them that it is all right to shout if things don't go your way. • Point 9. Have everything ready for the start of the lesson. This will help to get your child with SEND on task straight away thus setting the tone for the lesson. • Point 10. Be the adult. You are needed as the person who instills the boundaries, this is key for children with SEND.
Week 4	**Objective 4:** to be able to make visuals and other behaviour resources for children with SEND	• Introduce your training by reiterating the need and the value of visuals for children with SEND. • Brainstorm the value of visuals, traffic light systems and Now and Next cards with all staff. • Each class group to name one instance where a visual would be of benefit and aid behaviour. • Allow staff time to make visuals.
		• Value of visuals should include: Children with SEND need to know what their day holds for them and there should be no deviation from their routine. If there is to be a change you should be able to prepare the child for this through the use of visuals. • Discuss the use of Now and Next cards. Reiterate the value of structure and consistency.

Week	Training	Activities
Week 5	**Objective 5:** to be able to make good use of token economy	• Introduce your training by showing this clip: https://www.youtube.com/watch?v=1G2X6kngoP0 Note the use of the visuals as made in session 4 and also the use of an egg timer to show the length of time left. • As a whole staff discuss the value of token economy for SEND. Remind them of the need to use motivators for token economy to work effectively. • Task each class to devise an appropriate token economy system for a child with SEND.
	• Value of token economy should include: • Reinforces desired behaviour over time • Can provide positive reinforcement immediately following the desired behaviour • Token economy is structured in its own right which ensures it will be consistent • Can personalise the design of your chart to suit the child.	
Week 6	**Objective 6:** to be able to write social stories; to reduce anxiety-related behaviour	• Assemble all staff together and introduce your training on social stories for SEND using this clip. www.youtube.com/watch?v=NQq-JvVruag • Brainstorm some of the uses of social stories. • Give staff teams this scenario: you have a child who is on the autistic spectrum and who is about to move to a new class. You anticipate this will unsettle the child and want to reassure them before the move. • Write a social story to help your child deal with this situation.
	• The uses of social stories should include: • Teaching a child with SEND how to behave in a certain situation • Preparation for transition to new class, new teacher, new school • Introduction of new child to the class • Help the child to deal with their own emotions e.g. how to deal with anger without lashing out.	
Week 7	**Objective 7:** to understand the difference between a sensory shutdown and a temper tantrum and how to deal with both	• Introduce your training using this example of sensory shutdown www.youtube.com/watch?v=8WG7O3G2WZo • Challenge staff to design a fact sheet for dealing with a shutdown. Allow 20 minutes for this activity. • Show this clip to introduce a behaviour tantrum www.youtube.com/watch?v=eNYze6Z4M3A • Task your staff to produce a fact sheet for how to deal with a temper tantrum;
	Fact sheet to help identify a sensory shutdown should include; • sit on the floor with the child but not too close reduce the noise levels and ask all children and unnecessary adults to leave • avoid temptation to coax the child by talking to them • avoid touching them in a friendly way as this could be painful • remember in direct contradiction to the last point they may need deep pressure in the form of a hug • give the child time to calm down and then take them to a calming area	

Week	Training	Activities
		Fact sheet to help staff to deal with a temper tantrum should include: • Remember that behaviour is communication. Encourage the child to talk to you about the cause of their behaviour. • Use visuals to aid communication if needed. • Allow the child to take breaks before they become frustrated. • Try to avoid well known triggers if you know that a tantrum will be the result. • Remove the child from the room if possible or take them to a quieter part of the room as children do enjoy an audience. • Make a deal with the child; if you are aware that a temper tantrum may be on the way, pre-empt the behaviour. • If the child with SEND is violent remove the class.
Week 8	**Objective 8:** to be able to manage behaviour of children with SEND	• At a whole school staff meeting brainstorm reasons for poor behaviour from children with SEND. Produce a whole list of reasons why children may show challenging behaviour. • Remind staff to only pick the battles you need to win. You can't win every battle so choose one a day. • Remind staff of the value of positive behaviour management strategies. Preventing the behaviour by rewarding good behaviour is better than providing sanctions later. • Give your staff this scenario: you are about to take your class to the drama studio to prepare for a concert. Your child is displaying some emotions, for example, fear of moving rooms, excitement at the new activity, anxiety at change in routine. This spills over in to challenging behaviour and the child lashes out, begins shouting and running around the room. • Challenge staff to deal with this.
		Reasons for poor behaviour should include: • Inability to deal with emotions, for example, happy, sad, frightened, anxious • Communication, lack of understanding of the task • Seeking attention • Knowledge that this type of behaviour has previously worked and is therefore reinforced • Child is unprepared for an activity they were not expecting. A solution to the scenario should include always pre warning of any changes that are about to happen. In the event of a failure to do so the following is recommended: • Take the child to one side or if not possible remove the other children. Talk calmly and quietly to the child; tell them your expectation is that they will calm down. • Next, use the child's personal motivator. This is usually their favoured interest such as collecting bugs outside or time on an ipad. • Produce a 'Now and Next card' and an egg timer. Tell the child, 'Now we are going to calm down; next we are going to collect bugs'. Set the timer for 3 or 5 minutes depending on the child's attention span and the child will watch the timer and will calm down

Week	Training	Activities
		• Honour your promise; take them outside and to collect bugs or allow time on the iPad. This is not a reward as the child has had to wait. • Use a timer to show when the activity will finish. • When the child is calm use a visual timetable to explain to the child what is happening and tell them that they will return to their own room. Reassure the child and use feelings cards to talk about the emotions they have displayed.
Week 9	**Objective 9**: to find solutions to real scenarios	• Staff to work in class groups and use this specific example: a child in class is constantly ruining the continuous provision in EYFS, e.g. throwing paint in the sand and throwing water on the outside play area. The reason is the child is unable to make decisions and cannot decide which area they wish to visit. • Staff to discuss the behaviour and design possible solutions. • Share solutions with different class groups and share ideas.
		One solution to the scenario would include: • use of a visual timetable • use of 'Now and Next' cards • use of a timer • show the child the visual timetable with no more than two choices on it • child makes a choice • say 'Now you are doing this... next you are doing that' • use the timer and ensure the child stays on task for the allotted time • child moves to the next activity.
Week 10	**Objective 10**: to find solutions to real scenarios	Begin your training by reminding all staff there is no correct answer for children with SEND. Encourage staff to think about situations in different ways. Give your staff this scenario: • You have a child in your class who has been used to watching YouTube videos at home constantly to prevent them from displaying poor behaviour. • Challenge your staff to think of a creative way to wean the child away from constantly watching YouTube. • Conclude your training by sharing the different ides from each class.
		A solution to the above scenario might include this: • Make two visuals and place them just out of reach of the child: visual 1 is a picture of the child at work; visual 2 is a picture of the child watching YouTube. Use photographs of the child to make it real for the child. • Use your visual timetable and timer. 'Now you are doing this' and point to the photo of the child working. 'Next you can do that' and point to the picture of the child watching YouTube. • Set your timer for a few minutes and do not allow the child to come off task. • The first time you do this you may need to warn the class staff and children that there may be some noisy behaviour in the room. • It is imperative you stick to your guns. Increase the amount of time the child is expected to stay on task.

Fig. 115 Training plan: Full term on behaviour CPD for SEND

> **Name:** Paul Dix
> **Twitter handle:** @pivotalpaul
> **Website:** www.pivotaleducation.com
> Who are they? Behaviour specialist, CEO Pivotal Education
> **Why to follow them:** Expert with hard to reach children, podcast maker, all round behaviour expert.

The term's training plan could be adapted to impart any knowledge for SEND that requires updating. For example, when beginning a new topic in the creative curriculum you could adapt this plan to show how to adapt all your subject lessons for SEND around your topic. Your CPD sessions could include one for every area of the curriculum.

Time slot: A whole year of training

Overview

A whole year's training for SEND will allow you to work towards training your staff to overcome potential barriers to learning in a certain area. Choose your area of greatest need and structure your sessions in a sequential manner

Top tips for this time slot

As time is allowed to elapse between the sessions teachers can implement new strategies after each training session and evaluate their impact before the next session.

Example scenario

If you have a whole year to dedicate to training in an area of SEND, look to your cohort of children to see what to cover. Is there a pattern emerging? I am repeatedly asked for advice for children with ASC and ADHD. This suggests an increase in the numbers of children with these conditions in mainstream schools. It is acceptable to tackle both ASC and ADHD together in terms of training plans as they often benefit from the same strategies. I have chosen to do this as an example here. I recommend six hour-long sessions over the year, which equates to two sessions per term. This would give a good grounding for all staff.

Training focus	To enable teachers to effectively teach children with ASC and or ADHD
Who will be trained?	All teachers and TAs
Own research time required?	Allow time to research any new strategies and to seek out resources you need to show as examples.
Resources required	Now and Next cards, visual timetables, egg timer, traffic light systems PC, laminator, paper.
Budget required	None
Problems that may arise	Lack of resources to use as examples
Solutions to problems	Find examples on the internet to use as examples.
Any specific planning advice	Ensure all staff are trained for consistency throughout school.
Advantage of this training	Can make resources for specific children
Disadvantages of this training	Having enough resources available for all staff to make new resources.
Evaluation	Staff will have a greater knowledge of how to work with children with ASC/ADHD and the children will be calmer and more settled as a result.

Fig. 116 Overview training plan: Full year CPD on ASC and ADHD combined

Here is a suggestion for how to structure your six sessions. Don't assume any prior knowledge of your staff. Begin at the beginning thus ensuring everyone is up to speed with the current thinking on these two conditions and is aware of how to teach children with ASC or ADHD.

Remind staff that the signs and symptoms of ASC and ADHD are often similar and can be easily confused. For school staff the actual diagnosis is fairly irrelevant. Labels will not help you to teach a child; you need to teach the child in front of you rather than what the label describes. Each child with the same diagnosis will display different signs and symptoms and each child needs to be taught differently.

Week	Training	Activities
Week 1	Objective 1: for all teachers and TAs to recognise the signs and symptoms of ASC and ADHD	• Group your teachers and TAs in class groups and generate a five-minute discussion about what staff think ASC/ADHD looks like. Show this clip from the National Autistic Society 'What is Autism?' www.youtube.com/watch?v=d4GoHTIUBlI • Next, show your staff this clip from Howcast.com 'How to recognise ADHD symptoms in children'. • www.youtube.com/watch?v=1GIx-JYdLZs • In class groups discuss the two conditions and make a list of similarities of symptoms. • Bring your staff together as one group and follow this with a quick recap on the actual signs and symptoms using the handout provided at the end of the year plan. • Discuss the behaviours seen in children with ASC/ADHD. Generate a discussion on how you can best help the children to be fully included in the classroom.
Week 2	Objective 2: to understand the need for consistent classroom strategies for ASC/ADHD	• As a whole school staff spend five minutes discussing the benefits of structure and routine. Discuss how most children with ASC/ADHD need structure. Show this clip 'The Importance of Routine' www.youtube.com/watch?v=d4L85NOH9dQ • Show staff a variety of visuals in various styles using pictures for ease of understanding. • Show your staff this clip 'Using visuals when working with children with ASC'. This clip features a 'First and Then' card ('Now and next') www.youtube.com/watch?v=xoh49A_jrps • Give your staff time to make a Now and Next card.
	Benefits of structure and routine should include: • child feels safe • helps to promote independence • helps child to cope with everyday life • helps child to relax • helps child to feel happy.	
	Objective 3: to produce visuals for a specific child	• Provide resources to make visuals and dedicate the full hour for staff to make resources. • Staff to work in class groups and choose a child with ASC or ADHD they know will benefit from a visual timetable, a traffic light system or a Now and Next card.
Week 4	Objective 4: staff to learn new strategies to support children with ASC/ADHD	• Staff to work in groups of eight. • Each team to have a rectangular piece of paper. Fold the paper enough times to produce eight squares. In their teams each person should write one strategy to support the learning within the classroom for children with ASC/ADHD. • Swap the papers around the groups until all teams have seen all suggestions. You will now have generated a long list of tried and tested classroom strategies. • Show your teachers this clip 'How to teach children with ADHD' https://www.youtube.com/watch?v=JEAYVMFZLM4 • Discuss the key message 'positive attention'. Each class to think of one way to provide positive attention for children with ADHD.

Week	Training	Activities
	Positive attention should include; • plenty of smiles for the child; celebrations of every little success • praise for the child as soon as they sit down, even if it takes a few minutes for them to do so • an interest in their – interests • building up of a bond reassurance for the child that they are doing well at every opportunity • a gentle and caring attitude – children pick up on this • praise for children behaving well.	
Week 5	• Objective 5: to understand a sensory shutdown and how to deal with it	• Train all your teachers and TAs together. • Challenge each team to brainstorm situations which may result in a sensory shutdown. If staff can identify contributory factors they will be better able to cope with a shutdown or avoid it altogether. • Choose a spokesperson from each group to feed back to whole staff. • Task your staff to work in class groups and find solutions for sensory shutdown. • Show your staff this powerful clip The Autism Experience https://www.youtube.com/watch?v=-gSSkr-qFhc
	Situations which may result in sensory shutdown include: • crowded places • cluttered environment • sudden, loud noises • too much noise • dislike of hair brushing • dislike of hand washing • dislike of messy hands • dislike of texture of certain foods • lack of consistency • lack of routine • lack of structure. **Solutions to sensory overload** should include: • weighted blankets • fiddle toys • calming activities • Tacpac • visual supports • structure and routine consistency • own workspace • calm and quiet environment • chill out space/room.	

Week	Training	Activities
Week 6	Objective 6: to create a fact sheet to show understanding of social and emotional skills for ASC/ADHD	• Staff to work in class groups. • Discuss all the social skills that children take for granted that are difficult to master for children with ASC and ADHD. • Challenge each staff group to create their own fact sheet for teaching social skills. • At the end of the session swap sheets with other groups and read all ideas presented.
	Fact sheet should include: • How to take turns • How to join a conversation • How to understand facial expressions • How to remove themselves from stressful situations • How to respect personal space.	

Fig. 117 ASC and ADHD: Full year plan

Fact sheet for week 1	
ASC and ADHD signs and symptoms	
ASC	**ADHD**
Repetitive movements such as hand flapping (stimming)	Easily distracted
Focuses intently on one activity	Lack of response to the emotions of others
Some developmental delay	Calling out inappropriately
May be withdrawn	Fidgeting
Rigid thought processes	Running, jumping and being hyperactive
Possible inability to interact socially	Talking continually
Needs structure and routine	Lack of concentration
May have some sensory sensitivity	Inability to stay on task
May avoid eye contact	May avoid eye contact

Fig. 118 Week 1 fact sheet

Use this handout to accompany your second training session.

Fact sheet for week 2

The need for consistency in the classroom

- Use a visual timetable.
- Use Now and Next cards.
- Pick a style of visual resource and be consistent.
- Establish structure to the day.
- Establish a routine for the child with ASC/ADHD.
- Pre warn the change if there are to be any changes.
- Be firm but fair.

Fig. 119 Week 2 fact sheet

Use this handout to accompany your third training session.

Fact sheet for week 3

- The visual could be in the form of a column which is read from top to bottom.
- The visual could be horizontal and read from left to right.
- Use pictures, symbols or photographs, personalise for the child.
- Choose a style of visual for the child and use it consistently.
- They are portable so child can always have them to hand.
- Resources needed: card, Velcro, laminating pouches, Boardmaker and time to make visuals.

Fig. 120 Week 3 fact sheet

Use this handout to accompany your week 4 training.

Fact sheet for week 4

Support for learning in the classroom

Strategies for teaching children with ASC/ADHD should include:
- Structure
- Routine
- Consistency
- Extra thinking time
- Uncluttered environment
- Clear language
- Symbols
- Visuals
- Chill-out space/room
- Own desk
- Use of child's motivator for token economy
- Anything that works for the individual child.

Fig. 121 Week 4 fact sheet

Use this handout to accompany your week 5 training session.

Fact sheet for week 5

Information relating to sensory shutdown

Some children with ASC have sensory sensitivity and this makes their world seem rather chaotic for them. If they cannot deal with sensory information they receive they often become overwhelmed. This may result in a sensory shutdown.

- **Situations which may result in sensory shutdown** include: crowded places, cluttered environment, sudden, loud noises, too much noise, dislike of hair brushing, dislike of hand washing, dislike of messy hands, dislike of texture of certain foods, lack of consistency, lack of routine, lack of structure.
- **Solutions to sensory overload** should include: weighted blankets, weighted clothes, fiddle toys, calming activities such as calming music, Tacpac, visual supports, structure and routine, consistency, own workspace, calm and quiet environment, chill-out space/room.

Fig. 122 Week 5 fact sheet

Use this handout to accompany your week 6 training.

Handout for week 6

Social interactions

- Children with ASC and ADHD may have difficulty with social interaction and for this reason often spend their time isolated. As educators it is our job to try and help them to fit in with their peers. Unlike most children, those with ASC and ADHD need to be taught these skills.

Difficulties seen include:
- Seeming to be indifferent to other children
- Preferring to play alone
- Being unable to interpret body language
- Being unable to interpret gestures
- Being unable to interpret facial expressions
- Lack of imagination
- Lack of play skills
- Prefer the company of adults

Fig. 123 Week 6 fact sheet

Top tip

The main thing for ASC/ADHD is the practitioner's ability to think outside the box.

Adapting this training plan

This training plan can be adapted for any of the areas we have looked at in this book. Six sessions spread throughout the course of the year is ideal for keeping staff aware of the need for inclusion for all children. Similarly six sessions is ideal for training staff on behaviour issues. All you need is some dedicated time for research and the Internet.

- Give yourself one overall long-term target.
- Break your target in to six smaller targets.
- Plan and prepare your resources.
- Review progress after each session.
- Assess the impact of your training.
- Review your goal if necessary.

3 Evaluating the success of your CPD training

Before we begin to evaluate the success of your training, here is something important to remember about one-off training sessions: 'one off training days have very little impact on long term practice.' (@TeacherToolkit).

If you are completing some training for your staff in the area of SEND, do not expect too much from a one-day session. Although talking about CPD in general, @TeacherToolkit is correct. Much information can be passed on but the evaluation will not show a true picture unless the initiatives and activities have been tried and tested in the classroom. This is an important point to remember.

As we know, CPD for school members of staff varies in both quality and expense. Some of it is thrust upon us from above – namely the DfE in response to wholesale national initiatives. Often financial help is provided for this training, but quality remains an issue. Clearly we want staff to be interested in what they are being told and we need the training to hold their interest. There is little worse than a room full of teachers and TAs expressing boredom by talking and yawning.

Other CPD is led by school improvement or may be in response to a growing cohort of children who all have a specific need. Whatever drives the training, measuring the impact of it is important. We need to see that money, time and resources have been used wisely leading to the greater good of the children.

Why to conduct CPD SEND training

Here are five golden rules for CPD for SEND.

1. Good CPD helps certain cohorts of children to make better progress in their area of need.
2. Good CPD helps teachers to be more adequately prepared to teach children with challenging behaviours or complex conditions and learning difficulties.
3. Good CPD for SEND gives good value for money.
4. Good CPD for SEND focuses on the impact in the classroom over time.
5. Good CPD improves the classroom experience for all children and all staff, not just the child with SEND.

As the SENDCo, you need to have extensive knowledge of SEND yourself in order to help others. In general there are three reasons to conduct SEND training:

1. To close the gap for those with SEND
2. To do your best to remove all barriers to learning for those with SEND
3. For Quality First Teaching as per the Code of Practice, 2014.

Ofsted as evaluation

If you are the SENDCo and you have a choice in your own personal CPD, I would always suggest refining your data skills. Assessment and tracking pupil progress and data remains the backbone of your Ofsted inspection. You have to be able to prove that you know the level your SEND children are working at and that you are aware of how to help them achieve the next level. Once you know this information, you need to train your staff in data analysis. Data is everyone's responsibility, not just the SENDCo. Teachers must be able to explain the data too.

I was advised by my favourite Ofsted inspector and leadership consultant, @MaryMyatt, to make a one page summary to show how some children with SEND have progressed over the years. Data doesn't always tell the full story. Give reasons for any plateau, dips or spikey profiles and train your teachers to be able to do the same. After all, Ofsted is arguably the toughest measure of evaluation of your CPD you could possibly have.

However, improving the educational experience of the children should always be what drives your CPD. If you aren't doing it for the children, don't do it at all would be my advice. Don't do things purely in the name of Ofsted – they don't want you to change things for them. Ofsted want to see what you do day in, day out. What is the educational experience for the children? Never be tempted to lose sight of this fact when planning your CPD.

Reasons for evaluations

In Part 2, we have looked at various types of CPD. We have looked at different special educational needs and planned training for staff in various different time slots. Now there is a need to check that the training is effective.

The most common method of evaluating training is to supply a handout at the end of the session. We have all seen them and we have all filled them in.

I have supplied an evaluation sheet in part one. Here is an alternative evaluation template for a one-off training session for you to adapt for your own use.

School name (logo)	CPD evaluation sheet	Ofsted (logo) Outstanding 2015-16				
Read the statements below and rate your answers on a scale of 1 to 5 where 1= disagree completely, 2= agree a little, 3= mostly agree, 4= agree, 5= strongly agree						
The aims and objectives of the training were clear.		1	2	3	4	5
The training was relevant to my role in school.						
The handouts were clear and of value to me.						
The activities were engaging and stimulating and furthered my knowledge of SEND.						
The content was well-structured and well-paced.						
The trainer was knowledgeable about SEND and approachable.						
There was ample opportunity to ask questions.						
The objectives of the session were achieved.						
The information helped me to understand more about children with (insert your own training focus).						
Would you recommend this training to a colleague?						
Any further comments?						

Fig. 124 Evaluation sheet template 1

There are problems with this type of evaluation sheet. For example, it only provides you with a brief snapshot of what staff members have learned at the time. Other problems identified are:

- Sheets often completed in a rush as staff members want to go home.
- No time to reflect on the learning.
- No time to implement the strategies before evaluating the training.
- May be seen as a tick box exercise.

Other more effective ways of evaluating one-off sessions have been identified by my colleagues, e.g.

- 'I have done feedback on Post-its. It was a "what stuck with you" exercise.' (@samdaunt)
- 'Gauge the feeling of the room. Listen in on the conversations people are having and the things they are saying. Ask for verbal feedback.' (@thatboycanteach)
- 'Give two blank sheets "what went well" and "even better if" – feedback isn't restricted to set questions then.' (@thought_weavers)
- 'I ask three questions. 1. How did you find the presentation? 2. What did you learn? 3. What will you find useful in your practice?' (@reachoutASC)

Lynn McCann (@reachoutASC) is an autism consultant and I particularly like her method of evaluation because the delegates actually have to think about the training they have received. There are no clues and no tick boxes. Genuine reflection is required and this also helps Lynn to improve her own practice.

Here is a further evaluation sheet for you to adapt for your own use. There is very little need for staff to think hard when completing this one. The advantage is that you should have many completed evaluations. The obvious disadvantage is that they will be completed at speed and will not be as useful as those requiring more thought.

Session feedback

Date:
Trainer's name:
Course title:

1. The course title accurately matched the content.	Yes	No
2. The trainer had extensive knowledge of the course content.	Yes	No
3. The course presentation was systematic and organised.	Yes	No
4. There was ample time for questions.	Yes	No
5. The handouts were relevant and useful.	Yes	No
6. Would you recommend this CPD to others?	Yes	No

How will you use this training?
Thank you for completing the evaluation.

Fig. 125 Evaluation sheet 2 template

The final evaluation sheet template I am providing for you, provides delegates with the opportunity to reflect on their learning. Deep thought is required for this evaluation sheet and it is possibly the most useful for the trainer.

ADHD CPD evaluation sheet

1. Describe the most valuable item of information you learned about ADHD today.

2. What can you do now that you were unable to do prior to the training with regard to ADHD?

3. How will you use today's training in your classroom with your children with ADHD?

4. Do you feel more confident to work with children with ADHD after this training?

5. How will you disseminate today's ADHD training to your staff?

Thank you for completing the questionnaire.

Fig. 126 Evaluation sheet template 3

Evaluation sheets are not the only method of deciding upon the success of your training. Best practice is considered to be when some time has been allowed to elapse after the training before making an informed decision and feeding back.

These methods could include:

- **Formal observations** – the children with SEND in the class should be more settled and their barriers to learning should be removed.
- **Peer observations** (non judgemental) – it should be clear to your colleagues that you have been on training to further your knowledge on children with SEND.

- **Interview and observe the children without SEND in your class** – are they learning more? Is the class more settled as a result of your training?
- **Video your teaching and watch it back** – what are your pupils with SEND actually doing? Are they fully included in the lesson?
- **Interview other staff members in the room to canvass their opinion** – TAs should notice the difference and should report that your SEND training is having an impact.
- **Review your lesson plans and the wider curriculum** – armed with your new knowledge of SEND, the plans and curriculum will need updating to reflect your learning; new teaching resources will need to be made which will further the children's learning.
- **Conduct a work scrutiny** – the children with SEND should be producing improved work under your new guidance.
- **See if results improve** – the impact of your training will show in improved results for your children with SEND; there may also be a knock-on effect as other children are able to work in a calm atmosphere. As we know, a good lesson for children with SEND is a good lesson for all children.
- **Ask the parents** – your training for SEND may be having an impact at home: a calmer, happier child in school should be happier at home if the same routines are suggested and then followed up at home; also, a child who is learning coping techniques in school may be able to apply these techniques at other times when there is less structure available for them.

Planning next steps for CPD

If you are the SENDCo, it is good practice to evaluate your whole-school training on an annual basis. Take a good look at your cohort of children with SEND. Check what is working for them and determine what further training may be required for the coming year.

Evaluation of current knowledge

Use this checklist to evaluate your training. Although this checklist is designed for ASC it can easily be adapted and expanded to evaluate your training in all areas of SEND.

Check	Yes or no?
Do all staff have basic training for children with ASC?	
Do all staff understand the need for structure and routine?	
Are all staff aware of the need to give warnings of changes to routine?	
Are visual timetables regularly used throughout school?	
Do teachers consider seating and group work when thinking about children with ASC?	
Are all staff aware of the difference between a sensory shutdown and a temper tantrum?	
Are all staff aware of how to check the environment to minimise sensory overload?	
Is there somewhere for a child to go to in order to escape the hustle and bustle of the classroom?	
Are strategies in place to train staff who start mid-term and miss the whole school training?	
Does structure and routine continue at lunch times and other non-supervised times?	
Are behaviour strategies such as 'now and next' cards regularly used?	
Are all staff members aware of the need to give fewer choices?	
Are staff members aware of the need to avoid sarcasm?	
Are all staff members aware of the need to keep language clear and simple?	
Are all staff members aware of the need not to take aggressive behaviour personally?	
Are teachers aware that every child on the spectrum is different and should have a tailored curriculum?	

Fig. 127 Evaluation of current knowledge

If you complete an activity such as this you will have up-to-date knowledge of the training and development of the teachers in your school relating to children with SEND. More importantly, you will be aware of where there are gaps in the knowledge of your staff.

Also, as SENDCo do you have access to staff appraisals and performance management reviews? If so, check whether any members of staff have requested specific SEND training? This will be your starting point when planning your next steps for SEND training. You are now in a position to be able to plan how to address those gaps in staff knowledge.

Use these steps as a guide to help you plan your CPD cycle for your annual SEND training.

Steps	Activity
Step 1	Evaluate the needs of your cohort of children with SEND.
Step 2	Evaluate success of classroom strategies. 'EBI'
Step 3	Complete check list to evaluate staff knowledge in areas of SEND.
Step 4	Check appraisals and performance management reviews for SEND training requests.
Step 5	Decide on training needed, which areas of SEND.
Step 6	Provide training, internally or through bought-in professional consultant.
Step 7	Evaluate training.
Step 8	What is the impact in the classroom?

Fig. 128 Planning your annual CPD training

Disseminating the training

Possibly the last thing you need to do after receiving your training is to disseminate the information you have learned. You are only as good as the team you work with so do remember, for consistency in the classroom, you need to share your new-found learning.

Where appropriate share what you have learnt with:

- Whole school team
- Teaching staff
- TAs
- Class team working directly with you.

There are a number of ways you can do this and you need to choose the most appropriate method for the training.

- Peer mentoring
- INSET days
- Email
- Quick feedback at staff meeting.

For further details on these see Part 2, Chapter 1.

Ten top tips for disseminating CPD

1. Build up a bank of resources relevant to the CPD. For example, when looking at the area of ASC or ADHD choose one set of symbols for making your visuals and ensure the whole school is consistent in their use.
   Order plenty of Velcro™. You will need it. There is never enough!
2. Ensure all teams within school are actually using visuals in the same manner for the children on the spectrum. Consistency is key.
3. Ensure all teams within school are using the same set of objects for 'objects of reference'. Again, consistency is key.
4. Ensure behaviour strategies are followed by everyone and everyone knows where and how to seek help if required.
5. Consider dedicating a room in which to house your school's resources. There is no point in reinventing the wheel. Someone could have previously made the exact resource you require.
6. Share all resources with all staff members and ensure everyone has access to the pre-made resources.
7. Avoid passing on your knowledge at the end of the day, or worse still at the end of the staff meeting when staff are too tired to absorb the information.
8. Avoid talking 'at' your audience who may be silent due to lack of involvement.
9. Avoid training staff for whom it bears no relevance or interest. This will breed resentment.
10. Choose the best person to disseminate rather than just senior leaders. They are leaders rather than specialists in all manner of things related.

A final point to remember about dissemination is that it is a vital part of your CPD. If you want to bring about a lasting change in your school, either a particular teaching strategy, a behaviour initiative or changing the way staff behave, you need to consider your dissemination method carefully.

Research

I cannot finish a chapter on CPD without mentioning research. Many teachers and some TAs are now undertaking their own action research projects. There are certain advantages to this including:

- It gives the teacher some autonomy over their own CPD
- It allows a teacher to develop an area of interest of their own choosing
- Teachers who undertake research feel more confident to challenge authority in their area of research
- It encourages teachers to work collaboratively.

I asked the tweeting teachers their reasons for engaging with research, and these were the best replies I received:

- 'It makes you challenge your own assumptions.' (@DamsonEd)
- 'It helps you to challenge pedagogical orthodoxy in your own context and develop criticality when interpreting the research of others. And it can be hugely rewarding.' (@matthiasenglish)
- It 'helps you move towards a position of knowledge production as opposed to relying on knowledge consumption. Vital when developing the skills to meet complex SEND where existing resources etc. don't always fit need.' (@SimonKnight10)

As a result of teacher research, there are some obvious benefits for the school including:

- An improvement in pupil performance
- Improved staff development in the teacher's area of interest
- Improved sharing across local schools
- Allows the school/teacher to contribute to the wider knowledge in the researched area.

Teacher research is a powerful form of CPD; however, it must be supported by leaders and governors to be successful. When it is successful, there are clear and positive benefits for our students. That is of course our ultimate aim.

Bibliography and further reading

'Achievement for All' (AfA) Schools Programme, (2009) www.afaeducation.org/programme_schools

Barkley, R. A. (2010) *Taking Charge of Adult ADHD*. Guilford Press.

Baron-Cohen, S. (2008) *Autism and Asperger Syndrome*. OUP.

Bennett, T. (2015) 'New behaviour tsar Tom Bennett's top ten tips for maintaining classroom discipline' TES (www.tes.com/news/school-news/breaking-views/new-behaviour-tsar-tom-bennetts-top-ten-tips-maintaining-classroom)

Booth, T. and Ainscow, M. (2011) *Index for Inclusion: Developing Learning and Participation in Schools*. Centre for Studies on Inclusive Education (CSIE).

Carpenter, B. (2015) *Engaging Learners with Complex Learning Difficulties and Disabilities*. Routledge.

Causton, J. & Theoharis, G. (2013) *The Principal's Handbook for Inclusive Schools*. Brookes Publishing.

Chivers, C. (2015) 'Behaviour management and ITE' and 'Inclusion is just doing your job' (chrischiversthinks.weebly.com).

Coe, R. et. al (2014) 'What makes great teaching? Sutton Trust.

Collingwood, J. 'ADHD and Gender' www.psychcentral.com.

Crombie, M. (1991) *Specific Learning Difficulties (Dyslexia)*. Jordanhill.

Das. J. P. (2009) *Reading Difficulties and Dyslexia: An Interpretation for Teachers*. Sage Publications.

DfEE (1997) 'Excellence for all children: meeting special educational needs'.

DfE (2014) *Performance – P Scale – Attainment Targets for Pupils with Special Educational Needs*. Crown copyright.

DfE (2015) 'Special Educational Needs and Disability Code of Practice: 0 to 25 Years.' Crown copyright.

DfE (2015), 'Special needs expert to head new assessment review'. DfE (www.gov.uk/government/news/special-needs-expert-to-head-new-assessment-review)

DfE (2015) 'Supporting pupils at school with medical conditions'. Crown copyright

Gedge, N. (2016) *Inclusion for Primary School Teachers*. Bloomsbury Education.

Goswami, U. (2015) 'Children's Cognitive Development and Learning'. Cambridge Primary Review Trust.

Grandin, T. (2014) *The Autistic Brain*. Rider.

Gross, J. (2015) *Beating Bureaucracy in Special Educational Needs*. David Fulton.

Hartley, R. (2010) 'Teacher expertise for special educational needs: filling in the gaps' Policy Exchange.

Harwell, J. M. & Jackson, R. W. (2008) *The Complete Learning Disabilities Handbook: Ready to use Strategies and Activities to Teaching Students with Learning Disabilities*. Jossey Bass.

Hodkinson, A., & Vickerman, P., (2009) Key Issues in Special Educational Needs and Inclusion. Sage Publications.

IPSEA (Independent Parental Special Education Advice), 'EHC (Education, health and care) plans' (www.ipsea.org.uk)

Martin-Denham, S. (2015) *Teaching Children and Young People with Special Educational Needs and Disabilities*. Sage Publications.

McCann, L. (2016) *How to Support Pupils with Autistic Spectrum Condition in Primary School*. LDA.

McCann, L. (2016) *How to Support Pupils with Autistic Spectrum Condition in Secondary School*. LDA.

Mittler, P. (2000) *Working Towards Inclusive Education: Social Contexts*. David Fulton.

NUT: 'SEN for less able readers' www.teachers.org.uk

Ott. P. (1997) *How to Detect and Manage Dyslexia*. Heinemann.

Packer, N. (2014) *The Perfect SENCO*. Crown House Publishing.

Parsons, S. & Branagan, A. (2010) *Language for Thinking*. Speechmark Publishing Ltd.

Reiff. M.I. (2011) *ADHD: What Every Parent Needs to Know*. American Academy of Pediatrics.

Richards, G. and Armstrong, F. (eds) (2011) *Teaching and Learning in Diverse and Inclusive Classrooms: Key Issues for New Teachers*. Routledge.

Rose, J. (2009) 'Identifying and Teaching Children and Young People with Dyslexia and Literacy Difficulties: An Independent Report from Sir Jim Rose to the Secretary of State for Children, Schools and Families'. Crown copyright.

Tutt, R. & Williams, P. (2015) *The SEND Code of Practice 0-25 Years*. Sage Publications.

Wakefield. A. (1998) in *The Lancet*. Retracted article. http://www.thelancet.com/journals/lancet/article/PIIS0140-6736(97)11096-0/abstract

Walton. E. (2016) *The Language of Inclusive Education: Exploring Speaking, Listening, Reading and Writing*. Routledge.

Warnock, M. (1978) 'Special Educational Needs: Report of the Committee of Enquiry into the Education of Handicapped Children and Young People'. Crown Copyright.

Further reading

'ADHD A guide for UK teachers' – the Living with ADHD website: www.livingwithadhd.co.uk

'Food Dye and ADHD: Food colouring, sugar, and diet' www.webmd.com

P scales and performance descriptors: DfE (2014): *Performance – P Scale – Attainment Targets for Pupils with Special Educational Needs* (https://www.gov.uk/government/publications/p-scales-attainment-targets-for-pupils-with-sen

Bibliography and further reading

The Policy Exchange Research Note:http://www.policyexchange.org.uk/images/publications/teacher%20expertise%20for%20sen%20-%20jul%2010.pdf

'The Science Behind Dyslexia' www.bdadyslexia.org.uk

'What are the three types of ADHD' www.healthline.com

Research from The Speech and Language Therapist Sasha Bemrose 2013 (http://www.afasiccymru.org.uk/download/training/Links%20between%20SLCN%20and%20behaviour%20-%20Sasha%20Bemrose.pdf

Index